D0811531

ENGLISH MOUNTAIN SUMMITS

ENGLISH MOUNTAIN SUMMITS

NICK WRIGHT

Photographs by Iain Wright

ROBERT HALE · LONDON

FIRST PUBLISHED IN GREAT BRITAIN 1974

ISBN 0 7091 4560 8

Robert Hale & Company
63 Old Brompton Road
London S.W.7

MADE AND PRINTED IN GREAT BRITAIN BY
THE GARDEN CITY PRESS LIMITED
LETCHWORTH, HERTFORDSHIRE
SG6 1JS

CONTENTS

AUTHOR'S NOTE

The routes outlined or indicated in this book do not necessarily imply that a right of way exists.

ILLUSTRATIONS

(*The relevant entry or entries in the text are indicated by capitals*)

MAPS

ACKNOWLEDGEMENTS

I am particularly indebted to:
Betty Light and my wife for typing the manuscript; my son Iain for the photographs; those who encouraged me to put on record something of what I have found in English mountains; and those who assisted me by checking facts, comparing notes and exchanging views.

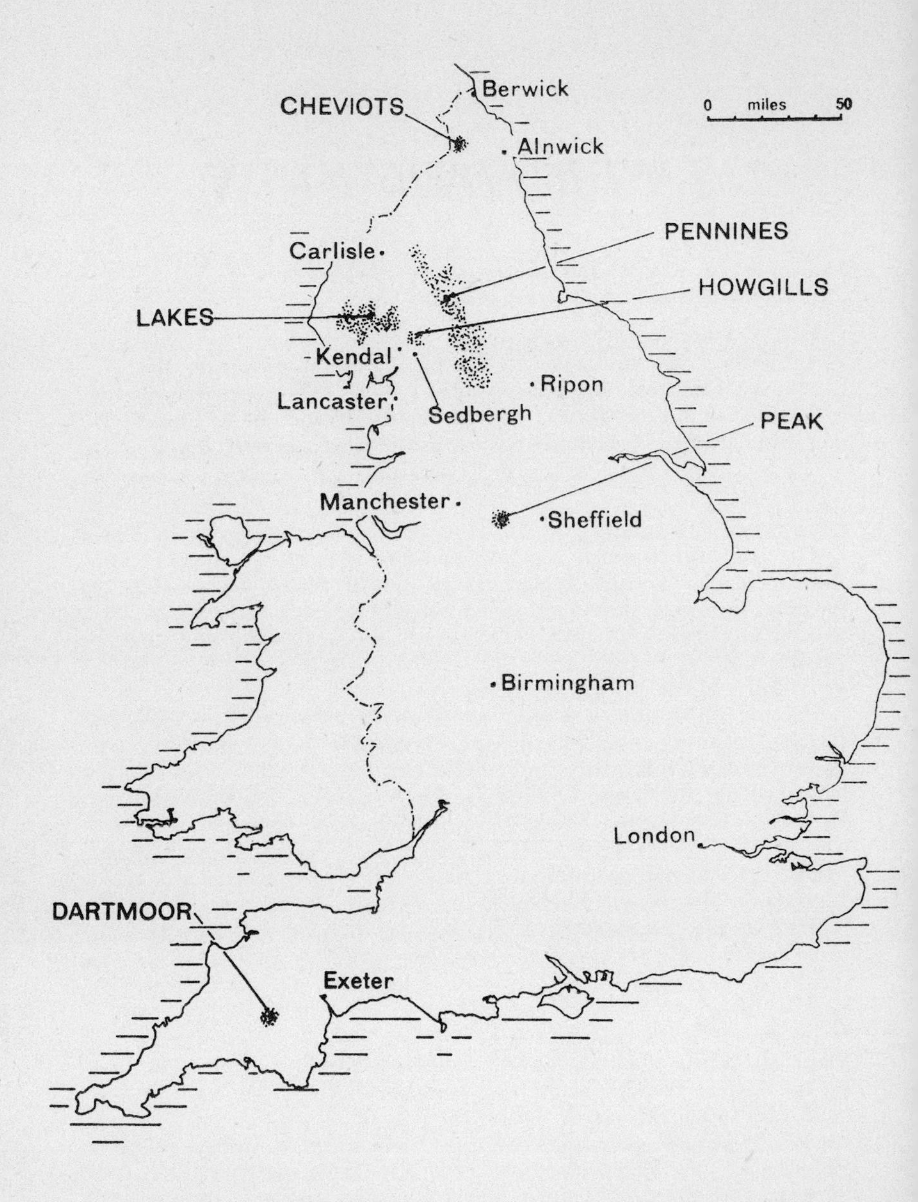

Berwick
CHEVIOTS
0 miles 50
Alnwick
PENNINES
Carlisle
HOWGILLS
LAKES
Kendal
Ripon
Lancaster
Sedbergh
PEAK
Manchester
Sheffield
Birmingham
London
DARTMOOR
Exeter

I

INTRODUCTION

'Where break the windy dawns on mountain heather
Where hills of granite cleave grey skies above
. . .
There walks the spirit of the land we love.'

P. H. B. Lyon

Mountains in England? The face of the Zermatt guide broke into a broad grin and he made a gentle undulating motion with his hands. Perhaps he was only interested in peaks above 12,000 feet or perhaps he knew that English mountains offered little scope for a man of his profession. But he obviously knew they existed and the gentle motion of his hands was at least a realistic description of some parts of the rolling Pennines.

Despite the guide's views, I would not exchange the Lakes and the Pennines for the Swiss Alps. Although, when weary of the pressures of London, my mind regularly turns to the mountains, it is not to the Alps, the Dolomites, the Pyrenees, the mountains of Kenya or the Hindu Kush, all of which have provided me with exercise and entertainment at various times. On such occasions my mind turns to the mountainous areas of Northern England and I remember the many happy hours I have spent walking there, looking at the distant horizons, seeing the birds and flowers and the occasional sheep, feeling free of all the troubles of this world and thinking how good it was to be alive and feel the mountain wind on my face.

No doubt I am biased. I was born on the flat West Lancashire plain where, on clear days, one could see the line of the Pennines on the eastern horizon stretching from Rivington Pike in the south to the Bleasdale Moors in the north. Best of all was the view of the Bleasdale Moors when they were covered in snow and, even more exciting, on one exceptional day, the appearance in the north-west of a mysterious black cone, Black Combe on the west coast of Cumberland. Perhaps because they were not in evidence on wet, gloomy days or because the happiest times of my schooldays were spent walking in the shadow of Pendle Hill, I was led to associate the northern hills with the good things in life. The Alps and such places, to me at any rate, are for limited summer vacations where one spends a week getting acclimatised in the hope that the weather will permit an ascent of one or two summits before it is time to return home.

English mountains are quite different. They are about 250 million years older than the Alps or Himalayas and in that time have lost the dirty, grey, glacial moraines which are such a feature of some Alpine scenes. Shaved by the vast ice cap which formerly extended to southern England, and eroded by wind, ice and water since then, they have been reduced to manageable proportions. Yet they offer endless variety of scene and, because of their latitude, often display a wild, forbidding and unruly nature to those who visit them. However, with proper care, any fit person can tackle the ascent of any one of them while, by judicious use of a motor car, some of the easier summits can be made accessible to the smallest toddler or the oldest pensioner. What is more, with the exception of some of those unfortunate enough to live in the south-east, anyone in England can go to see a mountain and return home within the compass of a single day.

Lest anyone think that I have underestimated these mountains or conclude that they are not worthy of serious attention, let me hasten to add that they are of interest to the rock climber as well as the mountain walker and that some ascents involve considerable effort and others scrambles over rough rock which may be too much for those who dislike exposed situations on high ground. Moreover, their ascent in unsettled weather or wintry conditions involves sufficient risks to ensure that it is not undertaken lightly with impunity. Such risks belong to mountains and those who know them would not wish it otherwise. However, the basic skills and experience necessary for those who wish to tackle English mountains without excessive risks can be obtained, without difficulty, at little or no cost. Guides are not necessary. Scafell Pike is free to anyone who cares to attempt it, whereas the average person's attempt on the Matterhorn, as long ago as 1966, cost something of the order of £20.

Someone is sure to say that I have omitted to mention the weather in the foregoing comparison. Everyone knows that the Lake District is the wettest part of England and that no one goes to the northern mountains without being prepared for wet weather. It is not so well known that the Alps and other areas also have their problems in that respect and that the walking season there is very short. English mountains can be attempted at any time of the year but the Alpine season does not start before the end of June and lasts for only a few months. Moreover, good weather in that short period is by no means guaranteed. I have encountered a blizzard in the Dolomites in July, rain for several days on end in the Pyrenees in August, torrential rain on a summer day in Kenya and ten days in Zermatt in July without a clear view of the Matterhorn, while two Cumberland lads who made a trip to Khatmandu in 1971 were prevented by floods from reaching the Everest foothills and never saw the mountains.

None of the hills I saw from my birthplace qualified as a mountain and I did not see one until, at the age of twenty, I went to the Lake District. Since then I have been trying to make up for the opportunities I missed in my early years and I took care to encourage my children, at an early age, to develop a preference for the mountains instead of the conventional seaside holiday. This done, it became my responsibility to organise holidays calculated to maintain their preference. Initially it was a question of using a car to enable them to get to the easier summits. Later, the problem was to find the most convenient routes up some of the higher peaks. I make no apology for making full use of all the short cuts and mechanical assistance available, although I realise that it will not meet with approval in many quarters. The single man can be choosy and may, if he wishes, operate in terms of ascents from sea-level rather than from a convenient mountain pass, but the man with young children needs all the help he can get if he is to reach and return from a summit in safety. He cannot hope to take his children up the major peaks but he can start them off at the earliest age on Drumaldrace and Dodd Fell Hill. Between these and Scafell Pikes is an infinite variety to suit every taste.

My planning was all well worth while and taught me a lot about the geography of the British Isles, but it became obvious to me that, although some walkers had a very detailed knowledge of the popular areas of the Lake District, few knew the more remote areas, whether of the Lake District or the Pennines, and none claimed to have walked all the English mountains or even to know how many there were. Moreover, I was frequently surprised at the general ignorance on a more local scale. For instance, the man in Sedbergh who knew the Howgill Fells but did not know their names; the guide book which said that Wild Boar Fell was the highest point in Yorkshire; the landlady who said that Killhope Law was the highest mountain in Northumberland; the Durham people who had not heard of Scaud Hill and had no idea what the highest summit in Durham might be; and my Westmorland friend who was sure that Sca Fell in Lancashire. Accordingly, I decided to compile a complete list and to make a point of walking them all myself.

Before compiling a list it was first necessary to decide on the definition of a mountain. Dictionaries are not always helpful. They have a tendency to say that a mountain is higher than a hill and a hill of less size than a mountain. Even less helpful is the Encyclopaedia Britannica. It refers to 'the Mountain' as being the left wing of the Whig party in the early nineteenth century and the only reference to hills I could trace was to sand dunes. However, the *Shorter Oxford English Dictionary* gives the following:

Mountain. A natural elevation of the earth's surface rising notably above the surrounding level.

Hills. A natural elevation of the earth's surface rising more or less steeply above the level of the surrounding land. Formerly the general term, including mountains; but now restricted; e.g. in Great Britain confined to heights under 2000 feet.

This to my satisfaction, and I hope to everyone else's, establishes a mountain in England as being something of 2000 feet or more in height.

I am glad the definition was not 'in excess of 2000 feet' as this would have excluded one of my favourites, Causey Pike, which is precisely 2000 feet high. It does exclude Illgill Head, the summit above the Wasdale Screes, which is recorded as 1978 feet, Thack Moor west of Alston in Cumberland at an altitude of 1999 feet, my friend Black Combe (1969 feet) and a host of other desirable locations. They should not be neglected merely because they do not qualify for inclusion in the list of mountain summits.

However, a decision on the height of a mountain does not resolve all the problems. Mountains do not occur as individuals. They do not all look like Great Gable as seen from Wastwater, and Great Gable looks quite different when seen from the other side. Mountains are often grouped together and linked by ridges and I would not care to attempt to define where one ends and another begins.

One cannot rely on the names given on maps. Maps do not always agree on names. For instance, the Bartholomews Road Atlas names the mountain to the west of Alston as Middle Carrick, whereas the 1 inch Ordnance Survey gives the name as Grey Nag. Names have sometimes been given to areas which are obviously on the side of a mountain, while some summits are not named and others have more than one. Ever since I read that the nearest inhabitants to K.2, the second highest mountain in the world, had not bothered to give it a name I concluded that names in themselves were not sufficient.

A. Wainwright, in his excellent guides to the Lake District, seems to have a feel for the precise limits of some of the mountains and suggests that the distinction between a hill and a mountain depends on appearance. Others speak of 'real' mountains, while the physicists who wanted a perfect mountain for the purpose of assessing the mass of the earth had to go to Schiehallion in the middle of Scotland. After much thought I concluded that I must avoid any definition which was a matter of opinion and adopt some rule which could be applied in a purely mechanical way. My solution was to count all those summits on the 1-inch Ordnance Survey maps which were 2000 feet or more in height and were enclosed by an individual contour line or a contour line broken by a crag.

The 1-inch Ordnance Survey map was an obvious choice as the basic guide. One cannot use a smaller scale for walking and the 6-inch to the mile maps are too detailed and too expensive for the normal walker. While I am very fond of the 1-inch Bartholomew map and have used the Lake District edition for much of my walking there, I have to admit that the Ordnance Survey maps are more precise.

The system is simple to operate—if one has good eyesight or a magnifying glass—but it produces some odd results. Some heights are left out which, when seen 'on the ground', appear obvious candidates for inclusion, while other heights of little significance are included. When one adopts a simple standard rule such as the one I have described one must expect a few unusual cases to arise. The explanation lies in the base line adopted by the Ordnance Survey and the contour interval. A couple of diagrams will perhaps illustrate the point.

The first diagram shows the contours and side elevation of two points which, under the system adopted, would rank as two

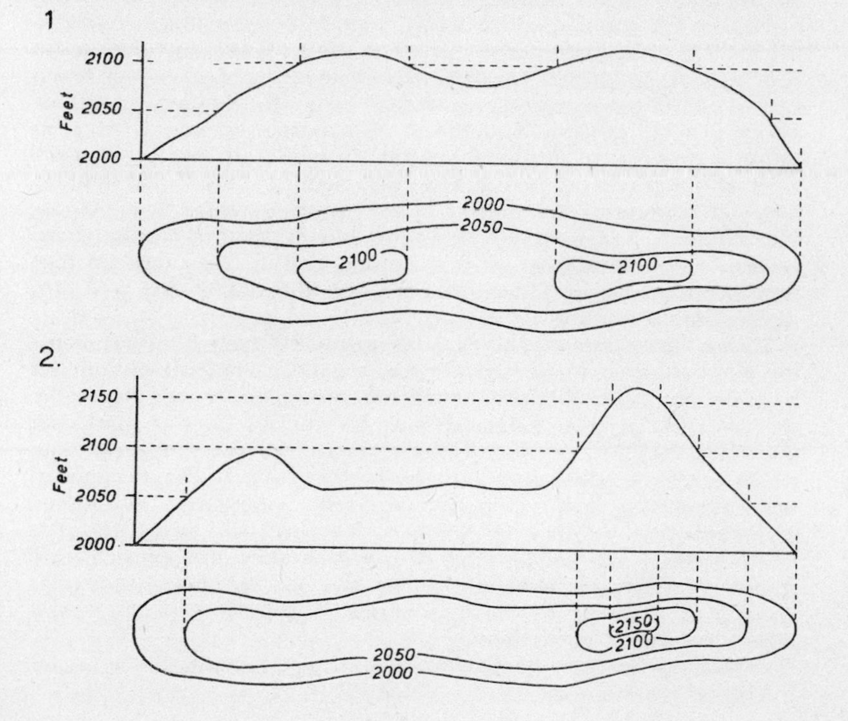

summits, while the second illustrates a case where there is only one summit. An example of the latter will be found at the trig point north-west of Burnhope Reservoir in County Durham, while Tynehead Fell provides several examples of the former.

I do not think a few odd results matter. There will be anomalies whatever system is adopted and it is well worth while to accept a few results which appear a little ridiculous in order to have a purely factual system instead of one which relies on opinion. After all, the primary objective is to identify areas meriting exploration.

My original list was compiled from a five miles to the inch Bartholomew's Road Atlas which readily identified all areas exceeding 2000 feet in height, although the scale was much too small for it to be used for walking. Using the Road Atlas as a guide, however, I found it easy to pick out the mountainous areas on the 1-inch Ordnance Survey maps and to compile what I hope is a complete list of summits of 2000 or more feet in height.

Before leaving this subject of identification it seems desirable to mention the possible effect of adoption of the metric system. The 6-inch Ordnance Survey maps are gradually being converted to the metric scale with contours at 10-metre intervals and metric maps on a 1 : 50,000 scale are expected to appear sometime in 1974 to replace the popular 1-inch maps. 2000 feet is equivalent to 609·6 metres and the question arises whether, after adoption of the metric system, a mountain will be defined as something in excess of 609·6 metres in height or whether someone will opt for 600 metres or perhaps 1000 metres. A standard of 600 metres would bring in quite a number of additional summits while, if the 1000-metre level is adopted, our mountains will be eliminated, the highest point in England being 71 feet below the 1000-metre level. Whatever happens, I fear the 2000-foot contour is destined to disappear. Its removal, you may say, will at least get rid of the nonsense that basis produces on Tynehead Fell, but any alternative may well produce a similar result in some other area.

When the Ordnance Survey have produced metric replacements for all the 1-inch maps and the Oxford Dictionary definition has been revised, it will perhaps be time to produce a revised list of the mountain summits of England but, for my lifetime at least, the 2000-foot level will remain. Having regard to recent dispute as to when is the true anniversary of the battle of the Boyne, because of the eleven days 'lost' when the Gregorian calendar was adopted in 1751, it may well be that the 2000-foot level will persist for very much longer. One comforting thought is that the existing grid references will continue to be valid on the new metric maps, so that those who continue to think in terms of 2000-foot summits will always be able to locate them.

My researches have revealed a total of 345 summits in six areas:

* But see Appendix V.

* *

BACKSTONE EDGE (Pennines). High Cup Nick

(*above*) BACKSTONE EDGE (Pennines). Stake Beck

(*below*) BRAM RIGG TOP (Howgills). Howgills from the M.6

Dartmoor, Cheviots, Howgills, Lakes, Peak and Pennines, the location of each area being shown on the map on page 10. Appendix I gives a summary by counties—as they stood before April 1974—and Appendix II a summary by the six main groupings. The counties, of course, are in the process of reorganisation and boundaries which have stood for 1000 years have just been changed. But, as with the 2000-foot contour, it will no doubt be a long time before they are accepted. I certainly hope that no one is going to move the Three Shire Stone from Wrynose.

Summits are arranged in alphabetical order with the 1-inch Ordnance Survey sheet number at the head, together with the grid reference and the altitude. Where the summit is near the edge of a sheet, as so often happens, the number of the adjacent sheet is also quoted. In this connection it should perhaps be mentioned that the Lakeland summits, which appear on Sheets 82, 83, 88 and 89 of the standard series, all appear on the 1-inch Lake District Tourist Map. Sheets 83 and 89 also include some Pennine summits but Sheets 82 and 88 cover only Lakeland summits. It is therefore advantageous to use the 1-inch Tourist Map for the Lakeland summits, partly because it is cheaper to buy one map than two, but primarily because it gets over the problem of coping with summits on the edge of a sheet. For instance, the Helvellyn ridge is close to the western edge of Sheet 83 and Saddleback is on the edge of Sheet 82. Summits appearing on the Lake District Tourist Map accordingly have an asterisk after the Sheet number in the standard series. It should be noted, however, that the sheets in the standard series are in some respects clearer than the Tourist Map. In the event of any dispute, therefore, reference should be made to the standard sheet. Altitudes are as stated on the 1-inch Ordnance Survey map or, where a spot height is not recorded there, the height of the encircling contour line. Names also, with one exception, are as recorded on the 1-inch Ordnance Survey. If a summit is named it is normally treated as a separate mountain. If it is not named, and cannot be treated as a subsidiary of the nearest named mountain, it is given the nearest name on the map.

Routes given, with one exception, assume the walker may wish to park his car near the starting point and return to it. There are many occasions when it would be more interesting to end the walk at a different point, but this is not normally convenient for the average walker and it would be quite impossible to set out all the possible variations which could be attempted in that way. Such an arrangement makes one dependent for transport on a friend or the public transport services, with all the problems of timing which this entails, or one must carry additional equipment and seek accommodation at the end of the day. This is out of the question for the man with a young family. Accordingly the routes are designed on the basis of a return to the starting point—an arrangement which is now recognised as desirable by planners when considering the future of our footpaths.

Although each entry includes an indication of one or more routes to the summit, the routes have not been set out in precise detail. Those who attempt the mountain summits of England need to be able to read a map and will, I am sure, prefer to have merely an indication of a route and be left to find their own way. Until they are capable of doing this they should not attempt any but the straightforward summits. Those who wish to develop their capacity in this respect, will find some notes on map reading in Appendix III and a few notes on clothing and equipment in Appendix IV.

Given adequate experience, ascent of every one of the summits listed is within the capacity of any reasonably active walker. Routes which present special problems are indicated in the text and it should be appreciated that some of them cover remote areas where there is little prospect of getting assistance if anything goes wrong and that there are tremendous variations in the type of walking encountered. Smooth easy surfaces such as those found on the Howgills, High Street or the Dodds are a remarkable contrast to the jagged rocks of Scafell Pikes, the slate of Skiddaw, the wild swamp of Yockenthwaite, the rough grass and bog of Scaud Hill and the granite of Yes Tor. This is what makes them so attractive, as also do the seasonal variations. Who can forget the autumn tints of Lakeland, the golden gorse of the Cheviot valleys in spring, a winter's day on Kinder Scout or the Pennines, a walk in the snow on High Street, or the sun on a Lakeland stream?

These summits were sought out primarily for the entertainment of my family, although I must confess that the younger element had largely gone their separate ways before the project was completed. The rocks of central Lakeland tended to be more attractive to them than the grassy summits of the Pennines. As far as I am concerned, however, when I try to compile a short list of my favourite summits, I find that half of them are places I might never have visited had I not set out to find and climb all our English summits. If any justification is required for it, this will surely be sufficient.

II

MOUNTAINS A–Z

For the significance of an asterisk after the sheet number see page 17.

ADAM SEAT

1. *Sheet 83*. Reference 472091. Westmorland. 2180 feet.*

This is the first of seven 'Seats' in this list of English summits, the others being Burnhope, High, Hugh, Lady's, Rogan's and Seatallan. Lest anyone suppose that these are lofty viewpoints from which Adam, Hugh or Rogan sat and gazed on some glorious panorama, let me explain that the derivation of the word means 'spring pastures'. The excursion to Adam Seat, therefore is to the place where Adam's cattle and sheep were put out to pasture in the spring and the best viewpoints are not to be found on the actual summit.

There are really only two routes to Adam Seat, one from the north at 469107, the end of the road which runs to the south-western end of Haweswater, and one from the south at Sadgill (484057) in the Long Sleddale valley. Whichever is adopted the excursion should, if possible, include the high ground running from Adam Seat over Harter Fell, The Knowe and Brown Howe to Kentmere Pike and on to the viewpoint of Goat Scar above Long Sleddale, all of which can conveniently be covered in half a day.

Whether the start is from north or south, the route is up the Gatescarth Pass to 474092 where a somewhat indistinct path strikes roughly south-west to the cairn on Adam Seat. From this point there is a gentle rise to Harter Fell to the north-west and then a pleasant walk, first south and then south-east, over the Knowe, Brown Howe and Kentmere Pike to Goat Scar.

Those starting from Sadgill can then continue slightly west of south to Shipman Knotts and down to 477049, whence a path runs east to Sadgill. Those starting from Haweswater, however, will be well advised to retrace their steps to Harter Fell and descend from there to the Nan Bield Pass and round Small Water back to their starting point. Given a choice, the latter route is to be preferred as it provides fine views of the Harter Fell crags and avoids the road walk above Sadgill. Moreover, it is readily capable of extension, if required, by proceeding from the top of the Nan Bield Pass north-west to High Street, returning to Haweswater over Rough Crag or Kidsty Pike.

The Sadgill route should take about four hours, while the Haweswater route should take $4\frac{1}{4}$ or six hours according to whether the route is by Small Water or Kidsty Pike.

ALLEN CRAGS

2. *Sheet 82.* Reference 237085. Cumberland. 2572 feet.*

Allen Crags are situated just north-west of Esk Hause at the beginning of the Glaramara ridge. The shortest route is from Seathwaite in Borrowdale, proceeding due south over Stockley Bridge and up Grains Gill. By this route the summit cairn of Allen Crags should be reached in about two hours.

An alternative and more secluded route is from Stonethwaite up the Langstrath valley. This is one of the quietest valleys in the Lake District and provides a very pleasant walk. The direct approach out of the Langstrath valley following the upper part of the stream is very steep and a diversion from point 247087 by way of Angle Tarn may be considered worth while. Time from Stonethwaite would be about three hours.

Allen Crags may also be approached by way of Glaramara, from Wasdale by Sty Head, or from Langdale by way of Rossett Gill, but the preferable routes for the walker who operates from a car are those from Seathwaite or Stonethwaite, returning down the Glaramara ridge or by the alternative valley. Inexperienced walkers should avoid the direct return from the summit of Glaramara to Stonethwaite as there is not a recognised path and some rocky scrambling is encountered. One and a quarter hours should be allowed for the return to Seathwaite over Glaramara and two hours for the return to Stonethwaite, whether direct or via Thornythwaite Fell.

AUCHOPE CAIRN

3. *Sheets 70 and 71. Reference 895194. Northumberland. 2419 feet.*
4. *Subsidiary summit at 891199. 2382 feet.*

These two summits, lying $1\frac{1}{4}$ miles south-west of The Cheviot, are not named on the 1-inch Ordnance Survey map but it is convenient to refer to them by the name Auchope Cairn, which lies between them. The cairn presumably has some connection with General Auchope, killed in action at Magersfontein during the Boer War, whose statue stands in Town Yetholm.

The summits are on the Pennine Way, over 240 miles from the southern end at Edale but only eight miles from the northern end at Kirk Yetholm. However, an ascent from Kirk Yetholm, other than by those who are walking to Edale, is hardly to be recommended. The round trip would require seven hours which could be better employed in taking a shorter route and including a walk on The Cheviot and its associated summits. There are three convenient starting points for such a walk: Cocklawfoot (854186) at the end of the minor road which runs from about a mile south of Town Yetholm along Bowmont Water; Longleeford (949220) at the end of the road from Wooler along the Harthope Burn; and Hethpool (895281) in the College Burn valley on the minor road starting from Westnewton, 5½ miles on the B.6351 road east-north-east of Wooler.

The route from Hethpool takes seven hours, of which 1½ can be saved by obtaining permission from the College Valley Estate Office in Wooler to take a car as far as the road junction at 888252. Beyond that point the road continues down the valley for a further 1½ miles and then degenerates—or improves, according to one's point of view—to a delightful path which runs to the end of the valley and the Pennine Way at 874202. From here one turns in an easterly direction along the Way up a gentle slope followed by a much steeper climb to the first of the Auchope Cairn summits. The second and main summit is almost half a mile further on to the south-east over boggy ground past the authentic Auchope Cairn.

Cocklawfoot provides a less satisfactory starting point as it has no valley walk comparable to the College Burn, involves retracing one's steps for the return and requires 6½ hours for the round trip. The route is by the track over White Knowe to the border crossing above Uswayford at 872160 and then north-east along the Pennine Way, first to the southern and then on to the northern Auchope summit.

From the southern and higher summit a short branch off the main Pennine Way goes east to the main Cheviot summit. Certainly the route is to the east, but, at the time of writing, there is little indication on the ground. Possibly Pennine Way walkers with enthusiasm for the Cheviot are rare. When one looks at the wild and desolate country which marks the way to far distant Edale, their feelings are readily understood. However, the route to the east is the one for those who wish to explore the plateau of The Cheviot, those returning to Cocklawfoot having ultimately to return to the southern Auchope summit and then retrace their steps to Cocklawfoot, while those returning to Hethpool should end their exploration at Braydon Crag (894215) and continue down the slope to a point west of Dunsdale where, after wading across the cold waters of the Lambden burn, they can take the road which rejoins the main College Valley road at 888252.

Longleeford, however, is the preferable starting point. It provides the shortest route (about 5½ hours), includes a valley walk which compares favourably with the higher reaches of the College Valley, avoids any retracing of steps and permits of a convenient extension to Comb Fell and Hedgehope Hill on the return. The route is along the Harthope Burn, one of the loveliest streams in the country, to its source on the southern slopes of Cairn Hill and then either around the slopes of Cairn Hill to the Auchope summits or, for those who like to simplify their navigation, to the sandstone shelter at the summit of Cairn Hill (904195) and then half a mile west to the main Auchope summit. After exploring the summit plateau of The Cheviot, Longleeford can be reached by descending from the subsidiary summit at 914208 along the line of cairns leading to the Harthope Burn. Alternatively, the return can be made from Cairn Hill across the head of the Harthope valley to Comb Fell (919187), then to Hedgehope Hill (943198) and down to Longleeford. This extension adds only about one hour to the round trip.

BACKSTONE EDGE

5. *Sheets 83 and 84. Reference 725276. Westmorland. 2292 feet.*

Backstone Edge lies nearly two miles north-west of the Pennine Way at High Cup Nick where it crosses the western edge of the Pennines on the section from Langdon Beck in Teesdale to Dufton in the Eden valley. The nearest approach from a road is from Dufton (691251) along the Pennine Way and then up the steep rocky path which leads to Narrowgate Beacon (737260 on Sheet 84). However, those who will not otherwise have an opportunity to see the wild beauty of the Pennine Way in this area may well decide to tackle it from Langdon Beck (854313) or from slightly lower down the Alston–Middleton-in-Teesdale road at 860304. It is a ten-mile-walk from Teesdale to Backstone Edge but, given the attractions of the route, no one need complain if time restricts them to returning by the same path. At least eight hours needs to be allowed for the ascent from Teesdale but the round trip from Dufton takes less than four hours if the return journey follows the old mine track running south-east from 719281.

Alternatively one can reach Backstone Edge from 717313 on the road which runs from the village of Knock to Great Dun Fell. The route lies over Knock Fell and High Scald Fell and is of particular interest to those who wish to make a round trip embracing Meldon Hill, 2½ miles north-east of High Cup Nick. Five hours will be required.

For those approaching from High Cup Nick the best route is by way of Narrowgate Beacon, then north-west so as to avoid the three tarns. Like so many trig points in the Pennines, that near the summit is not visible until close at hand. It is also, from the map readers' point of view, most inconveniently situated on the edge of Sheet 83. Narrowgate Beacon is on Sheet 84 and the hurried walker may well fail to observe that the high ground bends in an arc across the edges of the two sheets, the highest point being at the north-western end.

Whichever route is used, all who go to Backstone Edge will be well advised to allow in their planning of the walk a little extra time for a look at High Cup Nick. This great ravine is one of the wonders of the British Isles. It is a place for the photographer, but even that magnificent picture of the stone wall climbing almost vertically for the best part of 1000 feet up the side of the gorge does not give an adequate impression of the scene. The picture became familiar to many when it appeared on a calendar depicting North Country scenes but it is normally only the moorland walker, crossing the Pennines from Langdon Beck in Teesdale or ascending from Dufton in the Eden valley, who gets a full appreciation of the High Cup Nick scene. Pennine Way walkers now swell the numbers of those who cover this area but, even so, only comparatively few people have seen this marvellous sight.

High Cup Nick is a dry valley formed at the end of the Ice Age between 10,000 and 15,000 years ago when the ice on these high moorlands melted and a torrent of water poured over the western slopes into the Eden valley, cutting back into the hard dolerite of the Whin Sill to form an enormous waterfall. The cutting back is not like the gentle arc of Hardraw Force but is a long narrow cut with the sheer cliff of the dolerite band of the Whin Sill, a 300-million-year-old volcanic extrusion, revealed in a vast elongated horse-shoe near to the top. Walls which separate the sheep runs seem to climb almost vertically up the sides and that magnificent wall which appeared on the calendar, although no longer unbroken, is still sufficiently in evidence to form a worthy monument to the men who built it. Little, however, remains of the once vast torrent which used to flow over the easternmost point of the arc as the waters from this moorland area now largely drain by Maize Beck and the Tees to the North Sea.

Another view of the dolerite rock will be found in Stake Beck which flows less than half a mile away to the north-east. Below the white bridge a little to the north at 749270 the water flows over a smooth, jet black, shiny slab of rock and, further south, huge chunks of it lie in the bed of the stream. Somewhere down in the valley below High Cup Nick there must be blocks of this material which fell down when High Cup Nick was formed. Possibly some are in the walls and others covered by smaller debris. They would make an interesting subject for further exploration. Fortunately weathering of this material is slow, as evidenced by the pillars which stand out around the rim, and High Cup Nick should remain very much as it is today for many years to come.

BANNERDALE CRAGS

6. *Sheet 83.* Reference 335290. Cumberland. 2200 feet.*
7. *Subsidiary summit: Sheet 82.* Reference 329296. 2100 feet.*

Bannerdale Crags are about 1½ miles north-west of the Saddleback summit. They can readily be reached on the descent from Saddleback by way of Scales Tarn or Sharp Edge by ascending the Glenderamackin valley to 327292 and then proceeding due east for about half a mile.

For those who want a short half-day walk, or those who want to visit Bannerdale Crags on the way to Saddleback, there are two lines of ascent, one from near the inn at Scales (343269) and one from near the inn at Mungrisdale (362304). The former follows the Souther Fell route to 348272 and then the path going north-west to the Glenderamackin valley or reaches the valley by diversion from the Scales Fell route. In either case, the Glenderamackin valley must be ascended to 327292 and an easterly course taken from there to the main summit.

From Mungrisdale the route is a little more direct, the footpath from the inn running about due west along the river Glenderamackin and then ascending the south shoulder of The Tongue to 332303 on the ridge which extends from Bowscale Fell in the north to Bannerdale Crags in the south-east. Saddleback appears on the skyline as altitude is gained. On reaching the ridge, a short diversion to the north leads to Bowscale Fell, and a fairly level walk almost due south for half a mile brings one to the low mound studded with rocks which is the subsidiary summit at 329296. A continuation for three-quarters of a mile to the south-east brings one to the small slate cairn marking the main summit of Bannerdale Crags at 335290. There is a similar cairn above the steep slope facing Saddleback.

The advantage of the ascent from Mungrisdale is the possibility it offers of a round trip by dropping down the south-western slope to 327292 and following the Glenderamackin back to the inn. The round trip, including the diversion to the Bowscale Fell summit, should not take more than four hours.

On a visit to Bannerdale Crags in April 1970 there was snow and ice down to 1800 feet. A hard white covering made walking easy and the view of a small party winding its way up the wide expanse of virgin snow on Saddleback reminded one of our expedition in the Alps. An ascent in such conditions is an experience not easily forgotten.

BASE BROWN

8. *Sheet 82.* Reference 225115. Cumberland. 2120 feet.*

What a name to inflict on any summit, particularly one dwarfed by Great Gable! Base Brown, on a ridge running north-east from Green Gable on the west of Borrowdale, with Sourmilk Gill on one flank and Sty Head Gill on the other, could readily be ascended by those who descended from Great Gable in this direction. If there were a direct descent from it to Seathwaite it would no doubt bear a well-worn track and be known to thousands. However, as the ascent involves a diversion from the Sourmilk Gill path, such as is not welcomed by those who have just had the thrill of an ascent of Great Gable by the Traverse route, it probably sees few visitors.

But it is well worth a visit, particularly for those who cannot reach the Lakes from home until sometime in the afternoon. For such people, Base Brown can be a welcome appetiser. It looks east across Borrowdale to Glaramara and west to the dark crags of Brandreth and Grey Knotts and, despite its limited altitude and its position at the heart of Lakeland, can provide very extensive views ranging from Skiddaw, Saddleback and Scafell round to the Buttermere Fells.

Ascent from Seathwaite involves a steep scramble by the side of Sourmilk Gill, starting through the archway of the farm buildings at 236122 and ascending the hillside some way to the left of the old plumbago mine. Across the wet ground at the top of this first scramble is a line of cairns which points the way below the Base Brown crags to the head of the Gillercombe valley. Beyond the cairns is a well-worn path which should be followed until just below the crest of the rise at the end of the valley where it turns right to Green Gable. Proceeding in the opposite direction, a gentle rise over grassy moorland scattered with rocky outcrops brings one to the summit cairn of Base Brown, a cairn much larger than would be expected by those who have seen the round green slope of Base Brown from Sty Head tarn. Those who tire of the track along Gillercombe can take a short cut up the side of Base Brown at the point where the path drops a little and swings to the right (about 221117) to join the easier route of ascent shortly after it leaves the track to Green Gable. It is tough going, particularly for anyone who has just motored up from London, and not to be recommended.

On the return to Seathwaite a more attractive short cut presents itself in the shape of a short scree run just to the north of the main footpath. One could, of course, continue on the Green Gable track and have a moderate extension of the walk by returning over Green Gable and down Aaron Slack and Sty Head. But those pressed for time will probably wish to return down the Gillercombe valley and Sourmilk Gill. The round trip from Seathwaite on this route takes just over two hours and anyone newly arrived from the south will not complain at seeing the Gillercombe valley twice.

BELLBEAVER RIGG

9. *Sheet 84. Reference 763351. Cumberland. 2035 feet.*

A most interesting name, meaning the hill by the river where there are beavers. The South Tyne starts on the western slopes but the Tees, having descended from Cross Fell for a distance of over four miles, is a sizeable stream when it washes the southern slopes and is presumably the river where the beavers are supposed to be.

There is a parking space for two or three cars at Darngill Bridge (774371) and the obvious route of ascent from that spot is from the milestone about half a mile to the south. A high cairn marks the summit and is reached after little more than a mile of walking through boggy ground over Slack's Rigg and Tynehead Fell. A second substantial cairn lies a short way south at the head of the slope leading down to the Tees.

There is an even easier ascent from the west from the road which runs from Garrigill over Tyne Head to the Nature Conservancy station at Moor House. Cars cannot be taken beyond the gate at 757385 but it is a pleasant walk along the road and ascending from 753353 presents few problems and is reasonably dry.

BINK MOSS

10. *Sheet 84. Reference 877242. Yorkshire (N.R.). 2028 feet.*

Bink Moss lies in the desolate heather-covered country to the east of Mickle Fell and the Warcop artillery range. It is difficult country for walkers as some of the paths marked on the map are little used and in parts difficult to find, while walking where there are no paths can be very arduous.

Two paths pass within three-quarters of a mile of the Bink Moss summit, one to the west, which could well be one of the old 'green' roads of the Pennines, and the other to the east. The western path starts from 882214 on the west of Hargill Bridge on the B.6276 road from Brough to Middleton-in-Teesdale and runs beside Hargill Beck and then north past Bink Moss to connect with the Middleton-in-Teesdale to Alston road a mile or so from Langdon Beck, while the other starts from 887218 just east of Hargill Bridge and runs east of north to Holwick, three miles north-west of Middleton-in-Teesdale. Paths from 879224 on the western path connect with that on the east so that the eastern starting point can be used for the western route—a matter of some interest to car drivers who will find more room for parking there.

The easiest line of ascent is by the path on the west side of the summit to the top of Hagworm Hill (865244), turning due east at that point to the Bink Moss summit about three-quarters of a mile distant. Up to Hagworm Hill the path is fairly good but it more or less disappears beyond the summit and is not recommended as a route from the north.

There is no cairn on Bink Moss but the remains of a shooting box will be found near the highest point.

If activity on the Warcop range permits it may be convenient to extend the walk by returning to Hagworm Hill and proceeding west-north-west to Long Crag (843253), returning south-west to Staple Moss (857236) and then back to the starting point by way of the path along Hargill Beck.

BIRKHOUSE MOOR

11. *Sheet 83.* Reference 363159. Westmorland. 2350 feet.*
12. *Subsidiary summits at 365165. 2318 feet.*
13. *362157. 2300 feet.*
14. *361156. 2300 feet.*

Birkhouse Moor is the north-eastern end of the Striding Edge ridge. Thousands of walkers pass it by on their way to Helvellyn but, taken as part of a round trip from Patterdale embracing Striding Edge, Helvellyn and Catstye Cam, it makes a very enjoyable variation for the descent to either Glenridding or Patterdale at little, if any, cost in time. It can be used in both directions for those who wish to escape the stream of walkers on the usual route from Patterdale to Striding Edge.

For those who wish to have a more modest walk, Birkhouse Moor can be tackled in a round trip from either Patterdale or Glenridding, the easiest route being to follow the Striding Edge path from 383157 to the top of the ridge at 360155, from which point a fairly level walk in a north-easterly direction takes one over two of the subsidiary summits and the highest point to the cairn on the 2318-foot summit. The return to Glenridding is from a point just north-east of the main summit, the path following the line of the stream and reaching the road at 377167, from which point one can proceed into Glenridding or take the footpath in a south-easterly direction to the starting point west of Patterdale—a round trip of about three hours.

BIRKS

15. *Sheet 83.* Reference 382145. Westmorland. 2040 feet.*

Birks is on the ridge which runs north-east from St. Sunday Crag to the south-western end of Ullswater. Those who approach St. Sunday Crag from Patterdale will normally take it in their stride by ascending by the footpath through Glenamara Park from 386157, a little way along the Grisedale road. Those who reach St. Sunday Crag from the opposite direction will find it well worth while to walk down the ridge to Birks and the rocks above Black Crag for the views over Patterdale and Ullswater. The rocks are a better viewpoint than the small cairn on the summit.

BIRKS FELL

16. *Sheet 90. Reference 918764. Yorkshire (W.R.). 2001 feet.*

Birks Fell has no connection with the Birks above Patterdale but lies about five miles north-east of Pen-y-ghent on the ridge which separates the upper reaches of Wharfedale from Littondale. Malham Cove is about eight miles to the south and Langstrothdale 1½ miles to the north. In short, Birks Fell lies in the most interesting part of the Yorkshire Dales, an area which can safely be recommended to any lover of the English countryside.

There is a footpath from 935774 on the Buckden–Hawes road across Firth Fell to 906741 at Litton, and Birks Fell can most readily be reached by following this route. Starting from Littondale or Wharfedale, whichever is the more convenient, the path should be followed to the summit of the ridge and the ridge should then be followed for about a mile in a north-north-westerly direction. The summit is marked by a cairn, the positions of the various tarns being a useful guide to its location. The ascent from Wharfedale takes about 1½ hours and that from Littondale rather less.

BLACK BROW

17. *Sheet 83.* Reference 381102. Westmorland. 2100 feet.*

Black Brow lies between Dove Crag and Little Hart Crag and is on that path between the two of them which runs closest to the crags above Dovedale Beck. There is a tendency for it to be ignored because the path a little further south, which passes the magnificent cairn at 378099, is so much better known. Access to Black Brow, therefore, is by the direct approach to Dove Crag up Scandale Beck or by the route over Snarker Pike and Red Screes as described in the entry for Dove Crag. Alternatively, it can be crossed on the return route from Dove Crag to Patterdale by Scandale Pass and Caiston Beck. It is not a summit of great significance and is not marked by a cairn, but it is there and is an excuse for more detailed exploration of this interesting area of Lakeland.

BLACK FELL

18. *Sheet 83. Reference 648444. Cumberland. 2179 feet.*

Black Fell lies north of the highest point on the Alston–Penrith road. It makes a very pleasant walk from Hartside Cross (648419) at an elevation of 1903 feet and there is good parking for cars close by. The route follows the main ridge of the Pennines over Hartside Height in a direction which is almost due north and the trig point marking the summit is reached after a pleasant walk of about 1½ miles over grassy moorland.

The walk can be extended to Tom Smith's Stone and Grey Nag but there is a severe patch of bog on the north side of Black Fell which may prove too much for young children unless conditions are exceptionally dry.

BLACK SAILS

19. *Sheet 88.* Reference 283008. Lancashire. 2443 feet.*

Black Sails has no connection with Black Sail, the pass connecting Wasdale and Ennerdale. It is the summit between Wetherlam and Swirl How in the most northerly part of Lancashire.

The best approach is from Coniston, taking the path along Church Beck. That from the Sun Inn on the left side is preferable to the one which follows the opposite bank from the minor lane turning off the Coniston–Ambleside road about 100 yards north of the bridge. Both paths lead to the Miner's Bridge, a solid stone arch by some waterfalls. About twenty yards further on, the path forks, that on the left going past the white Copper Mines Youth Hostel and on to Levers Water, while that on the right contours around the slope, behind the row of partly ruined cottages, to the stone tower of the old copper workings south-west of the Lad Stones ridge at 288991.

Those who take the former route can continue by a fairly well-defined path on the right side of Levers Water to the bottom of Prison Band at 278008, just less than half a mile east of Swirl How. From this point a well marked path runs just north of east above the Greenburn valley to Wetherlam. About a quarter of a mile along this path is a short line of cairns, the largest one of which marks the best point of departure from the path to the Black Sails summit about 200 yards to the south. The actual summit is a rocky outcrop on which there is a cairn of moderate size.

Those who prefer a little rock scrambling to the steady progression up a recognisable path will, if the weather is clear, find the alternative route preferable. Just past the stone tower below Lad Stones is a bridge across the Red Dell stream—not entirely reliable, but still negotiable in the autumn of 1971—which leads to a built-up track going to the old mine workings at the southern end of the High Fell ridge almost due east of Levers Water. From the mine workings, a few paces bring one to the top of the ridge and this can then be followed over low crags interspersed with patches of grass until the Black Sails summit is reached. Black Sails offers views of Wetherlam to the east, Swirl How and the ridge to the Old Man on the west, and Coniston Water to the south, and, to the north, Pike of Blisco and the Langdale Pikes, with the flat cone of High Raise beyond and Skiddaw and Saddleback in the distance.

From Black Sails it is an easy matter to descend to the path above Greenburn valley or, if the weather is clear, to head directly for the main Wetherlam summit. There is a patch of bog before the final rise but the path can be joined at this point and provides a tolerable crossing. A subsidiary summit at Hen Crag lies about 400 yards to the south and, after admiring the extensive view to the north and east, the ridge running to the south can be followed for the return to Coniston. This, the Lad Stones ridge, is less rocky than the High Fell ridge leading to Black Sails and enables one to take full advantage of the views to the south and east. There is an indication of a path, marked by a number of small cairns, and a larger cairn marks the most convenient descent down the east side of the ridge to join a wide grassy path leading back to the fork above the Miner's Bridge. Those who wish to continue for a little while longer down the main ridge in order to get better views of the derelict scene around the Copper Mines Youth Hostel can do so, there being convenient routes down on the grassy eastern side of the ridge for some distance beyond the main cairn.

The round trip from Coniston requires about 3½ hours. It is an ideal half-day's excursion—probably the finest half-day's walk to be found in the Coniston area or in the whole of Lancashire. Ascent of the Old Man of Coniston will no doubt continue to be preferred by the vast majority who visit this part of Lakeland and the recognised routes to that summit will obviously be chosen by the inexperienced, but the seasoned walker would probably find ascent by way of Black Sails and Swirl How more rewarding. Certainly there is no need to limit the walk to Black Sails to a half-day. Prison Band gives ready access to the main Coniston Fell ridge and all the Coniston Fells are readily accessible from that point.

BLEAKLOW HEAD

20. *Sheet 102. Reference 093959. Derbyshire. 2060 feet.*

BLEAKLOW STONES

21. *Sheet 102. Reference 115964. Derbyshire. 2060 feet.*

These two summits are the highest points on the Bleaklow plateau. Said by some to be the only true desert in England, this area, although within four miles of the town of Glossop and even nearer to the main roads which pass north and south of it, can be a very wild and remote place. Those who venture on it need to take all the precautions associated with a mountain walk.

Bleaklow Head lies on the Pennine Way and the obvious route to it is to follow the Way from 088929 on the Snake Road (A.57) between Glossop and Sheffield or from 057980 on the B.6105 road between Glossop and the Woodhead Reservoir. Bleaklow Stones is 1¾ miles east-north-east of Bleaklow Head across the almost level plateau so that a return trip to both summits can be accomplished by the Pennine Way route in a little over three hours provided conditions are reasonably dry.

A more enjoyable and, if anything, shorter route would be to walk from the Snake road via Higher Shelf Stones as described in the entry for that summit, while a more extensive and spectacular route would be to approach from the Derwent reservoir. The latter is attractive in that it provides views of the rocks on the eastern edge of the plateau and an alternative return route. Starting from the road at 154927, where the river Westend runs into the westernmost point of the reservoir, a good forestry track can be followed, crossing the river by a bridge at 145936 and continuing to the open moor at 137948, Grinah Stones, an impressive sight, come into view for a brief spell soon after the bridge is crossed and again when the open moor is reached. From that point a narrow but well worn track runs up the east side of the stream to a crossing point marked by three posts high on the opposite bank. At this point it is best to leave the indistinct path which continues high on the west bank of the stream and climb to the top of the slope when Grinah Stones will again come into view. It is then merely a question of heading directly for Grinah Stones. At that point a well-worn path can be picked up running along the southern slope of the plateau for a distance of 1¾ miles to Bleaklow Stones, with Bleaklow Head 1¾ miles further on. Energetic walkers in good condition would no doubt be able to reach Higher Shelf Stones, another mile further on, before returning across the summit to Bleaklow Stones. From that point an east-north-east course should be set for Barrow Stones, descending from there to the Derwent just below its junction with Barrow Clough (142977), where there is a convenient crossing, and following the Derwent past Deer Holes and Slippery Stones to the reservoir and back to the starting point. The path is very wet at first but there is a broad track which can be followed after the first mile or so. About six hours should suffice for the walk with nearly another hour for the extension to Higher Shelf Stones. It could be walked in the reverse direction, an attractive proposition in one way because of the greater facilities for parking at the northern end of the reservoir, but the Westend starting point gives quicker access to the open moorland.

Bleaklow Stones, the most easterly summit in England, is a fine wild summit with a trident block of rocks at the top which makes a cairn superfluous. There is a well-shaped anvil in stone alongside and a number of other outcrops. The trident stones were disfigured by an early vandal in 1859 and acquired a few more marks in 1926 and 1965. It is to be hoped that these unfortunate examples will not be repeated.

There is not the same scope for vandals at Bleaklow Head, one of the highest points there being marked by a wooden post and the other by a cairn of moderate size.

BLENCATHRA

See SADDLEBACK

BLOODYBUSH EDGE

22. *Sheets 70 and 71. Reference 902144. Northumberland. 2001 feet.*

Bloodybush Edge is a round, green hill four miles south of The Cheviot and 2½ miles south-east of the Scottish border. The origins

BLEAKLOW STONES (Peak). Anvil

BLEAKLOW STONES (Peak). (*above*) Grinah Stones and (*below*) Trident

of the name are obscure. There is no 'edge' as understood by those who frequent the Lakes or the Peak District and no bush, but the proximity of the border is no doubt a guarantee that there has at some time been bloodshed.

The key to the approach to Bloodybush Edge is the ancient settlement of Alwinton, formerly a look-out post set up by the Percy family to give warning of raids across the border. It is in the lovely valley of the Coquet in an area of little used minor roads. Those who wish to tackle Bloodybush Edge in a day's excursion must first get to Alwinton and then proceed along a further ten miles of minor roads to Uswayford or take the minor road which crosses the river Alwin just east of Alwinton at 925063 and follow the Alwin valley for about five miles to Heigh (918117). Heigh is a remote, uninhabited spot, but the road is much better than would appear from the map.

Uswayford, which is in some ways more remote than Heigh, although with one or two dwellings, gives the shortest route to the summit. The path running south-east from the farm should be followed for about a quarter of a mile and a direct approach almost east from that point brings one to the summit in about forty-five minutes.

Heigh, although a little further away, is a better starting point as it gives the opportunity of a round trip taking in the Cushat Law summit. The route starts up the Yoke Burn and it is then a question of making use of a selection of forestry tracks until the open summit of Cushat Law is reached. It was certainly open in 1968 but the conifers were closing in and may well soon cover the whole area. From the Cushat Law summit it is merely a question of descending the north-western slopes and then keeping to the wire fence which runs west to Bloodybush Edge. Just over two hours will be required from Heigh. Anemones are plentiful on the grassy slopes in spring and the summit is marked by a trig point near a gate in the wire fence.

The direct return to Heigh, going due north down the slope to join the path from Uswayford, would not require more than one hour. Those with time to spare would be well advised to descend in a westerly direction to Uswayford and to continue beyond there to explore the Usway Burn and perhaps to walk to Windygyle. About seven hours should suffice for the round trip from Heigh to Windygyle, a magnificent walk in wild and beautiful country on which one may well not meet another soul—except, perhaps, the farmer at Uswayford.

BOW FELL

23. *Sheet 82.* Reference 245064. Cumberland/Westmorland. 2960 feet.*
24. *Subsidiary summits at 245069. 2800 feet.*
25. *245067. 2850 feet.*

Bow Fell forms part of that tremendous horse-shoe shaped ridge which starts at Sca Fell and goes round to Crinkle Crags. One is tempted by the outline on the Bartholomews map to plan a complete circuit but it would in some ways be a mistake to do so as there is far too much to see in a single day. Even so, Bow Fell suffers from the disadvantage of being regarded as a stepping stone to the peaks to the north or south of it rather than something to be ascended for itself alone.

It is readily accessible from Wasdale or Borrowdale by Esk Hause; by a longer but more beautiful walk up Eskdale by the Lingcove Beck route to Three Tarns; from Langdale by Rossett Gill or Hell Gill or, more directly, by The Band; or from the Wrynose Pass over Cold Pike and Crinkle Crags. The Crinkle Crag route from Wrynose is to be preferred since it avoids 1000 feet of ascent and descent as compared with the route from Langdale, thus providing more time to enjoy the walk on the summits.

There is convenient parking space slightly west of the highest point on the Wrynose Pass and the route strikes off on the north side of the road about point 275027, turning left to Cold Pike at a point south of Red Tarn and proceeding directly from Cold Pike to the first of the five Crinkle Crags. The route continues over the Crinkle Crags and Shelter Crags past Three Tarns to a sharp ascent to the Bow Fell summit, returning the same way. Two and a half hours should suffice for the outward journey and $1\frac{1}{2}$ for the return, but the attraction of the summit ridge on a fine day will no doubt impose some delay. For the most direct ascent from Langdale via The Band $3\frac{1}{4}$ hours should be allowed with a little over one hour for the return. Need one say more in justification of a preference for the Wrynose route?

Bow Fell's southern slopes seem to get much more attention than those to the north, possibly because the main access routes are from the south. An alternative explanation may be that the nature of the northern side is such as to prevent the hammering out of a clear path. Certainly one gains the impression that Bow Fell is much rougher than the main Scafell Pikes summit and that it is walked very much less frequently. Its main cairn, and also that on the northernmost summit, are very small affairs, particularly when account is taken of the readily available supply of building material.

Those who continue to the subsidiary summits will be well rewarded. The first of them has a much better cairn than the main summit, its main feature being two large slabs of rock placed like a pair of wings, and it provides a good view of that enormous inclined slab nearer the main summit which one observer has described as being 'the size of two football pitches'. This may be an overstatement, but the view is certainly impressive.

BOWSCALE FELL

26. *Sheet 83.* Reference 333306. Cumberland. 2306 feet.*
27. *Subsidiary summit at 340310. 2200 feet.*

Bowscale Fell lies due west of Mungrisdale on the north-east side of Blencathra. The footpath from the inn in Mungrisdale, which runs due west along the valley of the Glenderamackin and then ascends along the southern edge of The Tongue, is the obvious route of ascent. Leaving the path at its highest point (332302) the main summit lies a quarter of a mile to the north and the cairn marking the secondary summit a further half mile to the north-east. Time from Mungrisdale should be about 1¾ hours. The walk can conveniently be extended to Bannerdale Crags by returning to 332302 and then proceeding in a south-easterly direction.

BRAM RIGG TOP

28. *Sheet 89. Reference 668966. Yorkshire (W.R.). 2200 feet.*

Everyone has heard of the Pennines, the Lakes, the Cheviots, the Peak District and Dartmoor, but how many have heard of the Howgills, those fells which lie north of Sedbergh, shared between the West Riding of Yorkshire and Westmorland, and forming part neither of the Pennines nor the Lakes? They are quite different from the Lakeland and Pennine hills, their smooth, round, green tops unbroken by stone walls being much more akin to the Cheviots. From being relatively unknown, because of the construction of the M.6 motorway on their western side, they may soon become the best known mountain view in England. From the M.6, or preferably the Tebay–Sedbergh road where there is less traffic, they present a very imposing spectacle.

Bram Rigg is one of them. Its name means the broom or bramble ridge, but it is now covered in grass. There is a direct line of ascent from 636945 on the minor road running from Sedbergh, between the river Lune and the Howgills, to join the A.685 about 2½ miles south of Tebay. This route takes one across the Bram Rigg Beck on to the Bram Rigg ridge which ends at the summit—a rather disappointing top, without cairn or trig point.

The path continues from Bram Rigg Top south to the Calders summit at 671960, then descending to the south over Arant Haw and Winder to regain the Sedbergh–Tebay road at 642930, about a mile south of the starting point. A much better return trip, and a mile shorter than the Calders route, is to go north to the trig point on The Calf (667971), the highest point of the Howgill Fells. Looking back to Bram Rigg Top one sees it from a more favourable angle and can admire its lines against the sky before continuing to the north-west and then following the path down White Fell to the cross-roads at 633958, a mile north of the starting point. This shorter round trip should take about 2½ hours.

Such a walk may be adequate if one has only limited time available but it is a waste of effort to limit one's walking on the top of the Howgills to the short stretch between Bram Rigg Top and White Fell. From a distance the Howgills appear to be a succession of rounded hills separated by steep valleys, but closer inspection reveals that it is possible to walk nine of their eleven summits with only one short stretch below the 2000-foot mark. Fell Head and Great Dummacks are the two end points and, as they are separated by a distance of only three miles, one could ascend by any of the routes already mentioned and, at the expense of retracing one's steps, cover the stretch between Fell Head and Great Dummacks and return to the starting point within the space of five hours. A better plan would be to take the old 'green road' which starts by the stream at 633966 along the Sedbergh–Tebay road and passes behind Beck Houses to the open fell on Whins End. Leaving the path at about 640976 gives a moderately steep rise to the flat top of Fell Head. This must be crossed to the county boundary by the cairn at 655986 and a south-easterly course followed down the dip and up to Bush Howe, White Fell, The Calf, Bram Rigg Top and Calders. Great Dummocks is then about half a mile to the north-east. For the return it is best to retrace one's steps to The Calf and proceed down the White Fell path to the cross-roads at 633958 less than a mile from the starting point. This is a very pleasant descent, the roar of the stream and a peculiar crunch of the grass on the path may well be the only sounds to be heard. About 4½ hours should suffice for the round trip.

BRANDRETH

29. *Sheet 82.* Reference 218119. Cumberland. 2344 feet.*

Brandreth lies on the direct route between the top of the Honister Pass and Great Gable and is taken in their stride by the many walkers who use this route for the comparatively easy access it gives to the higher peaks. Nevertheless, it is worthy of an excursion for the views it provides of Ennerdale, Buttermere and the Gable and Sca Fell peaks. Allow about one hour from the top of the Honister Pass.

BRANSTREE

30. *Sheet 83.* Reference 478100. Westmorland. 2333 feet.*

This summit is not named on the 1-inch Ordnance Survey, which merely names Artle Crag on its north-east face. However, the Bartholomew's Map uses the name Branstree, as also does Baddeley's Guide, and this seems an adequate reason for departing from the normal practice of using only Ordnance Survey names.

The most direct ascent is from the road which runs to the southern end of Haweswater. Follow the path which goes over the Gatescarth Pass to Longsleddale, striking off to the north-east from its highest point. A small cairn marks the summit, the more striking cairn being that above Artle Crag which is to the north-east. Little more than one hour should be required for the walk and it can be extended in a southerly direction to Tarn Crag and Grey Crag, giving fine views into Mosedale and Longsleddale. Return to Mardale can be achieved by following the ridge from Branstree over Selside Pike and Selside End to the Old Corpse Road which strikes the main valley road at 480118.

BRAYDON CRAG

31. *Sheets 70 and 71. Reference 894215. Northumberland. 2353 feet.*

Braydon Crag, the most northerly summit in England, is one of five subsidiary summits around the central Cheviot plateau. Routes to the plateau are described under the entry for Auchope Cairn and it is only necessary to add that Braydon Crag is about 1½ miles due north of the southern Auchope Cairn summit and can be reached by keeping to the western edge of the plateau, thus avoiding the wet bog. Braydon Crag is the recommended point for starting the return to the College Valley.

Near the summit, which is marked by a cairn, there is a monument in the shape of an aeroplane propeller to the service of the U.S. Air Force in the years 1942–45. Parts of wrecked aircraft are to be seen near Braydon Crag and Auchope Cairn.

BRIM FELL

32. *Sheet 88.* Reference 271985. Lancashire. 2600 feet.*

Brim Fell is one of the Coniston Fells and is the summit next to the Old Man of Coniston on that lovely ridge which runs north from the Old Man to the Three Shire Stone on Wrynose Pass. There are five summits on the ridge spread over a distance of 2½ miles, so that anyone getting on the ridge can easily walk the length of it, although many of those ascending the Old Man by one of the direct routes to that summit may not be interested in proceeding further.

Apart from the direct routes to the Old Man, the ridge can be reached from the head of the Wrynose Pass (276027); from Coniston by way of Church Beck to Levers Water and then either by the path on the left side to 271996 or by the path on the right to Swirl How; from the Duddon Valley by way of Cockley Beck (247017) and Grey Friar or by way of Seathwaite Tarn to meet the westerly path from Levers Water; or from the Walna Scar Road to Brim Fell. 'Road' is a misleading term for this route from Coniston to just above Seathwaite in Dunnerdale. 'Pass' might be a better description, but Lancastrians use the term 'road' to cover a wider range of circumstances than usual and those who use it should understand that it is not suitable for four-wheeled vehicles beyond 288971 at the Coniston end or beyond the entrance to Seathwaite Reservoir at the Duddon end. Between these points it is a pleasant grassy track apart from a little competition with quarry traffic at the Coniston end. The path to Brim Fell leaves the road at 274966 and proceeds north-west, skirting Goat's Water and heading for the col between Brim Fell and Dow Crag. A right turn at the col takes one north-east to the large untidy heap of stones which marks the Brim Fell summit.

Alternatively, one could leave the Walna Scar Road at 258966 and approach Brim Fell by way of Brown Pike and Dow Crag. This might well appeal to those starting from the Duddon valley, although the path by Goat's Water will usually be preferred by those starting from Coniston.

Having reached Brim Fell and perhaps walked the ridge, the return journey to either Coniston or Duddon can follow the Walna Scar Road or make use of one of the alternative routes already listed for the ascent.

BROAD CRAG

33. *Sheet 82.* Reference 219076. Cumberland. 3050 feet.*

Broad Crag lies about 600 yards north-east of Scafell Pikes on the route to the summit from Esk Hause. Because of its proximity to the main summit it is given scant attention by most of those who travel the route from Esk Hause. In any other location it would be considered worthy of a special journey, but for the walker who has slogged up to that altitude and sees the steep rise to the main summit ahead, the prospect of a scramble over the hundred yards of rough rocks which lead to the Broad Crag summit is unwelcome. However, the diversion makes a useful break from the steady slog along the path and involves no hardship to the seasoned fell-walker who is prepared to use his hands and watch his step. There is no question of bounding from boulder to boulder as on the north-west face of Cross Fell. Broad Crag has sharp edged rocks and their size is not always an indication that they are stable. This gives one a feel of being in virgin territory, particularly when on the south-western side.

In 1971 the summit cairn, when seen from some angles, bore a remarkable resemblance to a square-nosed baboon. Unfortunately, some vandal has now reduced it to the usual standard heap of stones.

BROWN HOWE

34. *Sheet 83.* Reference 462083. Westmorland. 2300 feet.*

Brown Howe lies on the ridge running south from Mardale Harter Fell to Kentmere Pike and Goat Scar. A minor hump, it has no significance other than that of a link between other points on the ridge, but the whole amounts to a very pleasant walk with good views. There are a few wet patches but the going is easy.

From the main summit of Harter Fell the walk to Brown Howe takes twenty minutes and a further twenty minutes is required to reach Goat Scar, the best viewpoint over Longsleddale.

BROWN PIKE

35. *Sheet 88.* Reference 262967. Lancashire. 2237 feet.*

Brown Pike is the summit just west of the Old Man of Coniston on the six-mile ridge which branches from the main Coniston Fells at Brim Fell to provide the magnificent precipices of Dow Crag and gradually descend to Stickle Pike above Ulpha. There is easy access from the Walna Scar Road which runs from Coniston to just above Seathwaite in Dunnerdale, not, it should be noted, the wettest place in England. This distinction is reserved for the Seathwaite in Borrowdale.

The path to Brown Pike leaves the road at its highest point just west of the small but strongly built stone shelter which, although perhaps not sufficient for more than one person, would at least provide a welcome shelter for a short period. Compared with the leisurely ascent on the grassy track which is the Walna Scar road the final ascent seems very steep. The summit seems to be one huge cairn and a shelter on the steep eastern slope provides good views of Coniston Water and the country to the south. From this point one can continue along the ridge over Buck Pike to Dow Crag and thence to Brim Fell and the remainder of the Coniston Fells.

Those starting from Dunnerdale who wish to avoid returning by the same route can readily do so by proceeding from Brown Pike over Dow Crag to return by way of Seathwaite Tarn. More energetic walkers could continue over Dow Crag to Brim Fell and Swirl How returning either by way of Grey Friar and Cockley Beck or over Great Carrs to the Three Shire Stone on Wrynose Pass. Those starting from Coniston could return by way of Goat's Water or over the Old Man of Coniston.

The ascent of Brown Pike from the end of the well-paved road takes about 1½ hours from the Coniston side and slightly less from the Duddon side.

BUCKDEN PIKE

36. *Sheet 90. Reference 961788. Yorkshire N.R./W.R. 2302 feet.*

Rising at the back of Buckden in Wharfedale this summit, whose name means the hill over the valley of the bucks, can be reached along the North/West Riding boundary either from 945806 on the road from Buckden up Bishopdale to West Burton or from 986757 on the road from Kettlewell to Wensley. The Bishopdale route is much drier than the alternative, although it provides a somewhat sharper ascent, and should take about one hour, while the walk from the Kettlewell–Wensley road takes about 1½ hours. The latter route is easy going apart from the patches of bog which are encountered when one reaches the wall which runs over Tor Mere Top to the summit. Buckden Pike is marked by a cairn and a trig point, but they lie on the west side of the wall and are not visible if one approaches by the path running along the east side.

There must be magnificent views from the summit on a clear

day. My own visit coincided with hazy weather and I got no more than a brief hint of what the view of Langstrothdale could be.

BULLMAN HILLS

37. *Sheet 83. Reference 707374. Cumberland. 2002 feet.*
38. *Subsidiary summit at 704371. 2000 feet.*

These lie two miles north-north-east of Cross Fell. They can most easily be approached by following the Pennine Way from Garrigill and turning west across the Cash Burn at 715366.

There was little evidence of walkers on these hills in the summer of 1968. They are perhaps too insignificant and too far off the main route to Cross Fell to attract attention, but they make a pleasant excursion and provide good views to the north. For those who approach them from Cross Fell their green colour presents a sharp contrast to the grim summit of the higher mountain. Time from Garrigill would be about 2¼ hours, allowing for the crossing of the burn.

BURNHOPE SEAT

39. *Sheet 84. Reference 786376. Cumberland. 2452 feet.*

There is an easy ascent to Burnhope Seat from Darngill Bridge (774371) on the road between Alston and Middleton-in-Teesdale (B.6277). Little more than half an hour is required and the walk can conveniently be extended to include the summit of Yad Moss lying less than half a mile to the west. A further extension can be made along the ridge which runs north to Knoutberry Hill, a distance of about three miles. Although the two ends of this ridge are very boggy, there is good firm walking in between.

An alternative, but longer, approach is to take the track which leaves the B.6277 road at 814351 passing the neglected buildings of Grass Hill farm and continuing to the edge of Scaud Hill. From this point a flat boggy area must be negotiated and a compass will probably be required, but 1½ hours should bring one to the summit.

Burnhope Seat has a trig point slightly east of the summit, built on a large concrete base about a yard high with steps to the platform. The surveyors who had it erected may well have feared that a stone of the normal size would disappear in the bog! It is placed just on the Durham side of the county boundary at an altitude of 2449 feet and is thus the highest point in Durham.

BURTREE FELL

40. *Sheet 84. Reference 863433. Durham/Northumberland. 2000 feet.*

Burtree Fell lies east of the B.6295 road between Weardale and Allenheads. On the map the name is hidden down the south-west slope away from the summit. However, it is the nearest name and even nearer to the trig point at 868430 which, on the 1964 edition, was surrounded by a 2000-foot contour mark and thus qualified as a separate summit. A very rare example of an error on the part of the Ordnance Survey, which they corrected in the 1969 edition.

There is convenient parking space near the county boundary on the B.6295 road and a short walk almost due east along first a wall, then a wire fence and then a broken wall, brings one to the summit in the space of about ten minutes. The going along the wall is good but it is marshy further on and there is nothing to mark the actual summit.

From the summit one can see the trig point at 868430, but the area between is very wet with a number of small pools and not to be recommended. Those wishing for an extended walk would be better advised to take the route which runs south-west from 858432, below the flat top of this wild moorland.

BUSH HOWE

41. *Sheet 89. Reference 659981. Westmorland/Yorkshire (W.R.). 2000 feet.*
42. *Subsidiary summits at 660979. 2000 feet.*
43. *662978. 2000 feet.*

Bush Howe is one of the Howgill fells already referred to under the entry for Bram Rigg Top. There is a steep dip between the eastern end of Fell Head and the first of the summits of Bush Howe. This first rounded top, therefore, cannot be mistaken but the two subsidiary tops which lie on the ridge further south could easily be overlooked. The going is firm and the grass short—in fact ideal walking country.

CALDERS

44. *Sheet 89. Reference 670961. Yorkshire (W.R.) 2200 feet.*

Calders, another of the Howgill Fells, lies at the south-western end of the ridge which runs down from Bush Howe. The going is easy all the way and the walk from Bush Howe over The Calf and Bram Rigg Top should not take much more than half an hour. A moderately sized cairn marks the summit.

THE CALF

45. *Sheet 89. Reference 667971. Westmorland/Yorkshire (W.R.). 2219 feet.*

This is the highest of the Howgill fells but, apart from being the only one with a trig point, it has no distinguishing features. It is about thirty minutes' walk from Fell Head but could also be reached by paths which run up to White Fell, Bram Rigg Top or Calders from the minor road which runs from Sedbergh to Howgill. Those with limited time available will naturally find the round trip described under the Bram Rigg Top entry the preferable approach to The Calf, but those with more time to spare may be interested in the Bowderdale route. A minor road turns off southwards from the Kendal–Barnard Castle road (A.685) at 687055 and after a mile leads to a track going south past Bowderdale farm just east of the Bowderdale Beck. After crossing the stream it follows the valley up to the west of Yarlside at 678990 and then climbs fairly steeply to the central plateau of the Howgills, crossing it north of The Calf to descend by the White Fell ridge. As long as the weather is clear there should be no difficulty in deviating from the path at about 671975 to reach the trig point.

For the return journey, and to make the trip really worth while, a course should be set for 687982, the southern end of Yarlside, across the watershed between Bowderdale and Cautley Spout. This spot will give good views of the waterfall and a northerly course from there over Yarlside, Kensgriff and Randygill Top brings one down to the track at 677036 which leads back to the minor road off the A.685. The return journey includes a number of steep ascents and descents such as one would expect when one surveys the Howgills from a distance but the round trip should not take more than 5½ hours. Those who are really energetic, therefore, could undertake an extension from The Calf to embrace the high level walk between Great Dummocks and Fell Head and still get back to the starting point in under eight hours. Such would be well advised to reverse the Bowderdale part of the route so as to cover the undulations early in the day and reserve the smooth valley walk for the evening.

A shorter and more spectacular route would be to combine the ascent to The Calf with a walk up Cautley Spout. The path on the east side of the stream is quite steep but by going as far as the watershed with Bowderdale before turning west-south-west to The

Calf, then continuing over Bram Rigg Top and Great Dummocks with a wide sweep round the southern end of Cautley Crag, one could avoid the worst of the slope and complete a very interesting circuit in about three hours. An additional attraction of this route is that it enables one to make use of the good parking facilities available on the Sedbergh–Kirby Stephen road (A.683) near the path to Cautley Spout at 698969.

CALFHOW PIKE

46. *Sheet 83.* Reference 331211. Cumberland. 2166 feet.*

Calfhow Pike forms part of that magnificent ridge which runs for about seven miles from the Penrith–Keswick road to Dollywaggon Pike above Grasmere. There is good firm walking all the way and, while there may be the usual throng on Helvellyn, there is likely to be little competition for space further north.

Access to the northern end of the ridge is provided by a path from Hill Top Farm at 319232 which ascends in a very steep rise west of Clough Head. From that point, on a clear day, the route presents no problem, Calfhow Pike lying about one mile due south of Clough Head. Allow just under 1½ hours to get to Clough Head from the road and twenty minutes more to get to Calfhow Pike.

There is a path from Calfhow Pike to the Old Coach Road which runs around the north-eastern end of the ridge from Keswick to Dockray, but most walkers will probably wish to continue over Great Dodd and Stybarrow Dodd to descend by the Sticks Pass or, if they have convenient transport or accommodation in Grasmere, to carry on across the Sticks Pass and over Helvellyn to descend to the Grasmere road by Grisedale Tarn. Three and a half hours is required for the walk from Calfhow Pike via Sticks Pass and back through the Vale of St. John to the starting point near Hill Top Farm, and 4½ to 5 hours for the walk to Grasmere.

CAM CRAG

47. *Sheet 82.* Reference 257114. Cumberland. 2000 feet.*

Cam Crag lies one mile north-east of the main summit of Glaramara and it is convenient to use the name for the summit which stands above it to the west. The most direct ascent is from Stonethwaite (264137) by the path which runs to Tarn at Leaves (258123). From this point there is no recognised path but, by striking due south and keeping to the east side of Dovenest Crag, the summit can be reached in about 1½ hours. A clear day is essential.

By continuing in the same direction and contouring east of the crags at 255109 the main summit of Glaramara can be reached in a further forty minutes.

CARL SIDE

48. *Sheet 82.* Reference 255282. Cumberland. 2400 feet.*

Carl Side lies south-west of Skiddaw and is perhaps the best route of ascent for that mountain. From 256262 on the minor road which runs from the A.591 to Millbeck a footpath strikes in a northerly direction, bearing left at 257265 to ascend the south face. The going is firm and steep until the summit plateau and there is an interesting patch of white rock on the way and the views to the south can be magnificent. After a rest by the rocks at the summit to admire the grim slopes of Skiddaw, the walk can be continued on the narrow ridge which leads to Ullock Pike (244289) or directly to the south end of the Skiddaw summit ridge. Rather more than an hour is required for the walk to and from Ullock Pike but it provides such good views that even those continuing on to the main Skiddaw summit, which is less than an hour from Carl Side, should try to include it.

This direct ascent from Millbeck takes about 1¾ hours and there are alternative, and slightly longer, routes, using the forest road through Dodd Wood or following Mill Beck to the col between Carl Side and Skiddaw. Millbeck has the advantage of being the nearest point for anyone returning from Skiddaw down the south-east ridge but those who are not interested in this route might well consider the alternative of ascending from the north by way of Ullock Pike and Longside Edge. Paths leading to the ridge start from 235297 on the Keswick–Carlisle road (A.591) or from 236310 on the minor road running through Orthwaite to Caldbeck, the former involving a walk of about 2¼ hours and the latter one of 2½ hours to reach Carl Side.

CARROCK FELL

49. *Sheet 83.* Reference 342337. Cumberland. 2174 feet.*

Lying a few miles north of the Blencathra group, Carrock Fell is unusual among Lakeland summits because it carries the ruins of a hill fort. There is a reasonable route of ascent from the valley of the Caldew about a quarter of a mile west of the main road at Mosedale. At first the path is obscured by heather but the green line of it is clearly visible beyond and the only difficulty is the patch of scree about half-way up the steep part of the slope. There is a somewhat monotonous walk through the heather when the slope eases and the summit is not readily recognisable from this direction. Once the summit is reached the remains of the ancient hill fort are clearly recognisable and the summit itself is marked by a well-built high cairn. One and a quarter hours should suffice to reach the summit from the Caldew valley and the walk can be continued over Miton or Milton Hill (according to whether one uses the Keswick or Penrith sheet of the Ordnance Survey) and on to the Caldbeck Fells. The return may be made by descending just east of High Pike to the mine track which runs back via Colebrack or, preferably, down the beautiful Grainsgill Beck which flows into the Caldew at 327327. These latter routes can, of course, be used for the ascent but the quick ascent will generally be considered preferable.

CATSTYE CAM

50. *Sheet 83.* Reference 347158. Westmorland. 2917 feet.*

Catstye Cam lies just north of the route from Helvellyn to Patterdale which descends by Swirral Edge. Instead of following the path from Swirral Edge to the eastern end of Red Tarn one continues in a north-easterly direction up the slope and the summit is reached in a matter of a few minutes.

Alternatively, anyone wishing to avoid the popular Striding Edge route for the ascent of Helvellyn could take the Glenridding path past Greenside Mine and up Red Tarn Beck, climbing up the east slope of Catstye Cam and then proceeding by way of Swirral Edge. The ascent from Glenridding to the Catstye Cam summit would take about 2½ hours. The summit is a good viewpoint and its lovely conical shape makes it a well-known landmark.

CAUDALE HEAD

51. *Sheet 83.* Reference 413100. Westmorland. 2474 feet.*

Motorists driving south from Patterdale up the Kirkstone Pass, particularly in misty weather, may see an impressive mass of crags on the left-hand side. On looking at the map the name which makes the biggest impact is John Bell's Banner, but more detailed examination shows that the nearest summit is Caudale Head, immediately above the crags.

A path just north of the Kirkstone Inn strikes up the rocks of St. Raven's Edge, then follows the Edge roughly due north, and then bends slightly to the east over Pike How up the slopes of John Bell's Banner. At the point where it bends in an arc, about

414097, to go due east to Stony Cove Pike, the main summit of John Bell's Banner, those going to Caudale Head should continue due north to the cairn. It is west of the tarns and located on the slightly higher ground south of the crags.

The walk takes little more than an hour from the Kirkstone Inn and an obvious extension is to continue to Stony Cove Pike (418099) and then either north down the ridge to Hartsop Dod (412118) or east to Thornthwaite Crag and High Street. One could easily descend from Hartsop Dod to return up the Kirkstone road, but few will want to face the traffic and it is far better to retrace one's steps and enjoy the views from the higher ground.

CAUSEY PIKE

52. *Sheet 82.* Reference 218208. Cumberland. 2000 feet.*

'Causey' is said to mean the hill with a paved way. There is certainly a solid rocky path in the final stages of the walk to the summit, but the same may be connected with the fact that Causey Pike is the first summit on a high level ridge walk, one of the finest such walks in England.

Few who have seen the rounded hump which forms the summit will fail to recognise it whenever, and from whatever angle, it comes into view. Its popularity is perhaps best illustrated by the variation on the old folk song:

> Can she climb up Causey Pike?
> My Billy Boy.
> She can climb up Causey Pike
> Aye, and do it on a bike
> She can climb up Causey Pike
> My Billy Boy.

Some regular visitors to Keswick look on it as a reasonable Sunday morning stroll, but it is a mistake to go to the effort of reaching the summit without continuing on the ridge. There is convenient parking for one or two cars at the eastern end of Rowling End in the Newlands Valley and an initial sharp rise leads to the more gentle slope of the Rowling End ridge, followed by another steep rise to the summit. All points of the compass provide magnificent views from the summit on a clear day and the ascent from the Newlands valley should be accomplished in little over an hour.

From the summit the ridge runs slightly south of west over Scar Crags on to Sail, Crag Hill and Eel Crag. Then, after a rocky scramble down to Coledale House, and perhaps a paddle in the Coledale Beck, it can be continued over Grisedale Pike and down the ridge to Braithwaite, leaving a two-mile walk up the Newlands valley to get back to the starting point. About 3½ hours would be required, making about 4½ in all for the complete circuit. This, of course, is for those who do not linger for too long on the way. With views such as are encountered on this circuit much more time could be taken and, for the more energetic, the walk could be extended from Crag Hill to include Wanlope and Whiteless Pike with their fine views of Buttermere and Crummock. Grasmoor and Hopegill Head could also be fitted in, but there comes a time on a walk such as this when one gazes around at the magnificent panorama the area affords and decides that there is no point in going further until the time comes to return to civilisation.

The walk down from Grisedale Pike provides magnificent views of Skiddaw and, if one goes to the road which runs through Millbeck below Skiddaw, one can see at a glance the whole circuit from Causey Pike to Grisedale Pike. It makes a fine photograph.

CAW FELL

53. *Sheet 82.* Reference 132109. Cumberland. 2288 feet.*

This is one of the more remote Lakeland summits. The map shows the name against a spot height of 2187 feet at 123107 but, since this does not come within the definition of a summit, the name has been used for the higher point lying east-north-east about half a mile distant.

From the map the walk does not look particularly attractive. If one includes it in a wide circuit from Pillar and Haycock, Caw Fell comes as very much of an anti-climax and the approach from Ennerdale is to be preferred. From the western end of the lake a footpath runs along the southern shore for about half a mile and then leads to the top of Anglers Crag. A steep climb takes one to the imposing rocks which grace the skyline above the lake and, proceeding in a southerly direction, a steep scree slope leads to Crag Fell. Continuing south-east across the old mine track and up the long ridge brings one to Iron Crag (123119), a convenient halting place with fine views of Pillar and the Buttermere Fells.

A south-westerly route from Iron Crag, skirting round the top of Silvercove Beck, leads to an easy ascent to the summit of Caw Fell. It is a quiet, pleasant spot with interesting, although not spectacular views and a moderate cairn. The descent down Silvercove Beck to Ennerdale, however, although a little wet in places, is a fine experience. In its lower reaches the stream is very beautiful and there is an attractive waterfall just before the forest is reached.

The starting point can be regained either by walking along the southern shore or crossing the valley to the forest road which runs along the north side of the lake to Beckfoot and then taking the path which follows the shore, past the site of the Anglers' Inn. A round trip takes about 5½ or 5 hours according to whether the return is by the northern or southern side of the lake.

CHAPELFELL TOP

54. *Sheet 84. Reference 875346. Durham. 2250 feet.*

This is wild and desolate, wet and very boggy and, although the distance from the nearest road to the summit is only one mile, it is not a walk to be recommended. There is convenient parking space just before the quarry at the highest point of the minor road which runs from Langdon Beck to St. John's Chapel and the direct approach along the highest ground seems to be the obvious course to take. However, the going is very wet until the slope to the summit is reached and even worse on top.

No cairn or post marks the summit, nor is there any sign of any human interest in the place, and, while the bog is bad, it cannot compete with Yockenthwaite or Kinder Scout. Apparently it was formerly part of the hunting grounds of the Bishops of Durham. It is not fit for anything else!

THE CHEVIOT

55. *Sheet 71. Reference 909206. Northumberland. 2676 feet.*
56. *Subsidiary summits at Sheet 70. 891208. 2350 feet.*
57. *Sheet 71. 914208. 2656 feet.*

Details of routes to The Cheviot plateau are given under the entry for Auchope Cairn.

From the cairn at 895194 a walk in wet bog in an easterly direction brings one to Cairn Hill with its covering of short heather and a sandstone shelter on the top. Despite its name and altitude of 2545 feet it does not qualify as a separate summit. From the top, the Pennine Way, not marked in any way at this point, leads east-north-east for three-quarters of a mile to the trig point which marks the summit of The Cheviot. The trig point stands on a small peat hag in the middle of a sea of peat mud and one is forced to wonder how long it will be before the peat hag is worn away and allows the trig point to fall over and bury itself in the slime. A truly depressing spot for the highest point in the beautiful county of Northumberland.

The first subsidiary summit lies two-fifths of a mile to the north-east. It involves a walk through the slime surrounding the main summit to a somewhat drier area and is marked by a large cairn.

From the top, a line of cairns marks the normal route of ascent from Longleeford in the Harthope valley.

The remaining summit is 1½ miles to the west at 891208. There is mud for some distance from the main summit and then tussocky grass. Not the best of walking but the grass is better than the mud! A cairn on the crag marks the summit and gives fine views of Auchope Cairn and the head of the College Valley.

CLOUGH HEAD

58. *Sheet 83.* Reference 334226. Cumberland. 2381 feet.*

Clough Head is the name given to the most northerly summit on that magnificent ridge which runs from just south of the Penrith–Keswick road to Helvellyn and Dollywaggon Pike above Grasmere. There is some doubt about the name as it appears on the map in the clough north-west of the summit while the name White Pike appears on the ridge to the north-east of the summit. On some maps Clough Head is the name nearest to the summit while on others the nearest is White Pike. Clough Head, however, seems the most appropriate name.

The most direct approach is by the lane past Hill Top Farm—actually the Old Coach Road from Keswick to Dockray above Ullswater—which starts from the B.5322 road in St. John's in the Vale at 316231. A footpath starting just beyond the farm goes more or less due east for about half a mile, then turns south-east for another half a mile in a direct line for the summit, and then takes the steep part of the ascent in a line going almost due south, skirting the summit on its west side. The map shows it as continuing almost due south to Calfhow Pike and those heading for the summit at 334226 need to strike almost due east as the slope eases around reference 329224.

The summit is marked by a trig point and there is a useful stone windbreak close by from which there are fine views of Saddleback and the other fells in that group. About one and a half hours should suffice for the ascent from the valley road.

An easier line of ascent, for those who do not wish to extend the excursion down the ridge to the south, is to continue along the old coach road for about 2¾ miles to 351227 where it crosses the Mosedale Beck. From that point a path runs up the beck to the summit of Calfhow Pike, reference 331211, whence an easy walk along the ridge for just over a mile brings one to Clough Head. This route, returning directly from Clough Head down the footpath to Hill Top Farm, would make a round trip of three hours. A satisfactory afternoon's walk, but not to be compared with the magnificent walk south along the ridge towards Helvellyn.

COLD FELL

59. *Sheet 76. Reference 605557. Cumberland. 2041 feet.*

Cold Fell lies on the Pennines about twelve miles due east of Carlisle. It is the most northerly and also the most westerly of the Pennine mountains. To the north of it lie the Tyne Gap, the Roman Wall and nearly fifty miles of rolling country before the summits of the Cheviots are reached. South and east of it are some of the loneliest and wildest of the Pennine moors, the Pennine Way running down the valley of the South Tyne about four miles to the east.

There is no other mountain summit on Sheet 76 of the Ordnance Survey and one gets the feeling that Cold Fell is an outpost on the edge of a foreign land. Lanercost Priory, half a mile from the Scottish border, lies only six miles to the north and has a grim tale to tell of the raids it suffered.

Brampton on the Carlisle–Newcastle road (A.69) is the nearest town and the nearest point on a road is Forest Head four miles to the south-east. From 582575 an indistinct path runs almost due south on the southern side of the cottage garden wall to join what apparently is an old mining road running along the foot of the slope. This road is best followed for about half a mile to the south (581563) before striking up the slope of Brown Fell to the summit of Cold Fell less than two miles away. Access to this road is also available at a number of other points, e.g. Waygill Hill (553570) or Hallbank Gate (580596), but whichever is used, 581563 is the best point for the ascent. There is a large cairn at the summit surmounted by a trig point.

From the summit there are fine views of Grey Nag and Black Fell and all the rolling Pennine moors around them. To the west, the cooling towers of the Chapelcross Atomic Power Station, the Dumfries hills and the Solway estuary are in view and the Cheviots can be seen to the far north. It must be one of the finest viewpoints in the country.

COLD PIKE

60. *Sheet 88.* Reference 264035. Cumberland/Westmorland. 2259 feet.*

Cold Pike lies between the Three Shires Stone on Wrynose Pass and Crinkle Crags. It can also be reached from Great Langdale by taking the path which runs up Oxendale and then turns up Brown Gill, turning west to Cold Pike after passing Red Tarn. From either starting point it should be seen as a stage on a walk over

Crinkle Crags, and perhaps Bow Fell, rather than as an excursion in its own right. The summit is rocky with a number of cairns and it can be as cold as its name suggests.

COLDBERGH EDGE

61. *Sheets 84 and 90. Reference 829053. Westmorland/Yorkshire (N.R.). 2150 feet.*

The nearest approach is from the Kirkby Stephen–Muker road, one of the loveliest routes across the Pennines, and the name is probably strictly only appropriate to the southern escarpment. Since there is no name on the Ordnance Survey sheet against the summit it is convenient to use the name nearest to it, even though the actual summit is a grassy mound.

From point 825034 on Sheet 90, about one mile east of the county boundary, is an easy walk almost due north over gently sloping ground until the escarpment is reached. The only problem is the large expanse of rushes which covers a big area of the lower ground. Two medium-sized granite stones mark the summit which is on a direct line between Birkdale Tarn and the trig point on Nine Standards Rigg, the latter being about three-quarters of a mile distant in a direction slightly west of north.

No one should contemplate returning without proceeding first to Nine Standards Rigg. The going is rather rough, consisting of tufted grass, shallow gullies and bare patches of peat bog, and the excursion may appear a little pointless until the trig point is approached. At this point the standards which give the summit its name appear in view, somewhat like a menacing squad of Daleks on the northern skyline.

It is best to return from Nine Standards Rigg to the road by keeping to the western edge of the main summit until the prominent cairn on the rocky outcrop at about 824057 is reached. From that point the line of the old bridle way should be followed, first more or less due west and then south after passing through the limestone pavement on the eastern slopes of Tailbridge Hill. The going on this route is so easy compared with the traverse of the rushy expanse below the southern slopes that, certainly in wet weather, and possibly in all seasons, it would be preferable to take this route in both directions. The starting point from the road is reference 809043, a little way past the cairn on the north side.

Walking time for the round trip is just under two hours, but something extra should be allowed for a survey of the standards and for admiring the magnificent view to the Lakeland hills on the western horizon. This is at its best at sunset.

COMB FELL

62. *Sheet 71. Reference 919187. Northumberland. 2132 feet.*

Comb Fell lies near the head of the Harthope valley about 1¼ miles south-east of The Cheviot. There is an easy approach from the road which runs from Wooler down the valley of the Harthope Burn to Longleeford. Cars may be parked on the edge of the wood just before the surfaced road ends and a track follows the stream to the head of the valley. From there, a boggy area extends to the top of Comb Fell but there is some semblance of a path which enables it to be traversed without difficulty. The summit is disappointing and better views are obtained from Coldlaw Cairn, lying to the south-west a little below the main summit. From the summit there is an easy walk to the summit of Hedgehope Hill. Two patches of bog have to be traversed on the way up but the going on top is good. The Hedgehope Hill summit is marked by a large cairn on which a trig point is erected.

A direct descent to the Harthope Burn involves fording the stream before the path is regained, but this presents no problem. The round trip should take about 3½ hours but a little extra should be allowed if one wants to linger along the Harthope Linn and watch the trout. It is one of the pleasantest valley walks in this country and on the return to the main road, if the broom is in flower, the stretch which comes into view about 1½ miles beyond Longlee provides one of the finest views. As indicated under the entry for Auchope Cairn, the walk can be combined with an ascent of The Cheviot.

CONISTON OLD MAN

See OLD MAN OF CONISTON.

COOMB HEIGHT

63. *Sheets 82 and 83.* Reference 311327. Cumberland. 2058 feet.*

Coomb Height lies at the back of Skiddaw in the John Peel country. The most direct approach is up the Caldew valley west of Mosedale (point 357323) and then up the ridge which runs down to the junction of the Caldew and Grainsgill Beck. The summit is marked by a small cairn and a post. One and three-quarter hours should suffice for the walk to the summit from Mosedale and it can readily be extended to Knott, one mile further west, to Great Sca Fell three-quarters of a mile north of Knott, to Great Lingy Hill 1¼ miles east of Great Sca Fell, to High Pike one mile north-west of Great Lingy Hill and to Carrock Fell just over 1½ miles east of the midway point between High Pike and Great Lingy Hill.

A round trip of these summits from Mosedale should take about five hours, but the going is wet in places and steering by compass inevitable in the desolate area around Great Sca Fell. However, it is most unlikely that one will meet with other walkers on the way. To some, this will be looked on as a great advantage.

An alternative and equally isolated, although longer, walk would be to take the path from 254337 just below Orthwaite, reaching Coomb Height either over or by the southern slopes of Knott and returning by the path which runs from Great Sca Fell to 276364. The short road walk from there to the starting point would not be too onerous and the round trip would require about 4¼ hours.

CRAG HILL

64. *Sheet 82.* Reference 193204. Cumberland. 2753 feet.*

Crag Hill is on that magnificent ridge walk which is referred to under the entry for Causey Pike. It is at a central point with Sail to the east, Eel Crag to the north, Wanlope to the south and Grasmoor across the head of the valley to the west.

By walking up the Coledale Beck to Coledale Hause and then continuing up the valley which runs to the south for half a mile one could strike the path between Crag Hill and Grasmoor and ascend the former directly. Alternatively, one could reach the same point for a direct ascent by approaching from Buttermere over Whiteless Pike. But these routes are not to be recommended as a first choice when there is such ready access along the ridge. However, the latter route may be preferred by those operating from Buttermere and the former is of interest on days when mist hangs around the ridge in early morning.

Crag Hill has a broad rocky summit with a trig point and beautiful patches of alpine flowers in the early summer.

CRAGDALE MOOR

65. *Sheet 90. Reference 908822. Yorkshire (N.R.). 2050 feet.*

This is rough country and only experienced walkers should tackle it. The shortest approach is from Langstrathdale by way of Deepdale Gill, taking the track through the farm at 893797 up the west side of the gill and continuing due north. After a sharp rise to the cairn on the west of the slope, the stone wall marking the county boundary can be followed to 903822. From here one should head directly for the summit rather than follow the boundary fence in the worst of the bog. The going is through bog broken up by gullies of moderate depth but, by judicious selection of a route, one can get through it without getting wet and then take advantage of the firm hard going along the wall on the far side running towards the summit.

The wall is unusual as, near the summit, it comes to an abrupt end and is replaced by a fence. Possibly the builders ran out of funds or of readily accessible supplies of stone as the ground is quite firm enough to carry a wall. Whatever the reason, the line of the wall and fence is on the West Riding side of the minute cairn which marks the summit. Views from there are of desolate moorland, bare except for the trig point on Yockenthwaite Moor to the south.

An alternative approach is from the old pack horse road which runs from Stalling Busk to the Buckden–West Burton road (B.6160) at 944804. The road is not suitable for cars but provides good walking and Cragdale Moor can be approached from a point about a mile north of the highest point of the road in a route which skirts the edge of the flat, wet plateau.

This route can be continued to Yockenthwaite Moor, about a mile south of the Cragdale Moor summit, the return to the road being effected by the path which runs some distance south of the trig point to join the road at 936816, the end of the stone wall which lines the road up from Bishopdale.

The round trip from Deepdale takes 2½ hours while that from Stalling Busk would require 3½ hours. A round trip from 944804, including Yockenthwaite Moor, would take at least four hours, and possibly more if conditions were wet.

CRINKLE CRAGS

66. *Sheet 88.* Reference 248049. Cumberland/Westmorland. 2816 feet.*

67. *Subsidiary summit at 250046. 2733 feet.*

There are five Crinkles in all but only two of them qualify as separate summits. Routes of ascent are given under the entry for Bow Fell. In addition, the Crinkles can be reached from the top of Hard Knott Pass by skirting the slopes to the west of Mosedale Beck, crossing the head of the valley to Black Crag, and ascending the faint track which strikes off a little to the left. This makes a variation for those who like to have the hills to themselves, but the ascent from Wrynose is quicker—an important factor for those who wish to explore this magnificent ridge walk, perhaps the finest ridge walk in England, to the full.

CROSS FELL

68. *Sheet 83. Reference 688344. Cumberland. 2930 feet.*

Cross Fell, in company with Skiddaw, has the reputation of providing a long, monotonous walk. It is not really warranted. There are routes to cater for all tastes and the ascent of the highest of the Pennines is very worthwhile.

The easiest route uses part of the Pennine Way from Dufton to Garrigill. For the car owner, the walking can be cut to a minimum by driving to the end of the road somewhere near point 716317 on the route from Knock to the radar station on Great Dun Fell. From that point little effort is involved if one can find a dry route and is favoured with tolerable weather, there being an ascent of only 300 feet to Great Dun Fell, a drop and a further ascent of about 200 feet to Little Dun Fell and another drop and an ascent of about 450 feet to Cross Fell. On the way the source of the river Tees is crossed. The round trip back to the car can be accomplished in 2½ hours.

Those who prefer to walk from the valley could take the official Pennine Way route from Dufton, involving a round trip of nearly seven hours, but the preferable route would be to start from Kirkland (646325) and follow the old mining track to 672348, deviating from it at that point to take the path connecting with the Pennine Way north-west of Cross Fell. This route gives an exciting ascent over the rough boulders of Cross Fell's north-west face and the return can be effected by joining the path from Garrigill at about 697339 just above Tees Head. This is directed to Blencarn but there is a short cut to Kirkland about half a mile short of the village. The round trip should not take more than 4¼ hours. Those wanting longer on the high ground could continue from Cross Fell to Great Dun Fell and descend by the path which runs down to Millburn, from which point the return to Kirkland could again make use of the path by-passing Blencarn. Six and a half hours would be required.

A preferable route is from Hartside Cross (reference 647418) on the Alston–Penrith road. This starts one at an altitude of 1903 feet and provides a very pleasant walk in a southerly and then south-easterly direction over Fiend's Fell, Little Knapside Hill, Knapside Hill and Melmerby Fell to Cross Fell. After Melmerby Fell, on a clear day, the map can be dispensed with and a direct approach made to the well-known outline of the hill. Apart from the exciting scramble up the boulders on the north-west face and

BRAM RIGG TOP (Howgills). Howgills from Beacon Hill near Orton

BRAYDON CRAG (Cheviot)

(*overleaf*) FAIRFIELD (Lakes). Deepdale from Cofa Pike

(*above*) FAIRFIELD and HART CRAG (Lakes) seen from Kirkstone Pass

(*below*) FAIRFIELD and HELVELLYN (Lakes)

the long walk at a high level, the attraction of this route is the fact one does not see the radar mast on Great Dun Fell until one reaches the summit.

For the return, the best course is to retrace one's steps to Hartside Cross, giving a total of five hours for the day. But those who have strong objections to this can take a north-easterly course to Garrigill, taking in their stride, if they so desire, the Bullman Hills, Long Man Hill and Pikeman Hill. This will take a total of six hours and the road walk back to Hartside Cross can be avoided by telephoning the Alston garage for a taxi.

Cross Fell's summit is marked by a large cairn and a trig point. Otherwise the plateau, one mile long from east to west, is bleak and desolate, often snow covered, and gives one little inclination to linger. No longer does it carry the cross which gave it its name, erected there by inhabitants of Alston and Garrigill to ward off evil spirits. But it will always be one of the best-known landmarks of the Pennines and, as the highest point of the range, will continue to attract those who admire the high lands of Britain.

CUSHAT LAW

69. *Sheet 71. Reference 928138. Northumberland. 2020 feet.*

Cushat Law means the hill of the wood-pigeons. There were no wood-pigeons there in the spring of 1968 but the plantations of the Forestry Commission were creeping up its grassy slopes towards the cairn which marked the top. Possibly the confers already cover the summit and perhaps in due course we shall find that the wood-pigeons return.

The most convenient route of ascent is from Heigh, reached by the forest road which runs from near Alwinton. It is recorded under the entry for Bloodybush Edge, to which summit the walk can be conveniently extended.

DALE HEAD

70. *Sheet 82.* Reference 224153. Cumberland. 2473 feet.*

Dale Head is one of the Newlands Fells and lies at the head of the Newlands valley. From the head of Honister one could walk due north up the slope and reach the top of Dale Head in a matter of an hour. But no one who has the time and ability to walk the ridge which runs over Cat Bells and Maiden Moor should think of using the Honister approach. The usual route is to start from reference 248213 on the road from Keswick via Portinscale to Grange, walking along the ridge over Cat Bells, Maiden Moor, Eel Crags and round the head of the valley to Dale Head. There are fine views all the way and particularly from Dale Head where Honister and the Buttermere valley come into view. A particularly fine cairn marks the actual summit.

The return journey can be made via the Hindscarth ridge down to the Newlands valley or via Robinson, following the path which runs on the south side of the crags to run down Scope Beck to the west side of the Newlands valley. About five hours should suffice for the round trip via Hindscarth and nearly six hours if Robinson is included.

There is a lot to be said, however, for doing the walk in the reverse direction so as to have the benefit of the views over Derwentwater to Skiddaw on the return journey.

DARNBROOK FELL

71. Sheet 90. Reference 885728. Yorkshire (W.R.). 2048 feet.

Darnbrook Fell does not provide a particularly exciting walk but it lies in a most interesting area with Pen-y-ghent and Ribblesdale to the west, Malham and Gordale to the south and Littondale and Wharfedale to the east. It is a country of lovely green valleys and apart from Pen-y-ghent, flat, grim summits. Those who visit it should look for their main entertainment in the valleys and use Darnbrook Fell and Fountain's Fell, which lies in the same land mass just over a mile to the south-west, for a little gentle exercise.

The obvious line of ascent is by the Pennine Way from 853723 on the road which runs from Stainforth in Ribblesdale to Halton Gill at the head of Littondale. The Pennine Way runs south-east, then east across the north face of Fountain's Fell and is then about a mile from the summit plateau. A slight deviation from the route takes one to the three summits of Fountain's Fell and a more or less level walk of 1½ miles east-north-east of the main summit brings one to Darnbrook Fell. Time from the road for the return trip would be two hours to the main summits of Fountain's Fell and Darnbrook Fell, or three hours if the subsidiary summits of Fountain's Fell are included.

The valleys will speak for themselves, but those who are not familiar with the area can be recommended to see Malham Cove, Gordale Scar, Arncliffe church with its list of the men of Littondale who fought at Flodden, and the rock strata revealed by quarrying in the old Arco Wood quarry in Ribblesdale.

DEAD STONES

72. *Sheet 84. Reference* 794399. *Cumberland/Durham. 2326 feet.*

This summit is in the high rolling country between the heads of Weardale and Teesdale. Burnhope Seat marks the southern end of a ridge which runs north over Dead Stones, Nags Head and Knoutberry Hill to the road which goes up the Weardale valley to Nenthead and Alston. Cumberland and Durham meet on the ridge and the border is marked by a fence which forms a reliable guide to the route. About 50 per cent of the going is boggy but it does not present any real difficulty. Dead Stones is marked by a tall, thin cairn which is not visible from the south until close at hand, although visible for a considerable distance from the north. There is also a stone shelter there, roofed with slabs of the local stone.

Access to the ridge can be obtained from Burnhope Seat or from near Killhope Cross at 800433 on the Alston–St. John's Chapel Road (B.6293). Dead Stones can also be approached directly by taking the rough track which leads off the minor road running from Cowshill to the Burnhope Reservoir at 847396 and walking up the slope, past the trig point at 821400, to the main ridge at the summit of Dead Stones. This approach offers the possibility of a round trip taking in Burnhope Seat, Scaud Hill, Great Stony Hill and returning by the old road which runs east of Great Stony Hill to join the road to Cowshill just above the Burnhope Reservoir. Four hours should suffice.

THE DODD

73. *Sheet 84. Reference 792458. Northumberland. 2013 feet.*

Dodd means a rounded summit. Unfortunately, this does not apply to the summit of this particular Dodd and one has to struggle through bog in fairly deep gullies on an otherwise flat top when looking for it. The highest point is not marked.

This is wild and desolate country and the direct approach from 795445 in continuation of the descent from Killhope Law is very marshy and not to be recommended. However, the path from Coalcleugh (801452) is quite pleasant and one could get to the summit and return within an hour. Those requiring a longer walk could start from Carr Shield (803475) or from the end of the minor road at 786496.

DODD FELL HILL

74. *Sheet 90. Reference 841847. Yorkshire (N.R.). 2189 feet.*

This is more rounded than The Dodd but not so shapely as the Dods, those summits with only two *d*'s lying on the ridge which runs north from Helvellyn. Dodd Fell Hill stands a few miles south of Hawes, overlooking Wensleydale to the north-east and Langstrathdale to the south, and access to it is from the Pennine Way on its course between Hawes and Horton-in-Ribblesdale or from the road which runs between Hawes and Buckden in Wharfedale.

Those who want something shorter than the Pennine Way route should take the Hawes–Buckden road to 861847 and turn off on the Roman Road which is signed to Cam Houses. It strikes the Pennine Way in just over two miles, where there is one of the standard Pennine Way signs, and the easiest route from there to the summit is to follow the Pennine Way for about a mile and then to strike due east to the trig point. As with many of the Pennine trig points it is not seen, particularly when approaching from the south, until one is close at hand. The summit is of rough tussocky grass with patches of bog; hence the advice to make as much use as possible of the Pennine Way which, at this point, is a firm, smooth, green track.

DOLLYWAGGON PIKE

75. *Sheet 83.* Reference 345131. Cumberland/Westmorland. 2810 feet.*

Dollywaggon Pike is just off the route to Helvellyn which ascends from Grasmere by way of Grisedale Hause. It forms the southern end of a magnificent high level walk which runs north for a distance of six miles, the southern part being stony, while the northern part is largely grass. Sheer crags line the east side of the southern end and are best given a wide berth when there is a covering of snow or ice on the top or when there is a strong westerly wind.

The path from the south to Helvellyn is often crowded while Dollywaggon Pike, standing just off the Helvellyn path, is frequently clear of visitors. This seems odd as the Dollywaggon summit, with its cairn decorated with pieces of scrap iron, provides much better views than the Helvellyn summit. On a clear day they seem to take in most of Lakeland.

A return trip from Grasmere to Helvellyn taking in Dollywaggon Pike, High Crag and Nethermost Pike can be accomplished in six hours. But there are a number of alternative routes, an assortment of round trips being available from the Patterdale area making use of routes over St. Sunday Crag, up Grisedale, over Striding or Swirral Edges or by the Keppelcove path or Sticks Pass from the Glenridding valley. Striding and Swirral Edges are the only routes which involve a scramble.

Those who want something more adventurous can tackle the direct ascent of Dollywaggon Pike from Ruthwaite Lodge at the head of Grisedale which is recommended by A. H. Griffin in his book *The Roof of England.*

Times from Patterdale would vary between six hours for the longest route via St. Sunday Crag and Sticks Pass and four hours for the direct ascent to and from Dollywaggon by Grisedale.

DOVE CRAG

76. *Sheet 83.* Reference 375104. Westmorland. 2603 feet.*

Dove Crag is the name given to the summit above the crags which look north-east over Dovedale Beck. Scandale Beck drains its southern slopes.

When considering an ascent one is faced with two choices for a direct ascent and three choices for a ridge walk. Of the direct approaches, that by Scandale Beck from 377052 at the end of a minor road north to Ambleside is largely a pleasant valley walk and best reserved for a day of uncertain weather, while that from 403118 (the Botherswater Hotel on the A.592 Kirkstone road) or preferably 402134 (where there are better parking facilities), would be an easy first choice on a clear day. The path follows Dovedale Beck to strike the col between Hart and Dove Crags and provides a better view of the crags than any other approach. From the col a short walk to the south-east brings one to the cairn above Dove Crag and a continuation in the same direction past Little Hart Crag brings one to the marshy head of Scandale Pass. From this point a path runs down Caiston Beck bringing one back to the starting point in a round trip of about 3½ hours from the Brotherswater Hotel or four hours for the alternative starting point.

Apart from being on the well-known Fairfield 'horseshoe' stretching from Heron Pike round to High Pike above Rydal, Dove Crag is also accessible across Scandale Pass from the Red Screes–Snarker Pike ridge so that it can be included in any combination of three ridges. The starting points for the ridges are 365064 above Rydal for the Heron Pike ridge, 375054 for the High Pike ridge and the same point (using High Sweden Bridge) or 386054 for the Snarker Pike ridge. It is best to use one of the easterly ridges for the ascent so as to be able to take full advantage of the views as one descends from Fairfield down the Heron Pike ridge on the return, but it should be noted that use of the Snarker Pike ridge involves a fairly substantial drop to the Scandale Pass. Times required for the round trip would be 5½ hours for the Snarker Pike–Heron Pike route, five hours for High Pike–Heron Pike and four hours for Snarker Pike–High Pike. Dove Crag, with its cairn on a slab of rock, will be seen as a minor bump on any of the ridge routes and the Dovedale Beck route must accordingly be the preferred approach.

DOW CRAG (CONISTON)

77. *Sheet 88.* Reference 263978. Lancashire. 2555 feet.*

Dow Crag, a magnificent precipice, lies among the rounded Coniston Fells, due west across Goat's Water from the Old Man of Coniston. The best approach is by the track running from the Walna Scar road up the east side of Goat's Water, since this provides the most impressive view of the crags. A car can be taken up the road from Coniston as far as reference 289971 and the track to Goat's Water leaves the road a mile further on.

From Goat's Water, the track runs north to climb the col between Dow Crag and Brim Fell—another good viewpoint for Dow Crag—and then runs west and then south to the Dow Crag Summit. The summit is not marked by a cairn. It is doubtful if one could be lodged there. A cairn would in any event be superfluous on these massive rocks.

There is an easy descent down the ridge over Brown Pike to the Walna Scar road and the round trip can be done in as little as 2½ hours. But those who love to admire massive crags, whether from the bottom or for the view from the top, will take longer

This round trip can also be walked from 232968, the Duddon Valley end of the Walna Scar road. It is in many ways a better walk than that from the Coniston end, although a little longer. Those who approach from that direction may well be tempted to strike off over Brown Pike directly to Dow Crag but the circuit by way of Goat's Water will give one a better impression of the magnificence of Dow Crag.

DOW CRAG (ESKDALE)

78. *Sheet 82.* Reference 222066. Cumberland. 2300 feet.*

This summit is about 250 yards north of Dow Crag but there is a substantial drop between it and the ridge south-east of Scafell Pikes and Dow Crag is the nearest name on the 1-inch Ordnance Survey map. On the 2½-inch map the name is Pen.

Those who walk down the ridge south-east of Scafell Pikes with the intention of retracing their steps to the top will be deterred by the steep drop after the second of the subsidiary summits from proceeding further. Accordingly, it is best to get to Dow Crag from Eskdale. There are two ways: the east side of the river by the well-worn path which runs from Brotherilkeld (212012), or the west side by the path by Taw House from 203009. The latter provides the better views of the Esk waterfalls but involves some scrambling along the gorge and would be quite unsuitable for young children. Whichever route is used, the objective is the small cairn on a large boulder at about 222061 which marks a grassy route up the steep slope just west of Dow Crag. From the top of the slope one can either strike east directly up the steep rocks to the summit or continue to a point to the south of the cairn above Little Narrowcove which marks an easier, though still rocky, route to the small cairn perched in the rocky summit. It provides a wonderful viewpoint for upper Eskdale and the Scafell range.

From the summit one must inevitably return in a north-westerly direction to the col below the ridge which runs down from Scafell Pikes, at which point one has a choice of three routes. The first is to return more or less directly to Eskdale, preferably by continuing to Little Narrowcove and descending down that valley on the east side of Dow Crags. The second is to continue to Little Narrowcove and take the path up that valley to Scafell Pikes and return by Scafell and Slight Side. The third, and most interesting, is to contour in a westerly direction below Scafell Pikes to Mickledore on a walk which has a high percentage of grass interspersed with patches of rock and loose stones. The line will be obvious if it is surveyed from the Dow Crag summit. It does not present any serious difficulty and the direct route brings one to the Mountain Rescue Post at Mickledore, from which point one can descend to Lord's Rake and return to Eskdale by way of Scafell and Slight Side.

About five hours is required for the first of these routes, eight for the second, and seven for the third.

DRUMALDRACE

79. *Sheet 90. Reference 873867. Yorkshire (N.R.). 2015 feet.*

Drumaldrace is the Ordnance Survey name. On the Bartholomew map the name is Wether Fell.

This provides the easiest ascent of all the English summits. It lies just north of the Roman Road which runs from Bainbridge to Ribblesdale and, by taking a car to the junction of this road with the Hawes–Buckden road at reference 863854, one gets to within 1¼ miles of the top. A little over one mile of this is along the Roman Road, which is good firm going, and the walk to the summit is a matter of 200 yards with a rise of less than 100 feet. The summit is marked by a cairn.

Those who wish to make a longer excursion may walk the 4½ miles of Roman Road from Bainbridge or take a round trip of about six miles from Burtersett (891893), following the Countersett road to 905884 where it crosses the Roman Road, then taking the Roman Road to Drumaldrace and returning by the path which goes round the west and north sides of the summit to take a more or less direct line back to Burtersett.

EEL CRAGS

80. *Sheet 82.* Reference 235162. Cumberland. 2143 feet.*
81. *Subsidiary summits at 236170. 2050 feet.*
82. *235165. 2100 feet.*

These are the crags which lie between Maiden Moor and Dalehead above the Newlands Valley, the highest point of which is also known as High Spy. Routes to them are described under the entry for Dale Head. The ridge is quite wide, the walking easy, and there are good views into Newlands and Borrowdale and beyond.

Apart from the ridge routes there is a direct ascent from the Borrowdale valley just north of Grange and one a little less direct from Rosthwaite by the bridge at 252151 and High Scawdel.

ESK PIKE

83. *Sheet 82.* Reference 237075. Cumberland. 2903 feet.*

Esk Pike is the first summit on the ridge which runs south-east from Esk Hause to Bow Fell and the Crinkle Crags. It is observed at fairly close quarters by the many thousands who pass over Esk Hause and its south-west face is traversed by that section of them who reach Esk Hause by way of Bow Fell, but probably only a few of them reach the actual summit. This is a little way from the main path and involves a scramble over rough rock to a point where three small cairns on separate blocks of rock compete for the honour of being the highest point. That on the west wins, but only by a margin measured in inches.

Esk Pike can also be ascended directly by the ridge running north between Lingcove Beck and the River Esk. There are traces of a path in places and the walking is on dry grass interspersed with rocky outcrops, with little competition from other pedestrians. This ridge, with Yeastyrigg Crags on its eastern side, is the view one gets of Esk Pike from Eskdale, the perfectly proportioned cone seen on the skyline from lower down the dale, which could well qualify for the name Esk Pike, being Bow Fell.

FAIRFIELD

84. *Sheet 83.* Reference 358118. Westmorland. 2863 feet.*

Fairfield is often neglected because of the strong attraction of Striding Edge and Helvellyn a little further north. It stands just east of Grisedale Hause at the junction of three ridges, one running due south to Rydal Water, one running north-east to Patterdale and one, less well marked, running south-east to Dove Crag and then dividing into a ridge down High Pike to Ambleside and another leading to Red Screes overlooking the Kirkstone Pass and then continuing over Snarker Pike to Ambleside. Fairfield can therefore be conveniently fitted into a number of very pleasant circular tours.

Two ridge walks embracing Fairfield, one of them the 'horse-shoe', are given under the entry for Dove Crag. In addition, the Birks–St. Sunday Crag ridge can be taken from Patterdale, the return journey being made either by going south-east to Hart Crag and descending by the ridge between Dovedale and Deepdale Beck or by going west to Grisedale Hause and returning by the Grisedale valley. A minor variation on the latter route is to descend to the dip before Cofa Pike and then run down the scree track to a point east of Grisedale Tarn. About 4¼ hours should suffice for the round trip from Patterdale.

Another alternative is to start from Grasmere up the path by Greenhead Gill, past Alcock Tarn to the ridge south of Heron Pike. From here it is an easy walk up the ridge over Rydal and Greatrigg Man to Fairfield and a walk west to Grisedale Hause provides a choice between returning to Grasmere by way of the Old Pack Horse Road or over Seat Sandal. The round trip takes about 5½ hours, with a little longer for the return by way of Seat Sandal. However, those who get to the summit on a fine day will no doubt wish to extend their stay for as long as time can be spared by exploring the ridges towards St. Sunday Crag or Dove Crag. Those who get there in mist will find the number of cairns somewhat confusing and will need to take special care to get a safe route down.

FELL HEAD

85. *Sheet 89. Reference 650984. Yorkshire (W.R.). 2050 feet.*

This is the first of the summits encountered on the route over the Howgill Fells described under the entry for Bram Rigg Top. There is a small cairn on the crest as one approaches the top of the last steep rise, but the main summit is somewhat further east. The flat summit ridge has no bog and the walking there is all that could be desired. It is odd, however, to find that this part of Yorkshire is to the west of Westmorland, the boundary being marked by the cairn at 655986 on the east slope of Fell Head.

Fell Head can also be reached quite easily from The Calf as described under that entry.

FENDRITH HILL

86. *Sheet 84. Reference 877333. Durham. 2284 feet.*

Fendrith Hill is part of the high ground between Weardale and Teesdale and lies just south of Chapelfell Top. It is visible from Chapelfell Top and there is a tolerable route between the two. The bog becomes less difficult as one gets away from Chapelfell Top and for a time takes on the appearance of the salt marshes in the Ribble estuary, except that the mud is jet black instead of a dirty grey.

The easiest route back to the road is by way of the quarry about one mile to the north-west and then down the quarry track to meet the minor road at 862347. An ascent of Fendrith Hill by this route would present no difficulty.

Alternatively, one could approach Fendrith Hill from Swinhope Head (898334) on the minor road between Newbiggin and Westgate. A little over an hour should suffice for the return journey.

FIEND'S FELL

87. *Sheet 83. Reference 644407. Cumberland. 2082 feet.*

Fiend's Fell lies three-quarters of a mile south of Hartside Cross, the highest point of the road between Alston and Penrith. Its summit bears a trig point and it is the first stage of the high level route to Cross Fell. Fiend's Fell is supposed to have been the former name for Cross Fell. This seems quite probable, since the name Cross Fell derives from the erection of a cross to mark the departure of the evil spirits or to ward them off. But it does not explain why the name should be transferred to a point five miles to the north.

FLEETWITH PIKE

88. *Sheet 82.* Reference 205142. Cumberland. 2126 feet.*

The view of Fleetwith Pike from Buttermere is one of the best known views of Lakeland. To some extent the area lost its attraction for walkers when the road was built over Honister Pass, but, for those who want quick and easy access to Fleetwith Pike, the road to the top of the pass can be used to advantage. A car can deliver one there at a height of 1176 feet and a walk of an hour up the slope in a north-westerly direction brings one to the Fleetwith Pike summit. Such an excursion is not to be despised in Lakeland when weather in the early part of the day has prevented a longer walk.

For days when a longer walk is possible, it is best to start from Gatesgarth at the head of Buttermere and ascend by way of Warnscale Bottom or by Scarth Gap, reaching Fleetwith Pike in that case by way of Haystacks. There is a direct descent from a point just west of the summit, through a gap in the crags, north-west down the slope to Gatesgarth. Two hours should suffice for the round trip using the Warnscale Bottom approach and three hours if Scarth Gap is used. Those feeling like a longer return trip could descend from the summit by the path above Honister Crags to the top of Honister Pass and continue due north to Dale Head. From that point the route north-west could be taken to Robinson, returning to the Buttermere valley by the path to Hassness or the longer path due west to Buttermere village.

FLINTY FELL

89. *Sheet 84. Reference 772419. Cumberland. 2013 feet.*

This competes with Drumaldrace for the summit with the easiest ascent. From 768426 on the Garrigill–Nenthead road there is only seventy-three feet of ascent and a walk of half a mile. One point in its favour is the wild pansies which are to be found at the highest point of the road on the southern verge, but it loses the competition with Drumaldrace because there may be a bull in the field by the road.

Approaching by the footpath from Ashgillside on the Alston–Middleton-in-Teesdale road or by the old mine track from Nenthead is therefore to be preferred. One and a half hours should suffice for the round trip.

FOUNTAINS FELL

90. *Sheet 90. Reference 864716. Yorkshire (W.R.). 2191 feet.*
91. *Subsidiary summits at 868708. 2150 feet.*
92. *868697. 2000 feet.*

The most direct ascent is by the Pennine Way from 853723 on the road between Stainforth in Ribblesdale and Halton Gill in Littondale. At the head of the steep part of the ascent the Pennine Way goes to the south-east while the first summit with its large cairn lies slightly west of south at a distance of about 700 yards. About half a mile south-east along the line of wall west of Fountains Fell Tarn is the second summit. There is nothing to mark it but, to the east, is the highest Meteorological Station in England at which temperature records are taken and, a little north of that, a large cairn. The third summit, the most southerly summit in the Pennines, is about three-quarters of a mile almost due south from that point, marked by a prominent cairn and providing views of Malham Tarn.

Pieces of coal may be found on the main summit and are a reminder that Fountains Abbey used to obtain supplies of coal from this area. Fountains Abbey in fact owned the fell, which presumably accounts for the name, its territorial limit being marked by Ulfkill Cross on the western side. Beyond that point the land belonged to Sawley Abbey.

The Pennine Way could be used for the return journey but the alternative would be to continue down the long ridge and the footpath to the road at 856673, and then to Dale Head by the track which runs north from 846683 and back to the starting point along the Halton Gill road. The direct return trip would require about 1¾ hours and the round trip 3½ hours.

Darnbrook Fell, 1½ miles north-east of the main summit, can readily be included in any excursion to Fountains Fell but would not add much to the interest of the walk.

FROSWICK

93. *Sheet 83.* Reference 435086. Westmorland. 2359 feet.*

Froswick lies on the ridge, with crags along its eastern side, which separates the Kentmere valley from Hagg Gill and runs up to High Street. It can be approached by the Garburn Pass starting either from Troutbeck on the Windermere-Patterdale road, or from Kentmere. Near the highest point of the Pass a footpath runs almost due north over gently rising country until the ridge is reached. Its beginning is marked by a cairn about 1¼ miles from the

Garburn track and the first summit, that of Yoke, is nearly half a mile further on.

From just below the summit the path follows a narrow ridge above a line of crags to Ill Bell (slightly lower than Mardale Ill Bel but a much more interesting summit) and then to Froswick. Froswick is not nearly so imposing as Ill Bell but gives fine views of the Ill Bell crags and the crags below High Street. It is marked by a cairn.

The ridge continues for a further three-quarters of a mile and then joins the plateau which runs on to High Street. A short distance away to the north-west is the imposing beacon above Thornthwaite Crag. From this point one can return almost due south along the course of the Roman Road down Hagg Gill to Troutbeck, making a round trip of about five hours or continue to the High Street summit just over a mile to the north-east, and then return over Mardale Ill Bell south to Kentmere, a round trip from that point of about six hours.

GLARAMARA

94. *Sheet 82.* Reference 246105. Cumberland. 2560 feet.*
95. *Subsidiary summits at 240093. 2200 feet.*
96. *243097. 2350 feet.*
97. *245102. 2550 feet.*
98. *250108. 2550 feet.*

Glaramara is a familiar sight to the many thousands who walk in the upper part of Borrowdale but it is much less frequented than the routes over Sty Head or to Esk Hause. It is a fine looking mountain from the valley but in some ways is a disappointment when seen at close quarters. A ridge with slight undulations and a mixture of rock and marsh makes an interesting walk but hardly lives up to the picture one builds up on hearing the name Glaramara. The appearance of its summit does, however, lend credence to the origin of its name which is understood to mean the shieling in a clearing by a chasm.

The best approach is by way of Allen Crags, to which the route has already been outlined. The five summits are spread out on a ridge running for a distance of 1¾ miles in a north-north-easterly direction from that point and are all marked by cairns. They should be avoided in misty weather and are at their best in the afternoon sunshine.

The walk can be continued to the summit above Cam Crag, about half a mile further on, and then via Tarn at Leaves to Stonethwaite. There is no marked path for the first part of this route and for the inexperienced walker, and for anyone in bad weather, the path which descends from the main summit north-west to Seathwaite or the path proceeding in a direction slightly west of north to Thornythwaite Fell and then down Comb Gill will be preferable. These routes can also be used for the ascent, but the Allen Crags route is preferable.

The round trip from Seathwaite in Borrowdale via Grains Gill and Allen Crags would take about 4½ hours, while the round trip from Stonethwaite via Langstrathdale and Allen Crags, returning by Comb Gill, would take five hours.

GRAGARETH

99. *Sheet 89. Reference 688793. Lancashire. 2058 feet.*
100. *Subsidiary summit at 696804. 2000 feet.*

Gragareth lies on the ridge which runs along the Lancashire and Yorkshire boundary to Great Coum, a route described under the entry for Great Coum. The main summit lies to the west of the county boundary, although east of the trig point, while the subsidiary summit lies on the boundary. At the northern end of the main summit ridge, west of the boundary, is a prominent cairn. The summit ridge carries one of the highest dry stone walls in the country, all of it in very good condition in the summer of 1969.

The most notable features of Gragareth, however, are the Three Men on the western slopes overlooking Leck Fell House. They are at the top of a steep escarpment where building material is plentiful and are an imposing sight, dwarfing the other cairns and the bee-hive shaped shelter close by. Presumably they were constructed by the expert craftsmen who built the stone wall on the county boundary and the plentiful supply of stone at this point is a possible explanation for its unusual height. However the fact that the wall is of normal height along the Westmorland–Yorkshire boundary a little over a mile further north will suggest to some that its unusual height between Lancashire and Yorkshire has its origins in the Wars of the Roses.

GRASMOOR

101. *Sheet 82.* Reference 175204. Cumberland. 2791 feet.*

Grasmoor means the moor of the wild boar and its high grassy plateau and line of crags at the side remind one of Wild Boar Fell.

It lies due west of Crag Hill, roughly the mid-point of the high level walk from Causey Pike to Grisedale Pike, and can be included in this excursion at the cost of an additional hour's walking. There is a magnificent view across the valley to Gasgale Crags from the top of the crags on the north side of Grasmoor.

For a direct ascent of Grasmoor the shortest route for the normal walker is by Gasgale Gill, starting from point 159208 on the Cockermouth–Buttermere road and proceeding via Coledale Hause to ascend the east side. It is appreciably shorter than the route from Braithwaite up Coledale Beck, but the going is more difficult and the views are restricted to the narrow valley. The walk can readily be extended to other summits in the vicinity, if desired, and the return effected by a fine ridge walk over Hopegill Head, Gasgale Crags and Whiteside. The direct ascent and return by Gasgale Gill would take about three hours while an additional three-quarters of an hour would be required for the shortest return route by Hopegill Head and Whiteside. On a fine day, however, it would require a compelling reason to keep anyone moving on that time-scale in country such as this.

Experienced walkers who favour a more adventurous route can tackle the direct ascent up the north-west face from the bottom of Gasgale Gill. It is hard going, but not impossible.

GRAY CRAG

102. *Sheet 83.* Reference 429109. Westmorland. 2331 feet.*
103. *Subsidiary summits at 428114. 2250 feet.*
104. *426118. 2286 feet.*

Gray Crag lies almost due north from Thornythwaite Beacon. Its wide, grassy ridge makes a pleasant walk and gives fine views of Hayeswater and the steep rocky slopes on the west side of High Street. The most direct ascent is up the northern end of the ridge, which can be approached from Hartsop, just off the Patterdale–Windermere road. The path from Hartsop is a very pleasant walk along the Hayeswater Gill and the ascent to Gray Crag can be commenced from near point 420128 or from the dam just below Hayeswater.

However, since Gray Crag lies on one of several ridges which converge on Thornythwaite Beacon, the walker has a choice of many routes. The most obvious starting points are: Haweswater for an ascent by way of Mardale Ill Bell; Troutbeck for an ascent by Hagg Gill or preferably, as an extension of the walk to Froswick; Kirkstone Pass Inn for an approach by way of Caudale Moor.

GREAT BORNE

105. *Sheet 82.* Reference 124164. Cumberland. 2020 feet.*

Great Borne lies at the western end of the range which forms the northern side of the Ennerdale valley and used to provide a pleasant afternoon walk for anyone with an evening appointment for dinner at the Anglers Hotel. Alas, the Anglers Hotel is no more, but Great Borne survives and can be approached by way of the path which runs from 098167 on the road to Crummock Water. After about one mile on the path one can cross the stream and head directly for the summit, but this is steep going and it is preferable to go to the head of the pass above Floutern Tarn and ascend from that direction. A trig point marks the summit.

Having reached Great Borne the walker will naturally wish to sample the ridge walk to the east at least as far as Starling Dodd. The round trip as far as that point takes just over three hours but those with more time to spare will wish to continue over Red Pike and High Stile to High Crag, one of the best ridge walks in this country. A return trip to High Crag from the starting point above the Anglers Hotel site, following the ridge in both directions, would require nearly six hours.

Great Borne could, of course, be included in a walk of the ridge starting from Gatesgarth in Buttermere with an ascent of High Crag, but this is less satisfactory than the walk in the reverse order. A more satisfactory alternative would be to approach Floutern Tarn by the path which runs from Buttermere village to cross the stream at 168166, ascending to Great Borne from Floutern Tarn and following the ridge to descend to Buttermere either from Red Pike, High Stile or High Crag, according to the time available.

GREAT CALVA

106. *Sheet 82.* Reference 291312. Cumberland. 2265 feet.*

Great Calva, lying about two miles to the north-east of Skiddaw, is a round grassy hump with a high shoulder extending for the best part of a mile in an arc to the north-west. It can be approached by the Caldew valley from Mosedale on the Mungrisdale–Hesket Newmarket road in the east, by the Skiddaw House track from the Keswick–Penrith road in the south or by the track which runs down to Skiddaw House from near Bassenthwaite in the north. The latter route is the shortest of the three and has the added advantage of passing the Whitewater Dash waterfall. It starts as the road to Dash Farm at 249324, about two miles along the minor road from the A.591 to Orthwaite. At 263320, where the farm road turns to the east, the bridleway is followed to the south-east and across the bridge which spans the stream above the waterfall. From this point there is an easy ascent due east to the cairn on Little Calva and the flat high ground can then be followed round to the rocky outcrop and cairn on the Great Calva summit. The round trip takes about 3½ hours.

GREAT CARRS

107. *Sheet 88.* Reference 270009. Lancashire. 2500 feet.*

Carrs means rocks and Great Carrs is a rocky summit on the ridge which runs north from the Old Man of Coniston past Brim Fell and Swirl How to the Three Shire Stone on Wrynose Pass. It is crossed by anyone walking the ridge and may be used as the point of access to the ridge by those who reach it from the Duddon Valley by way of Grey Friar. The ridge provides good firm walking and first-class views and those who reach it should, if at all possible, insist on walking the full length of it.

GREAT COUM

108. *Sheets 89 and 90. Reference 701836. Yorkshire (W.R.). 2250 feet.*

Great Coum lies on a ridge which forms the boundary between Lancashire and Westmorland on the west and the West Riding of Yorkshire on the east, straddling the edges of Sheets 89 and 90 of the 1-inch Ordnance Survey. The best approach is from the minor road through Leck which crosses the A.65 Kendal–Skipton road at Cowan Bridge (636765). Those with limited time available may use a car to the end of the made up road just short of Leck Fell House. From there an ascent by the Three Men of Gragareth and the Gragareth trig point brings one to the high wall marking the county boundary and this can be followed along the ridge to Great Coum. A massive boulder marked 'W.S.1838' marks the three shire point at 702827 and was perhaps the determining factor in fixing it and there is a large cairn a little further north on the Yorkshire side. The summit cairn, however, is still further on just north of the wall after it swings to the east. Three and a half hours is required for the round trip back to the road, the return being achieved by retracing one's steps or continuing on the ridge to Crag Hill (693834) and then heading directly for the track at 688807 which runs back past Leck Fell House. Those with more time available would do better to park at Leck and walk up the road to Leck Fell House, ascending as before but returning via Crag Hill south-west down the slope to Ease Gill and continuing along Leck Beck back to the village. About 5½ hours would be required.

Alternatively, Great Coum can be approached from the minor roads which run from Ingleton up Kingsdale and past Dent to Barbon. An old track running from 724823 above Kingsdale to 679862 in Barbondale can be used for the approach, the shortest route being that from 724823 along the track to 707825 and then north-west to the wall along the county boundary. A return direct to the starting point would involve a round trip of less than two hours but the walk could conveniently be extended by continuing along the track towards Dent and returning up Deepdale.

GREAT DOD

109. *Sheet 83.* Reference 342205. Cumberland. 2807 feet.*
110. *Subsidiary summit at 349211. 2250 feet.*

'Dod' means rounded summit and Great Dod is an apt description for this one. 'Dod' in this case has two *d*s whereas the 'Dodd' of Dodd Fell has three. It lies on the ridge which runs north from Helvellyn to the Penrith–Keswick road. Approach routes for the ridge are outlined in the entry for Calfhow Pike and it is perhaps only necessary to add that Great Dod lies almost one mile south-east of Calfhow Pike and just over a mile north of Stybarrow Dod. It is a grassy summit with an enormous cairn located a little way from the highest point.

The subsidiary summit lies nearly three-quarters of a mile to the north-east close by the line of a footpath which runs from the main summit down Groove Beck to the Old Coach Road between Keswick and Dockray. Walkers who are striding down the ridge from Clough Head towards Helvellyn will hardly be attracted by it and it is best to cover it in a separate excursion. From 379219, on the minor road running north-west from Dockray, the Old Coach Road can be followed for half a mile to the footbridge over Groove Beck. From that point the footpath runs to the west on the hill-side above Groove Beck, but it is rather indistinct, there being no recognisable path for much of the way. However, the general direction presents no problem. There are patches of rock and a sizeable cairn just before the summit is reached, a somewhat more attractive spot than the main top. By continuing to the main summit one can follow the ridge over Calfhow Pike and Clough Head to return by following the Old Coach Road from about point 340236. A shorter return route is to go down the slope due north to the wet path which runs along Mosedale Beck, rejoining the Coach Road at 350227. This road provides a very interesting walk and those who are interested in bog may see a specimen of moderate difficulty in comfort by walking along the section of the Coach Road to the east of Mosedale Beck.

GREAT DUMMACHS

111. *Sheet 89. Reference 678963. Yorkshire (W.R.). 2150 feet.*

This is the last of the Howgill Fells, on the ridge walk from Fell Head over The Calf to the top of Cautley Crag, which is described under the entry for Bram Rigg Top. There is a ten-yard patch of bog in the slight dip between Calders and Great Dummachs but this can readily be avoided and the going is good all the way. From the top, there is a fine view of the loop in the Rawthey River due east of Cautley Crag.

Great Dummachs can also be visited by taking the route beside Cautley Spout to The Calf and then continuing south down the ridge to return to the starting point in a wide sweep round Cautley Crag.

GREAT DUN FELL

112. *Sheet 83. Reference 711322. Westmorland. 2780 feet.*

This is on the route from Knock to Cross Fell which is described under the Cross Fell Entry. Walkers will find it a depressing sight as it is disfigured by a tall radar station and its associated huts. The name means pasture hill but the sight of the iron dispels all thoughts of rural peace. An unusual hazard encountered there when there is a high wind and wintry weather are the large pieces of ice dislodged from the mast. The noise as they crash to the ground ensures that the masts are given a wide berth on such occasions.

GREAT END

113. *Sheet 82.* Reference 227083. Cumberland. 2984 feet.*
114. *Subsidiary summit at 225078. 2950 feet.*

Great End is the north-east buttress of Scafell Pikes. It is an awesome sight to the walker who approaches Esk Hause from Sty Head or Grains Gill, particularly when snow is lodged on its face, and the summit provides a magnificent viewpoint over Borrowdale and beyond.

It can readily be reached by any of the routes to Esk Hause or from the summit of Scafell Pikes, but the most direct route is from Seathwaite in the Borrowdale valley due south up Grains Gill. Stockley Bridge, a lovely spot for photographs, is crossed in less than one mile and after a further half mile the path inclines to the right away from the Glaramara crags to join the Sty Head–Esk Hause path south of Sprinkling Tarn. From Esk Hause the path running west to Scafell Pikes and south of the Great End crags is taken to 226080, where a path strikes off due north to the Great End summit.

The subsidiary summit listed, which is not really connected with Great End but does not have a separate name on the 1-inch Ordnance map, lies just south-west of the point where the path to the main summit diverges from the Scafell Pikes track. It is a jumbled heap of rocks and involves a diversion of only a few moments from the Scafell Pikes track.

A round trip from Seathwaite to the two summits would take four hours but, weather permitting, the walker will no doubt wish to continue to the Scafell Pikes summit and probably to return to Borrowdale by the Corridor Route to Sty Head.

GREAT GABLE

115. *Sheet 82.* Reference 212104. Cumberland. 2949 feet.*

Great Gable, the massive pyramid one sees from the head of Wasdale, has an extraordinary fascination for Lakeland walkers. Helvellyn is climbed more often, probably because it is more accessible, having main roads running east and west of it, and also because it is one of the few summits over 3000 feet in height. Great Gable, on the other hand, is in the rough hard core of Lakeland and from many directions, has the appearance of a 'real' mountain. It has also a number of rock climbs and such well known features as the Napes Needle and the Sphinx Rock. Many are content to make it their first choice for a walk whenever they visit Lakeland.

There are many routes to the summit, the most attractive to keen rock scramblers being the traverse route from Sty Head up the south-west face, while the easiest and also the most pleasant is perhaps the route from the top of Honister Pass over Brandreth and Green Gable. The traverse route should only be tackled by experienced scramblers. It starts from the top of Sty Head pass, running across the southern slopes of the mountain, past the rock climbing area and the Napes Needle, with awkward moments over patches of scree and, in one variation, a steep climb up the Westmorland Gully to reach the top.

With the possible exception of one of the ascents from the north-west from the head of Black Sail Pass by way of, or round the side of Kirk Fell, other recognised routes are all within the competence of the average climber. Taking them in a clockwise direction, the first is from the top of the Honister Pass by way of Grey Knotts and Brandreth and either over or round Green Gable to the well-worn path which goes up the north-east face from Windy Gap. This round trip need take no more than three hours.

Next come the ascents from Seathwaite in Borrowdale, either by Sour Milk Gill and the Gillercombe valley over Green Gable or by Sty Head Pass to ascend to Windy Gap by Aaron Slack from a point just short of Styhead Tarn or, alternatively, by continuing to the head of the pass and ascending up the south-east ridge.

From Langdale, the ascent would be rather longer but 5½ hours should suffice for a round trip from the end of the road in Great Langdale by way of Rossett Gill and Sty Head. Wasdale is a better proposition as, apart from the ascent from Black Sail Pass already referred to, it offers the possibility of an ascent by Sty Head Pass or a direct but grim approach up the ridge which faces Wasdale. The Wasdale side of Sty Head is longer but much more attractive than the Borrowdale side, having good views of the crags on either side and providing quite a gentle walk in the earlier stages.

Ennerdale has a direct route to Windy Gap between Great and Green Gable but it would require a 7½-hour round trip from the bottom of Ennerdale and the route would really only be of value to someone staying at the Black Sail Hostel. Buttermere, however, can offer a variation on the Honister route by an ascent from Gatesgarth up Warnscale Bottom to pick up the Honister path just south of Brandreth.

Out of all these alternatives the average walker from Borrowdale who wants something other than the direct route from Honister would probably find it best to start from Seathwaite, using the Sour Milk Gill route for the ascent and descending by the south-east ridge and Sty Head. Such a round trip would take about 3½ hours and could readily be extended to cover a return over Glaramara if required. For those starting from Wasdale, the Sty Head route is the obvious choice for the ascent while, for the return, instead of using the direct descent down the ridge facing Wasdale or the more difficult descent directly towards Kirkfell, it is perhaps best to descend to Windy Gap in the direction of Green Gable, continue for quarter of a mile north-west towards Ennerdale and then contour to the west to pick up the path running round Kirk Fell to Black Sail. This round trip would take 4½ hours, longer than the suggested round trip from Borrowdale but much more worth while.

The views from the Great Gable summit, for those fortunate enough to get there on a clear day, are magnificent but those who wish to see Great Gable itself will find it best to view it from

Lingmell or the slopes of Scafell Pikes, whence its crags can be seen to best advantage.

A rock near the summit cairn of Great Gable is the site chosen for the 1914–18 War Memorial to the members of the Fell and Rock Climbing Club.

GREAT KNOTT

116. *Sheet 88.* Reference 261043. Cumberland. 2200 feet.*

Great Knott is the minor summit about half a mile due north of Cold Pike overlooking Oxendale and the Langdale valley. It is not on the direct route between Cold Pike and Crinkle Crags but it only involves a very minor deviation. No doubt it could be reached directly from Oxendale, but it is doubtful if anyone reaches Great Knott other than when en route from the Cold Pike area to Crinkle Crags.

GREAT KNOUTBERRY HILL

117. *Sheet 90. Reference 788872. Yorkshire (W.R./N.R.). 2203 feet.*

This is the main summit of Widdale Fell which lies in that wild, remote area between Dentdale and Hawes.

There is parking space at Stone House in Dentdale (771859) and the best approach is by the minor road which runs from there up the left side of Artengill Beck between Great Knoutberry Hill and Wold Fell. The road dwindles to a path over the open fell at 793862 and, leaving it at that point, a walk of about three-quarters of a mile up the slope in a direction just west of north brings one to the trig point which marks the summit. These rolling moors have a much browner colour than the Pennines further north and, particularly when compared with the delightful scenes in the Dent valley, seem extraordinarily bare and desolate.

From the trig point it is possible to continue north-east past Widdale Great Tarn over very rough bog to the Widdale Fell summits at 798879 and 795880.

Winter is as good a time as any for this walk and the wildness of the scene is enhanced if the area is covered in snow.

GREAT LINGY HILL

118. *Sheet 82.* Reference 310340. Cumberland. 2000 feet.*
119. *Subsidiary summit at 303339. 2000 feet.*

Great Lingy Hill is about two miles due west of Carrock Fell in that deserted, rolling waste at the back of Saddleback. The ridge from Carrock Fell runs in a north-west direction and after 1½ miles one reaches a rough ridge of high land which runs north-north-east to High Pike and south-west to Great Lingy Hill. There is a shooting hut, as much of an eyesore on this landscape as any television mast would be, in a prominent position (312335) on the south-eastern slopes of Great Lingy Fell. Nearby is a wire-fenced sheepfold, an indication of the general lack of stones for the building of walls, a shortage which is emphasised by the fact that a cairn of only three stones serves to mark the main summit.

The secondary summit, about 700 yards due west of the first, has a somewhat larger cairn. On the whole the going is easy but there are a few wet patches.

There is a beautiful return route down Grainsgill Beck with its cascades of running water and there are a few old mines whose spoil heaps will attract amateur geologists. Recently, mining in this area seems to have taken a new lease of life and corrugated iron structures on the Carrock Fell mine now disfigure the area where Grainsgill Beck joins the Caldew. Energetic walkers may wish to continue to Knott, one mile south-west of the main Great Lingy Hill summit and to Great Sca Fell which lies just over a mile north-west of Knott, retracing their steps to Knott and continuing east down the ridge to Coomb Height and straight back to Mosedale. Five hours should suffice for the round trip.

In April 1970 the hut on Great Lingy Fell was operated as a shelter by the Mountain Bothies Association whose secretary was recorded in the register as Richard Dufty, of Brighouse in Yorkshire. More recently those requiring information have been directed to apply to Ian Mitchell, 7 William Street, Dunfermline, Fife KY12 8AS. There was a small reserve of food there and the hut had been occupied the previous night and on quite a number of occasions in the preceding month. Apparently the association exists to provide shelters at isolated sites in hill country for the use of walkers. A very worthy enterprise, which enables one to look a little more kindly on the blot on the landscape of Great Lingy Hill.

GREATRIGG MAN

120. *Sheet 83.* Reference 356104. Westmorland. 2513 feet.*

Greatrigg Man is the stony summit on the ridge which runs due south from Fairfield. There is a direct route to it from Grasmere via Stone Arthur but the preferable approach is as part of the ridge walks described under the entry for Fairfield. It is marked by a cairn of moderate size and is seen at its best from Hart Crag, especially when backed by the distant view of the Coniston Fells.

GREAT SCA FELL

121. *Sheet 82.* Reference 292338. Cumberland. 2131 feet.*
122. *Subsidiary summit at 290342. 2050 feet.*

This seems an odd name for a small hump seventeen miles north of Sca Fell, one of the finest of English peaks. It is not even great in area, but perhaps those who named it had never seen Sca Fell. The name in this case is supposed to mean 'hill with a shieling', which seems sensible for a hill of this type, even though the derivation seems a little obscure.

The main summit lies just over a mile due west from Great Lingy Hill and is marked by a minute cairn which is not visible until close at hand. As with Great Lingy Hill, the subsidiary summit, a little to the north-west, has an appreciably larger cairn. The circuit from Carrock Fell to Coomb Height, which has already been referred to under the entry for Great Lingy Hill, can readily be extended to include Great Sca Fell. It should be noted, however, that the gullies between Great Lingy Hill and Great Sca Fell are quite deep and that it is best to make a wide circuit under the slopes of Knott when travelling between the two.

An alternative route is the round trip from just south of Orthwaite as described under the entry for Coomb Height.

GREAT SHUNNER FELL

123. *Sheet 90. Reference 849973. Yorkshire (N.R.). 2340 feet.*

Look-out hill is the meaning of the name and it provides an imposing viewpoint on a clear day. It lies on the Pennine Way between Hawes and Thwaite and a long grim slog it must be for someone with a heavy pack who ascends by the ridge from the south. Thwaite is better as a starting point. A minor road, with a Pennine Way sign, goes due west off the Thwaite–Muker road a short

THE CALF (Howgills). Cautley Spout

(*left*) THE CHEVIOT.
The Summit

(*below*) DOW CRAG (CONISTON) (Lakes)

distance north of Thwaite and changes to a path as the open moor is reached. There is a steady rise for 1½ miles, a more level stretch for half a mile or so as the path turns south-west, another rise followed by a level stretch and then a rise to the trig point on the summit. On the whole the walking is quite firm but there are one or two wet patches on the high moorland.

For the return to Thwaite one has the choice of descending south-east past the prominent beacon at 855965 to the highest point on the Butter Tubs road and following it to Thwaite or retracing one's steps and keeping to the wild moorland rather than a fairly busy road. There is, however, an opportunity to extend the walk to Lovely Seat and to see the Butter Tubs if the first alternative is taken.

GREAT STONY HILL

124. *Sheet 84. Reference 824360. Durham. 2322 feet.*

Great Stony Hill is situated in the middle of the Durham summits which lie in an arc running clockwise from the south-east to the north-west of St. Johns' Chapel in Weardale. Possibly because it refers to the old mining area on the north-west slopes rather than to the actual summit, the name appears on the 1-inch Ordnance Survey about half a mile north of the summit. However, there are sufficient patches of stone on the higher slopes to justify the name.

The best approach is by the path starting from 822343 on the Alston–Middleton-in-Teesdale road (B.6277), there being a lay-by just north of Rough Rigg farm. The path heads directly for the summit and has some wet patches. Those who want something more substantial to walk on can use the track starting at 814351, a little further north, and running past Grass Hill Farm, south of Great Stony Hill to Weardale. On the Weardale side the track is well-paved for some distance beyond the junction with the road which goes through a gate and across the dam of the Burnhope Reservoir. However, it is very narrow, and those using it from the Weardale side would be well advised to park where they can turn round rather than try to take their car to the end of the paved stretch.

The track will provide dry walking and the ascent of Great Stony Hill is merely a matter of leaving the track at about 826357 and walking up a slope, largely of grass but with rock and stone patches, to the trig point on the top. It provides a magnificent view of the rolling country between Teesdale and Weardale and those interested in undertaking a major circuit of the area will be able to see one stretching along the skyline over Scaud Hill, Burnhope Seat, Dead Stones and the ridge over Lambs' Head down towards

Burnhope Reservoir. On descending from Lambs' Head past the trig point at 821400 the aim should be to reach the track which runs from the Cowshill–Burnhope Reservoir road at 848396 to reach the open moor at 843397. The road across the dam can then be taken to join the track passing just south of Great Stony Hill. Six hours should suffice for the round trip, whereas the return trip to Great Stony Hill from Rough Rigg farm would require only 1½ hours.

GREAT WHERNSIDE

125. *Sheet 90. Reference 003739. Yorkshire (W.R.). 2310 feet.*
126. *Subsidiary summits at 999755. 2200 feet.*
127. *004759. 2200 feet.*
128. *018736. 2000 feet.*

Whernside means the hillside from which millstones were quarried. Great Whernside affords more evidence of suitable material than does Whernside but, while it could be that the bigger millstones came from Great Whernside, the allocation of the prefix 'Great' to the latter, which is the lower of the two, most probably stems from its greater area. It has not the striking profile of Buckden Pike, Ingleborough or Pen-y-ghent and is really just a large piece of rolling Yorkshire moorland, but its subsidiary summit at 018736 has the distinction of being the most easterly summit of the Pennines.

There is a pleasant ascent to Great Whernside from Kettlewell by the path starting off the minor road at 975726 on the path marked to Hag Dike and going up the south-western end of the ridge. After walking the ridge past the main summit to the two subsidiary summits to the north and returning to descend the slope to that on the east, the return to Kettlewell can be accomplished by returning over the southern end of the ridge to the path which is marked on the map from 995727. Five hours are required for the round trip.

For the shortest route it is necessary to go to the highest point on the minor road from Kettlewell to Wensley (986757) and proceed to the ridge just east of the line of the wall which forms the boundary between the West and North Ridings. There is a good path through a gate in the wall a little to the east of the road and then south-west to a stile over the wall along the county boundary just below the summit ridge. From that point the ridge to the south is easily reached and can be followed past Black Fell Crags to the main summit at Long Crags. From here it is necessary to proceed about a quarter of a mile to the south and then strike east to the subsidiary summit about a mile down the slope. To reach the other summits it is necessary to return along the ridge to its northern end and, for the return, it is best to proceed to the prominent cairn beyond them and descend by the path which runs directly from there to the starting point. The round trip can be done in about 3½ hours and can be recommended as a welcome break on a journey between the Lake District and South East England.

On a recent visit a local farmer objected to the use of this more or less direct ascent. Possibly the answer is to follow the bridleway to the northern end of the ridge at 008765, but the well-marked track to the big stile over the wall among the county boundary suggests that the more direct ascent is a well used route.

Great Whernside provides a variety of walking, the northern summits being on fairly smooth grass while the main summit has large areas of rock and the eastern summit lies in an area of bog. The main summit is marked by a trig point and a large cairn while the most northerly summit is unmarked and the next one bears a large boundary stone built into a wall which has the letters YB on one side and KB and a cross on the other. There is nothing on the highest point of the easterly summit but it has a slim cairn nearly five feet high on its western slope which is not easily visible until close at hand. A small cairn about mid-way between the summit and the cairn at 008733 is a helpful guide on the way.

From all the subsidiary summits there are good views of the Angram and Scar House reservoirs at the head of Nidderdale.

GREEN GABLE

129. *Sheet 82.* Reference 215107. Cumberland. 2603 feet.*

Green Gable lies across Windy Gap from Great Gable, which exceeds it in height by a mere 346 feet. But there is all the difference in the world between the two and it is doubtful if anyone ascends Green Gable other than as a stepping stone to or from Great Gable. It lies on the route between Great Gable and the top of Honister, the easiest line of approach, and also on the route from Seathwaite up Sour Milk Gill and the Gillercombe valley.

GREEN HILL

130. *Sheets 89 and 90. Reference 702815. Lancashire/Yorkshire (W.R.). 2054 feet.*

131. *Subsidiary summit at 702821. 2050 feet.*

Green Hill forms one of the pleasantest stretches of the ridge which runs from Gragareth to Great Coum. The two summits are not marked, the local stone having been consumed by the wall along the ridge. The route is outlined under the entry for Great Coum.

GREEN SIDE

132. *Sheet 83.* Reference 355188. Cumberland/Westmorland. 2600 feet.*

Green Side is the grassy hump which lies east of Stybarrow Dod above the crags at the head of Glencoynedale. It lies just north of the Sticks Pass and anyone climbing to the Helvellyn ridge by that route could readily take Green Side in their stride. They would be unlikely to do so, however, as would those using Sticks Pass for the descent, since Green Side has very little to offer compared with the summits on the ridge. But, taken in conjunction with Hart Side to the north of it, and Sheffield Pike to the south-east, it offers the possibility of a pleasant half-day excursion.

Those who desire an easy route which is not too difficult to follow should start from Glenridding and proceed up the Sticks Pass to about 357183, leaving the path at that point to walk in a north-westerly direction up the grassy slopes to the cairn which marks the summit of Green Side. From there the walk can be continued to the north-east to Hart Side, returning above the crags at the head of Glencoynedale to approach Sheffield Pike from the west. The easiest return route to Glenridding is to head west-south-west from the Sheffield Pike summit to strike Sticks Pass at about 360179 and follow it down the valley back to the starting point. A more adventurous return is possible by striking south-east from Sheffield Pike, but this is steep and requires careful navigation to avoid the crags.

Those who prefer the less frequented routes may start from either Dockray (393214) or Dowthwaitehead (371208), heading south-west from the former and due south from the latter to the edge of the steep slope on the north side of Glencoynedale and then continuing up the valley and then east of the crags to Sheffield Pike. From Sheffield Pike a more or less direct line can be taken to Green Side and, after continuing to Hart Side, a short extension to the east makes it possible to return to either Dockray or Dowthwaitehead on the line of the outward journey. Those starting from the latter point may think it worth while to return via Dockray for the views of Ullswater, but all who get to Sheffield Pike will get views of that lake if the weather is clear.

GREY CRAG

133. *Sheet 83.* Reference 497072. Westmorland. 2093 feet.*

This is the most easterly of the Lakeland mountains, lying south of Haweswater and east of the head of Longsleddale. It is not on the maps of Baddeley's guide, let alone in the text, and is a very secluded spot.

It is an easy walk from Branstree, to which a route has already been given, the going being over Tarn Crag and quite easy apart from short wet patches at the bottom of the dip between Branstree and Tarn Crag and around Greycrag Tarn. The latter can be avoided by swinging a little to the east. Grey Crag does not provide such a good view as Tarn Crag as it is too far east of the Longsleddale valley. Its most prominent feature is the cairn on Harrop Pike at the north-eastern edge of the summit ridge.

As an alternative to the route from Branstree, Grey Crag can be reached from Sadgill in the Longsleddale valley by way of Great Howe or from Swindale Head (504126) along Mosedale Beck or by a much longer walk from 568128 on the A.6 road over Shap. Of these, the 3½-hour round trip from Swindale Head is easily the most attractive.

GREY FRIAR

134. *Sheet 88.* Reference 260005. Lancashire. 2536 feet.*

This is one of the most interesting of the Coniston Fells. It lies due west of Swirl How and there are routes to it from Great How Crags south of Swirl How, and from Great Carrs further north. For the walker who reaches the ridge at its southern end and proceeds over the Old Man and Brim Fell, the obvious route is to bear left from below Great How Crags to Grey Friar, returning via Great Carrs and Swirl How. There are good views of Seathwaite Tarn as one skirts Great How Crags but there is no clear footpath until the ridge connecting Grey Friar and Great Carrs is reached.

There is also a direct ascent from Cockley Beck in the Duddon valley up the north-western slopes of Grey Friar. It is not the sort of ascent to be recommended, but a descent by that route would be attractive for anyone who had reached the main Coniston Fell ridge from the Duddon valley by the Walna Scar road.

The summit is rocky and is marked by three cairns. It can provide good shelter from wind and rain, and fine views into Dunnerdale when the weather is clear.

GREY KNOTTS

135. *Sheet 82.* Reference 219127. Cumberland. 2287 feet.*

Grey Knotts is on the route between Great Gable and the Honister Pass and this is the reason it is so often visited. However, the views of Buttermere, Ennerdale and Borrowdale provided by the ridge from Honister over Grey Knotts and Brandreth are sufficient in themselves to attract those who have no interest in getting to the top of Gable. Little over an hour would be required for the return trip from Honister.

GREY NAG

136. *Sheet 83. Reference 666477. Northumberland. 2154 feet.*
137. *Subsidiary summit at 664480. 2050 feet.*

Grey Nag is the end of one arm of the summit ridge which starts from Hartside Height just north of the highest point on the Alston–Penrith road. The Bartholomews road map gives its name as Middle Carrick but the name Grey Nag is not in doubt if one refers to the Ordnance Survey. Cold Fell, the most northerly of the Pennine mountain summits, lies a few miles to the north-west.

From Hartside Cross the ridge runs north over Hartside Height to Black Fell, a pleasant walk over grassy moorland. The descent on the northern side takes one into a patch of severe bog which is the source of streams running down to feed the Eden on the west and the South Tyne on the east. Just after Woldgill Tarn, Tom Smith's stone is reached. This stone, at an altitude of 2071 feet, marks the border between Cumberland and Northumberland and a wall runs from the spot to the sheep pens near the main summit of Grey Nag. The trig point and cairn marking the summit are to the west of the wall and the subsidiary summit, which provides the better viewpoint of the two, is about 400 yards to the north-west.

The round trip from Hartside Cross requires about 3½ hours. Those who undertake it need to choose a spell of dry weather and to be prepared for some hard going through the bog. It is not merely a question of walking but rather of careful selection of the most practicable route. However, the walker will have the place to himself and will not see any signs of orange peel, waste paper or empty tins.

An alternative route, avoiding the bog of Woldgill Tarn, would be to take the Pennine Way route from about 696490 of the Alston–Brampton road, and strike up to Great Heaplow from about 694357, continuing over Whitley Common to the Grey Nag summit.

GRISEDALE PIKE

138. *Sheet 82.* Reference 199226. Cumberland. 2593 feet.*

Grisedale Pike is at the northern end of that magnificent ridge walk which runs over Hopegill Head, Eel Crag, Crag Hill, Sail and Scar

Crags to its southern end at Causey Pike. The walk is given in more detail under the Causey Pike entry and it is perhaps only necessary to add that the circuit could equally well be started from near Braithwaite at 228236 on the Whinlatter road by a direct ascent up the long slope to Grisedale Pike. Because of the angle of this slope and the fine views it provides of the Skiddaw range, however, it is best to approach Grisedale Pike by the route from Causey Pike.

For those who do not wish to tackle the 4½-hour round trip a shorter route is possible by taking the other path from 228236 which runs beside the Coledale Beck to Coledale Hause. The path is an old mining track with an easy gradient and a good firm surface and there are pleasant views all the way with impressive views of the crags below the south face of Grisedale Pike as the gradient steepens before Coledale Hause is reached. From that point the mountain is in full view and there is an easy ascent in a north-easterly direction to the summit. About three hours are required for the round trip.

Grisedale Pike is perhaps the most graceful of English summits. On a distant view Buckden Pike in upper Wharfedale has similar lines, but closer inspection proves Grisedale Pike to be far superior. It will bear inspection from most points of the compass and its modest cairn, sometimes decorated with fence posts, is not really in keeping with its merits.

HARD HILL

139. *Sheets 83 and 84. Reference 731331. Westmorland. 2225 feet.*

The name is supposed to mean the inaccessible hill and presumably relates to times long past when there was no road to the old mine near Tyne Head and beyond. Today, those with permission to use the road to Moor House may drive to within 1½ miles of its summit.

The hill lies in the Moor House Nature Reserve and permission to walk there should be obtained from the Warden. It can be approached from the Cross Fell ridge down the old mine track which runs from just south of Great Dun Fell past Moor House to Tyne Head, or it can be approached in the reverse direction. The latter is the best approach and involves leaving the car at Darngill Bridge (774371) on the B.627 Alston–Middleton-in-Teesdale road and walking over Tynehead Fell and Bellbeaver Rigg to the Tyne Head road, or parking at 757384 on the minor road to Tyne Head from Garrigill and then walking due south past Tyne Head. In either case the Tyne Head road should be followed to the bridge over the River Tees at 760338 and the path up Trout Beck taken to the south-west. Trout Beck is a pleasant stream and the walking easy and there is no problem in reaching the trig point on the summit if the line of the stream running into Trout Beck at 737323 is followed.

Those who do not mind getting their feet wet can then continue due north across the Tees over Round Hill and descend from its subsidiary summit to the end of the public road at 757384. From here there is a track across the South Tyne to a footpath leading to the B.627 road just above Darngill Bridge.

The round trip takes 4¼ hours from Darngill Bridge and 3½ hours from 757384.

HARRISON STICKLE

140. *Sheet 82.* Reference 282074. Westmorland. 2403 feet.*

Walkers tend to neglect the Langdale Pikes. They leave them to the rock climbers and tourists, preferring the wild valleys of Wasdale, Borrowdale and Ennerdale to the peaceful scene in Langdale.

Harrison Stickle is the eastern pike, eighty feet higher than Pike of Stickle and separated from it by a distance of half a mile, a dimension which will no doubt surprise those who are familiar with the view of the two summits from the south-east.

One of the most frequently used ascents is from the Langdale valley by the path on the west side of the Dungeon Ghyll stream, rising steeply to the more or less level ground between the two Pikes. After ascending the two Pikes it is convenient to go north as far as Pavey Ark and descend by the path which skirts the east side of Stickle Tarn and runs beside Mill Gill down to the valley. A little over three hours is required.

Alternatively one could ascend from Stonethwaite in Borrowdale by way of Langstrath and the northern section of Stake Pass, returning over Thurnacar Knott and High Raise and then down Greenup Gill, a round trip of eight hours, or one could take the Easedale Tarn path from Grasmere and ascend by way of Blea Rigg, Sergeant Man and Thurnacar Knott, a round trip of about 5½ hours.

Harrison Stickle is seen at its best from the top of Pike of Blisco or from just north of Bleatarn House on the road between the Langdale valleys, a much better view than one gets at close quarters.

HART CRAG

141. *Sheet 83.* Reference 368112. Westmorland. 2698 feet.*

Hart Crag lies on the ridge between Fairfield and Dove Crag about three-quarters of a mile north-west of the latter summit and the routes described under the Dove Crag entry are equally applicable to Hart Crag. In addition, there is a direct route from Bridgend in the Patterdale valley up the ridge between Deepdale and Dovedale to a point just north of Hart Crag.

The summit is rocky and is marked by a number of cairns. It is quite a contrast to the grass of most of the ridges in this area and prompts one to think of the approaches to Scafell Pikes.

HART SIDE

142. *Sheet 83.* Reference 359198. Cumberland. 2481 feet.*
143. *Subsidiary summit at 363195. 2350 feet.*

Hart Side is said to mean the side of the hill frequented by stags, but it is doubtful if it lives up to its name. Its twin summits, with outcrops of boulders and a few cairns have a few pools and marshy patches but their grassy slopes provide easy walking. They are best reached as part of an excursion to Green Side as described under that entry.

HARTER FELL (ESKDALE)

144. *Sheet 88.* Reference 218997. Cumberland. 2129 feet.*

Harter Fell means stag hill and there are two of them in Lakeland, one above Mardale near to the Martindale deer sanctuary and one between the Esk and Duddon valleys where deer are less likely to be encountered. The Mardale Harter Fell gives fine views of Haweswater, which now takes up so much of Mardale, but Eskdale Harter Fell gives better views of the Duddon and Wrynose Pass than it does of Eskdale, and Dunnerdale Harter Fell might be a more appropriate name.

Ascents are possible from the Esk or Duddon valleys and from the top of Hard Knott Pass which links them on the northern side of Harter Fell. The Duddon route starts from 235994 and, apart from the initial walk through the forest, is a straightforward ascent up the south-east slope, while the ascent from the Esk Valley starts either from the road which crosses the river near the Woolpack Inn or from the Eskdale side of Hard Knott Pass, the two paths joining at 207998 to continue south along the stream to 211993 and then ascend the south-western slope.

The route from Hard Knott Pass involves a direct approach in a south-westerly direction, at first over marshy patches interspersed with rock and finally a scramble over boulders and through gaps in the crags. It saves over 1000 feet of ascent as compared with the other routes and is a pleasant, easy walk. However, those who prefer to have alternative routes for the ascent and descent will find it best to ascend from the bottom of Hard Knott by the path running round the northern slopes and descend from Harter Fell to the top of the pass, walking down the pass past the ruins of the Roman fort to the starting point.

There are three high points at the top, the highest with a small cairn perched somewhat precariously on a pointed rock, one with a trig point and one a big rock with ample sitting room for a sizeable party. The latter provides good views of the Sca Fell ridge, the Duddon valley and Wrynose, Seathwaite Tarn and the Duddon Sands. Two hours suffice for the round trip from Hard Knott but one could easily spend a long time on the rocks at the summit.

HARTER FELL (MARDALE)

145. *Sheet 83.* Reference 461095. Westmorland. 2539 feet.*

Mardale Harter Fell is not an isolated peak like its namesake in Eskdale but forms the end of a ridge. Even so, the crags on its northern slopes make an impressive sight to those who view them from the southern end of Mardale. There is an easy ascent from the southern end of Haweswater by the Gatescarth Pass and thence over Adam Seat, and those who have been impressed by the magnificent crags which are in view for much of the way may be surprised to find what an easy grassy walk the summit provides. More important, if the right spot is chosen somewhere on the ridge north-east of the summit cairn, it provides magnificent views of Haweswater. Its summit is marked by two cairns.

A direct return to Mardale can be made by the Nan Bield Pass past Small Water, 2½ hours sufficing for the round trip, but the walk can readily be extended either north to High Street or south to Kentmere Pike as described under the entry for Adam Seat. That entry also describes an ascent from the Longsleddale valley.

HARTSOP DOD

146. *Sheet 83.* Reference 412118. Westmorland. 2018 feet.*

Hartsop Dod overlooks Hartsop and Ullswater and the shortest ascents are by the footpath from 403117, just south of Brotherswater Hotel, or that from 405126, alongside Brothers Water. Those who prefer to avoid a steep grassy ascent are recommended to take the path which starts from 402083, just north of the Kirkstone Inn. After a short scramble up St. Raven's Edge it continues along the

Edge over Pike How towards Caudale Head and then turns east to Stony Cove Pike. From that point it continues north over high ground to the small cairn which marks the summit of Hartsop Dod. This makes a very pleasant walk, particularly good views being obtained of Patterdale, part of Ullswater and the crags east of Fairfield.

The round trip back to Kirkstone requires just short of four hours. Those who have the time and the energy can extend it by descending the sharp drop east of Stony Cove Pike to Thornythwaite Beacon and beyond.

HAYCOCK

147. *Sheet 82.* Reference 145107. Cumberland. 2618 feet.*

Haycock, lying at the western end of the Pillar group, is off the beaten track and will appeal to those who like to be alone on the hills.

The shortest approach from a motor road is from 158064 on the north side of Wastwater, up Nether Beck by the path which crosses the dip between Haycock and Scoat Fell to the head of Ennerdale Water. From the highest point on this path a short walk south-west up the slope brings one to the cairn on the top of Haycock. About 3½ hours would be required for the round trip back to Wastwater but, on a fine day, most walkers would wish to extend the walk along the ridge towards Pillar in the north-east. There are two alternatives, the shorter being to turn south from Steeple over Red Pike and Yewbarrow for a round trip of about five hours and the other being to continue over Pillar to return by Black Sail Pass in a round trip of 6½ hours.

From the Ennerdale side the approach is much longer, but is not to be despised. Ennerdale has been changed by afforestation but it still seems a much more peaceful valley than Wasdale and those who wish to explore it can readily use it for an ascent of Haycock coupled with a walk along the ridge over Scoat Fell and Steeple or even as far as Pillar and Black Sail Pass. There is a parking site where the public road ends near Bowness on the northern side of Ennerdale and the forestry road can be followed along the lake to 131144 where the track to the south is taken across the Liza, and then either up the slopes east of Deep Gill, over Tewit How to the gap between Haycock and Scoat Fell or up the ridge between Deep Gill and Silvercove Beck to Little Gowder Crag.

Those using the former route will then have to ascend up a grassy slope to the Haycock summit and then return to proceed to Scoat Fell, Steeple and Pillar. Those ascending by Little Gowder Crag will have a slightly longer walk but will then be able to proceed down the opposite slope without retracing their steps.

For those wishing to limit their day, the ridge north of Steeple is a possible line of descent, but it limits the walking in the upper Ennerdale valley and it is better to continue to Wind Gap at 168118 and descend from there by the path which follows the upper stretches of High Beck. This would involve a round trip of about six hours, while the complete circuit over Pillar to descend by Black Sail Pass into Ennerdale just above the Youth Hostel would take 7½ hours.

The snag in the Ennerdale route is the long stretch of road along the valley so that, on a direct comparison, the Wastwater starting point is to be preferred. However, the alternative can be strongly recommended to those who wish to see the beauty of the upper Ennerdale valley.

HEDGEHOPE HILL

148. *Sheet 71. Reference 943198. Northumberland. 2348 feet.*

Hedgehope Hill, the most easterly of the Cheviots, lies south of the Harthope Burn and can be reached from Longleeford. A better approach, however, is to walk it as an extension of the walk to Comb Fell as described under that entry. The summit is marked by a large cairn on which a trig point has been erected.

There is little to be said in favour of the summit but anyone going there by way of Comb Fell will be amply rewarded by the walk along the Harthope Linn.

HELVELLYN

149. *Sheet 83.* Reference 342152. Cumberland/Westmorland. 3113 feet.*

Helvellyn, the highest point in Westmorland, is the most popular of English mountain summits when judged by the number of people who climb it, its popularity probably stemming from it being in excess of 3000 feet in height, the highest mountain readily accessible to the majority of visitors to Lakeland, and from having a variety of access routes which cater for all tastes. Anyone attracted by Striding Edge is more or less compelled to continue on to Helvellyn, even if only to return immediately down Swirral Edge, and this guarantees the summit a stream of keen walkers to leaven the procession of casual visitors, many of whom are perhaps making the only real walk of their lives.

Fortunately, the Helvellyn crowd is confined to a comparatively small section of that magnificent six-mile ridge of which Helvellyn is the highest point. Even at the southern end, the summits of Dollywaggon Pike and Nethermost Pike are often deserted and the northern end is sometimes looked on as the loneliest part of Lakeland. While, therefore, Helvellyn will not have a strong appeal to those who know the rugged heart of Lakeland, it is useful to have it as a link between Striding and Swirral edges and to absorb all the people who might otherwise be trampling a broad highway on more secluded summits.

Routes to the Helvellyn ridge from Patterdale, Glenridding and Grasmere have already been mentioned under the entry for Dollywaggon Pike. Additionally, Helvellyn can be reached by a number of old traditional routes from the Thirlmere valley, notably that from Thirlspot (317178) which ascends by the north-western slopes over White Side and Lower Man and that from Wythburn (326136) by Birk Side or, the shortest route of all, from Wythburn by Whelpside Gill. None of these routes is to be recommended. For anyone who cannot use one of the various approaches from Patterdale or Glenridding the best course would be to take a bus from Grasmere to Stanah (319189) and ascend the ridge by Sticks Pass. This would provide a delightful walk over Raise and Helvellyn down to Dollywaggon Pike and allow the Grisedale route to be used for the return to Grasmere. The walking time would be only 5½ hours and, while the walk up Sticks Pass might be found a little monotonous, it would be better than the drag up White Side and the longer ridge walk would repay the effort.

HELVELLYN LOWER MAN

150. *Sheet 83.* Reference 338154. Cumberland/Westmorland. 3033 feet.*

This is the next summit to Helvellyn along the ridge less than half a mile to the north-east. It is also on the route from Thirlspot and is thus more frequently traversed than many of the other Lakeland summits.

HERDSHIP FELL

151. *Sheet 84. Reference 794328. Durham. 2100 feet.*

Herdship Fell lies almost at the head of Teesdale between the river and the road to Alston. The best approach is by the mine road which runs from 783354 on the Alston road along the south side of Viewing Hill and Herdship Fell to Langdon Beck. By following this track to somewhere near 787326 and striking up the hill slightly north of east it should not be difficult to find the summit of Herdship Fell. One hour from leaving the Alston road should be sufficient, the summit being small and marked with three whitewashed pieces of metal—possibly as an indication for air surveys—and a metal hemisphere with a hole in the top like that found on the summit of Red Howe below Crinkle Crags.

There is no bog on top of Herdship Fell but it is wet and marshy and provides feeding for a large number of golden plover and a few curlews. While the Cow Green reservoir is much in evidence to the south-east, Herdship Fell itself has that desolate appearance peculiar to the old mining areas of Durham.

Returning over Viewing Fell involves a walk in bog, first in the dip between the two summits and then over most of the flat top of Viewing Fell, and could well take rather more than an hour because of the difficult going.

HERON PIKE

152. *Sheet 83.* Reference 356083. Westmorland. 2003 feet.*
153. *Subsidiary summit at 357087. 2000 feet.*

Heron Pike forms the southern end of the ridge which runs due south from Fairfield. It can be ascended direct from Alcock Tarn, which is reached by the footpath branching off at 346085 from that from Grasmere to Stone Arthur. This makes a pleasant walk.

Those who have the time to spare and suitable weather, however, will find it preferable to reach Heron Pike by walking the Fairfield horseshoe, or the alternative ridge over Snarker Pike, from Ambleside as described under the entry for Dove Crag. Such an approach gives one the benefit of the views to the south.

The main summit is marked by a small outcrop of rock and there is a small cairn on the subsidiary summit.

HIGHER SHELF STONES

154. *Sheet 102. Reference 089948. Derbyshire. 2037 feet.*

The name means high hill with stones. They lie south of Bleaklow Head and can be reached by a short diversion from the Pennine Way route between the Snake Road and Bleaklow Head. This diversion is well worth while, the summit overlooking the steep-sided Shelf Brook and Doctor's Gate and being marked by a number of jagged rocks which tower over the trig point.

Those starting from the Snake Road, however, will be well advised to keep off the Pennine Way, which tends to be very wet and muddy on the flat stretch just north of the road. Instead, they should head for the bend in Crooked Clough at 089936 and follow the path which runs on the eastern side. It is firm and reasonably dry when the Pennine Way is over ankle-deep in mud and leads to an easy crossing of the stream just north of the fork at 095945, from which point one can head north-west directly to the summit. By this route the summit can be reached in less than half an hour from the Snake Road—a worth while diversion for anyone travelling across the Pennines by this route.

Wain Stones and Bleaklow Head are about three-quarters of a mile away just east of north and Bleaklow Stones a further 1½ miles to the east across the wild plateau. In summer this is a routine moorland walk but in winter, with snow on the ground, it can be an exciting adventure. On a visit in February 1970 the rocks were covered with beautiful patterns made by snow driven into their faces by a strong wind and subsequently frozen. With their height enhanced by accumulations of snow and ice they completely dwarfed that part of the trig point pillar which stood above the snow.

HIGH CRAG (BUTTERMERE)

155. *Sheet 82.* Reference 180140. Cumberland. 2443 feet.*

There are two High Crags; this, which forms part of the Buttermere ring, and another which lies between Dollywaggon and Nethermost Pikes on the Helvellyn ridge. The latter is the higher of the two but my preference is for the former.

From Gatesgarth, at the foot of Honister on the Buttermere side, a path goes across the flat land above the lake and then heads south up Scarth Gap. At the highest point of the pass a path crosses the Scarth Gap path and goes up a steep incline to the summit of High Crag. The actual path may be indistinct because of the loose scree over which it wends its way as height is gained, but the general direction is obvious.

At the summit one is at the beginning of one of the finest ridge walks in the country. High Stile is less than one mile to the north-west and Red Pike is almost a mile further on over Chapel Crags. One can descend to the northern end of Buttermere by way of The Saddle on the north-east shoulder of Red Pike or by Scale Force to the north, or continue over a wide grassy ridge by way of Starling Dodd and Great Borne to return by the path running north of

Floutern Tarn to Crummock Water. The round trip back to Gatesgarth via The Saddle requires three and a quarter hours, while the longer route round by Floutern Tarn would take 5½ hours.

HIGH CRAG (HELVELLYN)

156. *Sheet 83.* Reference 343136. Cumberland/Westmorland. 2850 feet.*

This lies on the ridge between Dollywaggon Pike and Nethermost Pike south of Helvellyn. As with the two Pikes, it gives magnificent views of much of Lakeland and can readily be reached by a small diversion from any of the routes to Helvellyn.

HIGH PIKE (AMBLESIDE)

157. *Sheet 83.* Reference 374087. Westmorland. 2155 feet.*

This graceful peak, which just qualifies as a separate summit by virtue of the slight dip in the slope as the ridge continues north, is the first summit on the Fairfield 'horseshoe' when walked from east to west as outlined under the entry for Dove Crag. There is a small cairn at the top and the walk from 374054, just north of Ambleside, is pleasant and quite rocky. Full value for the effort involved, however, is only obtained by those who continue to Dove Crag and Fairfield to return down the Rydal Fell ridge in a round trip of about five hours.

HIGH PIKE (CALDBECK)

158. *Sheet 82.* Reference 319350. Cumberland. 2159 feet.*

High Pike is the most northerly of the Lakeland mountain summits, lying due north of Saddleback. It is convenient to include it in the walks covering Carrock Fell and Great Lingy Fell, as described under those entries. The walk to the summit is an easy stroll over grass, the summit being clearly marked with a trig point and cairn and having a solid slate seat nearby erected to the memory of Alec Lowson. This monument suggests that these remote summits may be more popular than is generally supposed. High Pike is certainly a pleasant viewpoint over the rural country to the north-west and the hills to the south and south-east, but it may also derive some of its popularity from the fact that it has a number of old mining areas on its slopes.

(*above*) HIGH WILLHAYS (Devon) and (*below*) HIGH WILLHAYS and YES TOR

(*above*) HILTON FELL (Pennines)

(*below*) HOPEGILL HEAD (Lakes) from Whiteside

HUGH SEAT (Pennines). Cotterdale

ILL CRAG (Lakes) across Little Narrowcove

HIGH PIKE HILL

159. *Sheet 90. Reference 803034. Westmorland/Yorkshire (N.R.). 2105 feet.*

This is the northern end of the ridge which overlooks the upper waters of the River Eden in its lovely valley south of Kirkby Stephen. The obvious route of ascent is from near the county boundary (812042) on the B.6270 road from Kirkby Stephen to Muker. A little west of the boundary, opposite the cairn which marks the bridle-way to the north, there is a green grassy patch which leads to a sheep track across the bog before the steep slope. From there a fairly sharp rise takes one to the broad flat summit which is marked by a neat slim cairn of moderate size.

The views from the summit are quite remarkable, the Lakeland summits, Cross Fell, the Howgills, Wild Boar Fell, Rogans Seat and Nine Standards Rigg being visible as well as the inn at Tan Hill.

The walk can be continued south along the ridge to High Seat, Mallerstang Edge, Hugh Seat and Sails on Abbotside Common.

HIGH RAISE (LANGDALE)

160. *Sheet 82.* Reference 281096. Cumberland. 2500 feet.*

High Raise lies on the ridge running north from the Langdale Pikes to Ullscarf. If one draws a line from Tarn Crag, the most easterly summit of Lakeland, to Iron Crag, the most westerly, and another one from High Pike, the most northerly, to Walna Scar, the most southerly, they intersect on its summit. High Raise can therefore be accepted as the centre of Lakeland, despite the claims of Esk Hause with its more strategic position.

High Raise is crossed on the route between Borrowdale and Harrison Stickle as described under that entry, but there is a lot to be said for keeping it as a separate excursion. Those starting from the Borrowdale area will find the best approach is from Stonethwaite (263136) up the lovely Langstrath valley, leaving the Stake Pass route at 265087 to head slightly north of east for three-quarters of a mile and then north-east to the summit. There is a trig point to the west of it. From here the walk can be continued to the north to return from 286105 by the path down Greenup Gill back to Stonethwaite, a round trip of four hours.

An alternative route is from Grasmere by Easedale Tarn, whose white waterfall is such a prominent feature of the view from the slopes below Heron Pike. From Easedale Tarn a path goes south-west to Blea Rigg and continues along Blea Rigg to Sergeant Man and High Raise. From High Raise one can go north to 286105 to return down Far Easedale Gill or over Gibson Knott and Helm Crag back to Grasmere.

Either of these routes can be extended to include Ullscarf, 1½ miles north of 286105. Both of them provide very attractive walks and the time on the high ground near the summit should provide a very comprehensive view of the Lakeland tops.

HIGH RAISE (MARDALE)

161. *Sheet 83.* Reference 448134. Westmorland. 2634 feet.*

High Raise is the name of the first summit beyond Kidsty Pike on the ridge which runs north from High Street to Loadpot Hill near Howtown on Ullswater. It barely gets a mention in Baddeley's guide, which devotes considerable space to the High Raise above Langdale. Of the two, many will prefer the one which overlooks Mardale.

For those who wish to walk the ridge the best approach is probably from Howtown on the south bank of Ullswater. A path runs south from there up Fusedale to reach the ridge just north of Red Crag at 453155 and a walk of 1½ miles due south brings one, after a gentle rise, to the summit of High Raise. The line of the old Roman Road can be followed on the return from High Raise and continued past Red Crag to Wether Hill and Loadpot Hill, and Fusedale can be regained by a path down the stream which has its source on the western slopes of Loadspot Hill. The round trip from Howtown should take about 4½ hours.

Those who object to retracing their steps, even on such fine walking country as the High Street ridge, can take a wider sweep from Howtown following the road past Martindale church and turning left at 434190 to take the road to Dale Head (434165). From this point a path goes south-west up Bannerdale in a wide arc to reach The Knott, from which point the main High Street ridge can be joined and the return effected over Ramsgill Head, High Raise, Raven Howe, Red Crag, Wether Hill and Loadpot Hill. This round trip takes only an hour longer than the Fusedale route, but may not appeal to those whose primary interest is to see the High Street ridge.

HIGH SCALD FELL

162. *Sheet 83. Reference 718287. Westmorland. 2256 feet.*

High Scald Fell, on the Pennine ridge a few miles south of Cross Fell, is readily accessible by those reaching Backstone Edge from

Dufton or by those approaching Backstone Edge from Knock Fell as described under the entry for Backstone Edge. The route from Backstone Edge is north-east to Great Rundale Tarn, a pleasant spot in this otherwise grim moorland, and then north-west to High Scald Fell. Those wishing to complete a short round trip from Dufton can return by the track which runs down Great Rundale Beck.

The summit is marked by a cairn and it provides views over the Eden Valley to the Lake District.

HIGH SEAT

163. *Sheet 90. Reference 803013. Westmorland/Yorkshire* (*N.R.*). *2328 feet.*

High Seat is the summit south of High Pike Hill on the Mallerstang Edge ridge and its ascent is merely a matter of walking due south from High Pike Hill on the ridge for about 1¼ miles. Its summit is not marked but it has two cairns on its slopes, one north of the summit and one south.

HIGH STILE

164. *Sheet 82.* Reference 169148. Cumberland. 2644 feet.*

This is the highest of the Buttermere Fells, less than one mile along the ridge from High Crag. What a ridge it is, giving views across the Ennerdale valley to the Pillar group on one side and across the Buttermere valley to the Derwent fells and Grasmoor on the other! The narrow rocky section continues beyond High Stile to end about three-quarters of a mile further on just before the steep rise to the rounded summit of Red Pike, but a broad grassy ridge continues from there to Great Borne above Ennerdale.

Apart from being reached from the High Crag or Great Borne ends of the ridge, High Stile can be approached directly from Buttermere by paths which start either from the village or from Gatesgarth and meet at 181149 to ascend by the line of crags north of Burtness Combe. This route provides better views than the other approaches and the fact that it strikes the main ridge at its centre point, necessitating retracing of steps if one is to walk the length of it, is no disadvantage in country like this.

HIGH STREET

165. *Sheet 83.* Reference 441110. Westmorland. 2719 feet.*

This flat summit, which carried the Roman Road north from Ambleside towards Penrith and the Wall and was subsequently used, it is said, for local horse races, is best ascended from Mardale. There are somewhat longer and easier routes to it from Hartsop by Hayeswater Gill and the Knott, from Kirkstone by St. Raven's Edge, Stony Cove Pike and Thornthwaite Crag and from Windermere by the Roman Road up Hagg Gill, but there is little doubt that the Mardale route is to be preferred. Even from Mardale there is a choice of three routes; the Nan Bield route, leading to High Street over Mardale Ill Bell, and the two ridges of Riggindale Crags and Kidsty Pike. Ascent by Riggindale Crags and descent by Kidsty Pike is probably the best choice.

There is parking for a few cars at the southern end of Haweswater and a path leads across the wet ground to the ridge which descends from High Street by Riggindale Crags to Haweswater. One path leads to the foot of the ridge while another leads to Blea Tarn and an ascent by a grassy slope to a point high up on the ridge. The former is preferable and leads to a magnificent ridge walk over the Rough Crag summit to High Street with fine views of Blea Tarn on the way. High Street summit, marked by a trig point, is a little way south of the point where the High Street ridge is first reached.

From this point, after having another look at Blea Tarn, one can continue north along the flat ridge to Ramsgill Head and then bear left to The Knott and on to Rest Dod, three-quarters of a mile further on, with its fine views over the deer sanctuary of The Nab above Martindale. Returning to The Knott and striking due east brings one to the familiar summit of Kidsty Pike and the return to Mardale can be achieved by continuing down Kidsty Howes to Haweswater and back to the road along the shore.

The round trip takes about 4½ hours.

HIGH SPY

See Eel Crags.

HIGH WILLHAYS

166. *Sheet 175. Reference 579891. Devon. 2038 feet.*

This summit is in the Dartmoor National Park and forms part of an artillery range. Okehampton is the nearest town and inquiries there in the spring of 1969 elicited the information that there is never any firing on Saturdays and that details of firing times can be obtained from the police and local Post Offices. What an excellent arrangement and what a pity it is that a similar system does not operate for the Warcop Range!

If one takes the road marked to the Dartmoor National Park which runs due south from the main street in Okehampton and follows it to the east gate of the camp at 592932, one finds a notice stating that there is no entry beyond the red and white posts when a red flag is flying on Yes Tor or a red lamp lit at night. Having checked that the range is open, one may take the road which turns sharply to the right at that point and follow it to where the good surface ends north-east of West Mill Tor at 589914. The rough track which runs from that point should then be followed for just under a mile to 586902, from which point it is an easy walk to the W.D. shelter on the east side of Yes Tor just below the highest point. An easy scramble from there up the rocks brings one to the highest point which is marked by a large flagpole and a trig point.

High Willhays, pronounced locally as 'High Willies', is three-quarters of a mile due south of Yes Tor, the walk there being over rough but dry moorland. There are two rocky outcrops on the summit, the first bare and the second carrying a W.D. shelter, but nothing to indicate that this is the highest summit in Devon and the most southerly and most westerly in England.

Those who take the trouble to visit this area will naturally wish for a longer excursion than that already described and can be recommended to sample the area of Hangingstone Hill (617861) and Whitehorse Hill (617854). There is a big area of bog—not so bad as Kinder Scout or Yockenthwaite as the gullies are fairly shallow—but bog all the same and there is a monument there, erected in 1909, to a Mr. Philpotts who made a track through the bog for the benefit of cattlemen and hunters. About a mile to the west of the monument to Mr. Philpotts at 603858 is Cranmere Pool, the centre of Dartmoor.

HILTON FELL

167. *Sheet 84. Reference 775235. Westmorland. 2249 feet.*

Hilton Fell, together with ten other summits, lies within the Warcop Artillery Range and this presents a problem of access. It is not easy to assess the full extent of the range. The 1-inch Ordnance Survey does not give any limit or even mention the range in its 1964 edition but, in the 1970 edition, goes so far as to mark seven 'Danger Areas'. These, for the benefit of those using earlier editions of the map, are centred on references 765265, 735234, 767202, 772239, 769163, 748179 and 795232. Unfortunately, there is no indication of the extent of each area. The Ordnance Survey's explanation is that it is unwise to indicate limits because the extent of the danger areas may change.

The range authorities do not appear to be too concerned about marking the actual danger areas but prefer to draw an all-embracing boundary and to keep everyone outside. This area covers about forty square miles and its borders roughly follow the line Murton–High Cup Nick–Cronkley Fell (839282)–Ley Seat (828203)–Lowgill Cottage (774152)–Hilton–Murton. Red flags are flown at a few points when the range is in use but, for the most part, because the range is so big, the authorities rely on warning notices reading:

'Danger W.D. Range, Shelled Area.
Beyond this point you proceed at your own risk'.

Such a notice, encountered without previous warning on a wild Pennine slope, is calculated to deter most walkers.

Security arrangements are obviously taken very seriously (as they should be) by the range authorities and, in 1970, they claimed that they had not had any casualties in the preceeding thirty years. On the other hand, they seem to be unnecessarily restrictive. It is very doubtful whether it is necessary to exclude the public from about forty square miles of the wildest part of the Pennines for the amount of firing which takes place. But it is obviously very much easier for the range authorities to have an all-embracing restriction on access than to confine the restriction to the area actually required, and this is perhaps one of the chief reasons for the present situation. What is annoying, however, is the fact that the standard arrangement is for firing to take place from Tuesday to Sunday inclusive, so that such access as is available is normally confined to the Monday of each week, conveniently (perhaps) calculated to be of the least possible value to walkers. Exceptionally, the range does not operate for two short periods in the spring and autumn when the local farmers round up their sheep. These periods are fixed by the farmers at annual meetings with the range authorities.

The authorities at the range H.Q. at Warcop will normally be willing to indicate when the range is not in use and they have assured me that there is no risk to the walker as long as firing is not in progress provided, of course, he refrains from touching any metal objects he may encounter.

Having established that there will not be any firing, a car may be parked at 735207 overlooking the entrance to the range area on the eastern outskirts of the small village of Hilton. A bridle path on the right bank of Hilton Beck takes one up a very beautiful valley, which often contains a herd of ponies, to reference 764233. From this point a steep ascent, followed by a walk over gently rising ground in an easterly direction, brings one to the large cairn of substantial stones which marks the summit of Hilton Fell at 775235.

The walk may conveniently be extended two miles east-north-east to Mickle Fell and 1½ miles south-east to Little Fell and the return to Hilton effected by the path which runs from 770207 along Swindale Edge back to the main valley.

Readers may be interested to know the reaction of the Ramblers Association to a suggestion that they negotiate with the range authorities for the free day to be changed from Monday to either Saturday or Sunday. Their local investigator said that week-ends are the busy periods at the Warcop Range because this is the time civilian volunteers are able to participate in exercises and it would therefore be difficult to persuade the Army to make any change. However, he volunteered the information that it was 'reasonably safe' to use the path along Hilton Beck when firing was taking place as firing was always into Roman Fell and Little Fell and it was only the 'very, very bad shot' which went over the sky-line. Could the Army authorities wish for anything more reasonable?

HINDSCARTH

168. *Sheet 82.* Reference 216165. Cumberland. 2385 feet.*
169. *Subsidiary summit at 215160. 2200 feet.*

Hindscarth, the hill of the hinds, lies in the middle of the Newlands or Derwent fells, between Dale Head and Robinson, about five miles south-west of Keswick.

It can be included in the ascent of Dale Head as described under that entry but the preferable route is to take the footpath from 232195 in the Newlands valley up Scope End (225184) and walk along the crags to the main Hindscarth summit, continuing over the subsidiary bump and returning via Dale Head and the Maiden Moor ridge.

Alternatively, one could include Hindscarth in the round trip from Gatescarth in Buttermere over Dale Head and Robinson as described under the Fleetwith Pike entry.

HONISTER CRAG

170. *Sheet 82.* Reference 213142. Cumberland. 2050 feet.*

Honister Crag dominates the Honister Pass and stands out to the north-east of Fleetwith Pike when one looks up the pass from the Buttermere valley. It can be reached without difficulty from the top of Honister Pass, via the Drum House, the return trip from the road taking only about 1½ hours.

Alternatively, being only half a mile east of Fleetwith Pike on the route to the top of Honister Pass, it can be included in the various ascents of Fleetwith Pike from Gatescarth described under the Fleetwith Pike entry.

Currently, one of the main attractions of Honister Crag is the magnificent viewpoint it provides for anyone who wishes to watch the traffic on the road up the pass. How different this scene is from those days in the early 1930s before the road was constructed. At that time the route was a rough pony track and there were times when ascent of the pass could involve an exhausting battle with wind and rain. Walkers who knew the pass in those days will never cease to regret the construction of the motor road, but will comfort themselves with the thought that the fears that the road over Honister would be followed by one over Sty Head have so far proved groundless.

HOPEGILL HEAD

171. *Sheet 82.* Reference 185223. Cumberland. 2525 feet.*

Hopegill Head, overlooking Whinlatter Forest and Coledale Hause, the head of the pass between Braithwaite and Loweswater, is thought by some to be a little frequented part of Lakeland. The distinct footpath along the ridge towards Whiteside and another over Ladyside Pike suggest that this is no longer the case.

Paths up Coledale Beck from 227236, from near Braithwaite, or up Gasgale Gill from Lanthwaite Green (159209) lead to Coledale Hause and it is an easy ascent from there to the Hopegill Head summit less than one mile to the north. Alternatively, using the same starting points, one can take a more direct approach by walking over Grisedale Pike or Whiteside. Yet another approach is by the path which runs from 169242 over the Ladyside Pike ridge to reach Hopegill Head from the north. The Whiteside approach is very steep at the beginning and parts of the ridge which runs from there to Hopegill Head can be very unpleasant in strong winds, while the Ladyside Pike approach involves a scramble up a crack in a steep rock face which is not recommended for children. All the other routes are straightforward.

Those reaching Hopegill Head from Braithwaite may like to make a round trip by proceeding south over Coledale Hause up Eel Crag and then round the ridge over Sail and Causey Pike to descend by Rowling End to Stair. Those starting from the Loweswater side can either go over Eel Crag, or along the stream between Eel Crag and Grasmoor, to Wanlope and Whiteless Pike, descending from there down its southern ridge and then heading north-west to reach Crummock Water and follow the road back to Lanthwaite

Green. The round trip from Braithwaite can be done in less than five hours while that from Lanthwaite Green takes just over four. Either walk can be extended by a diversion to Grasmoor, about a mile west of Eel Crag.

Hopegill Head presents its most attractive face to the west and is seen to best advantage from the Whiteside summit. It is not marked by a cairn but has a rocky outcrop at its highest point.

HUGH SEAT

172. *Sheet 90. Reference 809992. Westmorland/Yorkshire (N.R.). 2257 feet.*

Hugh Seat is the tip of that spike of the North Riding which intrudes into Westmorland south of the ridge running down the east side of the Mallerstang valley. It is separated from the main ridge by Black Fell Moss, the main source of the River Eden, while its eastern slopes feed the River Swale and the patch of bog to the south is one of the sources of the River Ure which runs down Wensleydale.

Matterstang means boundary mark and the solid square stone structure on the west slope of Hugh Seat just below the summit bearing the markings $\overline{\wedge}$ P 1664 and FHC 1890 suggest that there was more than usual interest in boundary limits in this area as also does the ten foot high square stone tower at 812996 where there is a sharp change in direction on the line of the county boundary.

Apart from this, Hugh Seat is of interest because it is said to be named after Hugh de Morville, one of the knights who murdered Thomas Beckett in Canterbury cathedral on 29th December 1170. He and his accomplices are understood to have remained in hiding for a whole year in his castle at Knaresborough, forty miles from Hugh Seat.

There is easy access to Hugh Seat by walking along Mallerstang Edge from High Pike Hill (to which a route has already been given) and then following the line of the county boundary around Black Fell Moss to the stone wind-break which marks the summit. The views are of rolling Pennine country with Ingleborough, Pen-y-ghent and Whernside in the distance to the south, Great Shunner to the south-east and Wild Boar Fell to the west. Beyond Wild Boar Fell the Howgill summits can be seen.

It is doubtful, however, if Hugh de Morville's cattle came to their spring pastures by way of the wild pass between Muker and Kirkby Stephen. They would be much more likely to use the route up Cotterdale, which leaves the A.684 Hawes–Kendal road at 843922 and, after passing through the hamlet of Cotterdale at 834940, continues up Mid Rigg on Abbotside Common in a fairly direct line to Hugh Seat. This is a pleasant introduction to the wild scene around Hugh Seat and may appeal to those who prefer an alternative route for the return since, from Hugh Seat, one can readily turn due south over the boggy watershed of the Swale and Eden to Sails and then return down its southern ridge to join at 823931 the path which runs from the Mallerstang valley to the A.684 road just west of the entrance to Cotterdale. Four and a half hours should suffice for the round trip.

ILL BELL

173. *Sheet 83.* Reference 437077. Westmorland. 2476 feet.*

The route to Ill Bell, the most imposing peak on the ridge between the Garburn Pass and Thornthwaite Beacon just south of High Street, is described under the entry for Froswick. 'Ill' means 'evil' and refers to its crags. They are such a distinctive feature that the mountain is not given any prefix to distinguish it from the Ill Bell which lies 1½ miles away to the north. This is Mardale Ill Bell which has crags overlooking Blea Water. Mardale Ill Bell is scarcely noticed as one walks the ridge to High Street whereas no one could miss the real Ill Bell. It has a rocky summit with a collection of cairns and makes a fine viewpoint.

ILL CRAG

174. *Sheet 82.* Reference 224074. Cumberland. 3000 feet.*

Ill Crag is about half a mile due east of the main summit of Scafell Pikes, and about a quarter of a mile south of the route to the Pike from Esk Hause. Because it is so close to the main summit without being on one of the routes, and because those who ascend Scafell Pikes often find the main summit sufficient in itself, Ill Crag is visited comparatively rarely. It is not even mentioned in Baddeley's guide.

There are several routes up Scafell Pikes and, once the main summit has been reached, the walk of three-quarters of a mile to the top of Ill Crag should not present any problem. For those who take the route which runs from Esk Hause just south of Great End to Scafell Pikes (described under the entry for Great End) only a short diversion of a quarter of a mile is involved, although there is no recognised path. However, if one leaves the Esk Hause path at a point due north of Ill Crag the going is not difficult, being over a layer of rock interspersed with small patches of moss so that, for some of the time, it is possible to step between the rocks—a welcome relief for the weary feet. After a fairly level walk of about 400 yards, ascent to the summit cairn involves a short scramble over loose and jagged rock.

Those who try to take a short cut from just below the Ill Crag cairn to the dip between Ill Crag and Broad Crag will encounter some laborious and precarious scrambling in the sharp faced rocks just before the dip is reached. For those who prefer an easier route it is best to return directly to the main path.

To see Ill Crag to best advantage, one needs to descend south-east from the main Scafell Pike summit to the ridge above Little Narrocove. With mist drifting over its south-western face, it is an awesome sight.

INGLEBOROUGH

175. *Sheet 90. Reference 741747. Yorkshire (W.R.). 2373 feet.*

The name means 'hill barrow' and the summit was a hill fort, perhaps inhabited in times when the climate was warmer than it is now and certainly occupied by the Brigantes as a centre of resistance against the Romans in the middle of the first century A.D. On the approach routes near Ingleton and Clapham are interesting limestone caves, partially open to the public, and on the southern slopes is Gaping Gill Pothole, 350 feet in depth. Potholers have for a long time been hoping to establish a connection between the Ingleborough cave near Clapham and Gaping Gill. By 1970, after strenuous efforts by caving frog-men, the gap had been narrowed to about forty yards.

Although the full extent of the cave near Clapham and the White Scar cave above Ingleton is not open to the public, enough can be seen to make them well worth a visit. Unfortunately, the readily accessible part of the White Scar cave does not include the vast bottomless lake which is said to lie underneath Ingleborough. Ingleton also has some fine waterfalls and close by, outside Settle, is the Victoria Cave inhabited by Neolithic settlers around 3000 B.C. Can any other mountain offer so much?

The mountain itself is one of the finest in the Pennines and a familiar landmark to all who travel in the neighbourhood. Charles Lamb mentioned it as one of the outstanding memories of his visit to Lakeland early in the nineteenth century and, until an accurate survey was made in comparatively recent times, it was credited with a height in excess of 5000 feet and considered one of the highest mountains in England. It forms part of the celebrated Three Peaks walk, the object being the ascent of Ingleborough, Pen-y-ghent and Whernside on the same day.

Ingleborough can be reached from the B.6255 road between

Ingleton and Ribblehead along the track which strikes due east from point 702732, about a mile from Ingleton and a little way below the entrance to the White Scar cave. There is convenient parking in what may have been an old quarry and a path from there leads to an unpaved road which runs between stone walls until access is gained to the open fell by means of a well-constructed metal stile. Where it is confined by the stone walls the track tends to be wet and muddy but, on reaching the open moorland, it develops into a lovely grassy track and, after passing the isolated farm some distance further on, it runs along what, in wet weather, is a delightful rocky stream. After a dry spell the stream disappears underground.

The steep-sided summit is in full view once the stone walls are left behind but there is an exhausting slog up a patch of bog and grass which precedes the three short steep stretches on rocky paths which lead to the top. There are two massive cairns on the flat summit and a well-constructed shelter with a direction indicator which was set up by the local Fell Rescue organisation in 1953. Morecambe Bay is visible to the west and north-west are the Lakeland Hills, while the Ribblehead viaduct and the entrance to the famous Blea Moor tunnel are on view to the north-east. Those more interested in past history can amuse themselves by looking for traces of the old hill fort.

The round trip from the quarry takes a little over three hours and, despite the difficult stretch of grass and bog before the final ascent, is a very pleasant excursion. Nevertheless, the longer route from Clapham on the A.65 road between Settle and Ingleton may be found preferable. A path goes through the woods along the Clapham Beck past Ingleborough Cave, turning left at 757716 to climb up through Trow Gill to the open moor. Gaping Gill is reached just over half a mile from the narrow exit from Trow Gill. From that point the path continues north-west to and along the ridge which runs north to the summit.

Instead of returning by the same route the walk can be continued in an easterly direction to Simon Fell, with its three separate summits, and the return to Gaping Gill made down the southern slopes of Simon Fell over the prominent viewpoint at 759749. From Gaping Gill the original route is followed down Trow Gill and along Clapham Beck to the village. Four and a half hours is required for the round trip, excluding any time which may be spent in the Ingleborough Cave, and the extra 1½ hours as compared with the ascent from Ingleton is well spent.

Ingleborough can also be ascended from Ribblehead by way of Simon Fell as described under that entry.

There also used to be a route from the inn at Chapel le Dale (744777) on the B.6255 road between Hawes and Ingleton. However, on a visit two years ago the access at this point was fenced off with barbed wire and there was a bull in the field. Possibly the answer is to use the bridle-way to Great Douk Cave which leaves the road a little way north of the inn. The advantage is a short route to the summit (about 2¾ hours for the round trip) with a view of the mountain from the start, but the other routes listed will prove more attractive.

IRON CRAG

176. *Sheet 82.* Reference 124119. Cumberland. 2100 feet.*

Iron Crag is the most westerly of Lakeland mountain summits and lies in a little known area south of Ennerdale Water. An ascent route from the western end of Ennerdale, with a return down Silvercove Beck, is given under the entry for Caw Fell. The walk could be done the other way round, but those who tackle it on a day when visibility is clear from the start will have a preference for the quick ascent of Crag Fell. The scattered rocks with the well-built cairn of red rock at the summit, and the views of the Pillar Group and the Buttermere Fells, make it a delightful picnic spot.

KENTMERE PIKE

177. *Sheet 83.* Reference 465077. Westmorland. 2397 feet.*

Kentmere Pike is the last summit on the ridge running south from Harter Fell (Mardale). A route from the southern end of Haweswater has already been described under the entry for Adam Seat.

The ridge provides a pleasant grassy walk but there is nothing remarkable about the Kentmere Pike summit. There is a trig point near the top and the wall which runs along the ridge provides useful shelter when there is a keen east wind. However, by continuing down the ridge in a south-easterly direction for a further three-quarters of a mile one obtains the reward of a fine view of the Longsleddale valley from the rocks at Goat Scar.

Those who approach the area from the south may ascend Kentmere Pike from either the Kent or the Longsleddale valleys. The former is a straightforward easy route by the footpath which is a continuation of the road to Brockstones (466053) while the latter gives three possible routes of ascent one from the highest point of the track from Sadgill to the Kent valley by way of Shipman Knotts and Goat Scar, one more enterprising going almost due east to the summit over Steel Rigg, and one a longer route via the Gatescarth Pass, Adam Seat, Harter Fell and down the ridge. The latter is the best proposition for a walk from Longsleddale since it provides a round trip with a return to the starting point by way of Shipman Knotts. As little as four hours should be sufficient.

KILLHOPE LAW

178. *Sheet 84. Reference 819448. Northumberland/Durham. 2207 feet.*

According to the landlady at the Allenheads inn, this is the highest hill in Northumberland. She completely ignored the half share of Durham and the claims of The Cheviot, but in so doing was only following the custom of other inhabitants of the English hill country. A farmer on Wiswell Fell near Whalley always claimed that his fell was higher than Pendle Hill, while the inhabitants of West Yorkshire used to credit their famous Three Peaks with heights far in excess of anything in the British Isles—and got away with it until comparatively recent times.

The recognised route up Killhope Law is by the track which starts from 851465, a little north of Allenheads, and continues up the north-east slope. However, those wishing for a quicker route may go to 815458 on the Allenhead–Nenthead road, follow the track to the disused mine, and then continue straight on to the summit. Apart from a small patch of bog at the top, the going is easy and in little over half an hour one can be examining the massive cairn which marks the summit together with a trig point, a very tall pole, and a small pool. The cairn was undergoing repair in July 1969 and was not the usual dry-stone construction but a solid job of stone and mortar, obviously intended as a very permanent feature. Allenheads obviously thinks very highly of it and it would be a pity to tell the landlady anything about The Cheviot.

KILLHOPE MOOR

179. *Sheet 84. Reference 801440. Northumberland/Durham. 2150 feet.*

This summit lies about 1¼ miles west-south-west of Killhope Law and after ascending that summit it seems quite natural to follow the county boundary in that direction. Unfortunately, it is boggy practically all the way, marshy in some places but with fairly deep gullies in others. The gullies do not compare with those of Kinder and the going is not so bad as on Yockenthwaite Moor, but it would be bad enough in wet weather. To the experienced walker in fair weather, however, it presents no serious problem.

There is nothing to mark the summit but close by is an old fence post covered in rusty wire which appears to be the meeting point of the three counties of Northumberland, Durham and Cumberland since it marks the junction of what had formerly been fences running south and north-west along the line of the Cumberland boundary. A walk along the remains of the latter fence brings one to the Nenthead–Allendale road at 795445, from which point it is a pleasant walk back to the starting point at 851465, the scene at the bridge over the tributary of the West Allen river at 809456 being worthy of special note. Those wishing to avoid the bog could, of course, reach the summit by a half-mile walk from the road at 795445, which is already at an altitude of 1999 feet.

KIDSTY PIKE

180. *Sheet 83.* Reference 448127. Westmorland. 2560 feet.*

This summit can conveniently be used for the descent from High Street after ascending by the Riggindale ridge as described under the High Street entry. The crags on its southern side give it a distinctive appearance and the summit, with its small cairn above the rocks, provides a fine viewpoint which comes as a marked contrast to the flat grassy walk from High Street. One could, of course, ascend Kidsty Pike directly from Haweswater but this would not have the interest of the Riggindale route and would seem laborious by comparison.

KINDER SCOUT

181. *Sheet 102. Reference 086876. Derbyshire. 2088 feet.*
182. *Subsidiary summit at 077894. 2051 feet.*

Kinder Scout is a plateau of peat with rocky outcrops and with an area of about four square miles in excess of 2000 feet in height. About half of it falls within the 2050 contour line, much of it cut up by gullies or groughs varying from one to over ten feet in depth, so that location of the slight mound which is the highest point of Kinder Scout—and also the highest point in Derbyshire—can be a matter of some difficulty. It is usually a question of walking on a compass bearing and then searching for some identifying mark. In 1960 the search led to a bare mound of peat on which was spelled out in flat stones the word 'Top' and the figures '2089'. In 1972 the search led to a slight mound covered with vegetation and marked by a stone cairn about thirty inches high. Possibly the top layer of the bare mound of 1960 has been blown or washed away in the intervening years or perhaps it still exists as a potential challenger to the location of the present cairn.

It would be only too easy to question whether the cairn is precisely on the highest spot. Walkers who reach it are probably so happy to find a distinguishing feature in this wild waste that they accept it without question. If the cairn were on a solid foundation and stones plentiful walkers would no doubt build it up until it became a much more prominent landmark. Fortunately this is not likely to happen. Stones can normally only be found by digging in the beds of the gullies, which are shallow at this point, and such additions as are made to the pile are quite possibly offset by its gradual sinking into the peat.

However, there must be a possibility that the cairns on the rocks about a quarter of a mile north-east of the present summit may one day be assembled into a single large cairn which, given its solid base and the more plentiful supply of building material, may eventually reach such stature as to be clearly visible.

Walkers on Kinder on a December day in 1972 when questioned about the highest point either said 'Take your pick', or words to that effect, or had no hesitation in saying that the highest point was the trig point on Low Kinder. Anyone standing at the summit on a clear day will certainly be tempted to think that he is looking up to the trig point and will need all his confidence in the Ordnance Survey before he accepts that he is standing eleven feet above it.

Problems of identification do not arise for the subsidiary summit. It bears an Ordnance Survey trig point mounted on a solidly built block of stones a yard or so high and is notable for having a broken trig point pillar at its base. But the Ordnance Survey, having solved this problem of location, have created another one by the discrepancies between the latest edition of Sheet 102 and Sheet 111, the Peak District Tourist edition and earlier editions of Sheet 102. The 1970 edition of Sheet 102, showing the M.62 motorway and the Booth Wood and Scammonden reservoirs, gives a height of 2051 feet for the trig point at 077894 which, being outside the 2050 countour line encompassing Kinder Low, Crowden Head and the 2088-feet top, for the purpose of this account ranks as a separate summit. 2031 feet is the spot height at 076896 and does not appear on the 1970 edition of Sheet 102. On the previous edition the figures 2031 appear without the spot! In future editions the problem will be resolved by putting contour intervals in metres. Accordingly, those who wish to have this record of an extra summit on Kinder should get a copy of the 1970 edition without delay.

How fortunate for those primarily interested in summits that there should be two on Kinder, since it compels them to see more of the plateau than they otherwise might. From Upper Booth (102854) a round trip to the main summit could be encompassed within a little more than 2½ hours—and would be quite enjoyable—but how much

(*above*) INGLEBOROUGH (Pennines). Potholers near Quaking Pot, below Ingleborough

(*below*) KINDER SCOUT (Peak). The summit

KINDER SCOUT (Peak). (*above*) Noe Stool and (*below*) Kinder grough

better it is to think in terms of two summits or, better still, a complete circuit of the Kinder plateau with minor diversions to the summits. This has only become possible since 1954, prior to which time Kinder was an enclosed grouse moor. As early as 1897 a legal action was fought to secure the right of way up William Clough. More spectacular, perhaps, was the mass trespass in 1932 which resulted in a number of ramblers from Manchester receiving prison sentences. They would feel well rewarded for their efforts if they could see the large numbers of well equipped walkers who now walk around Kinder, even in conditions of snow and ice. Such walkers have pounded out a track which completes the circuit of Kinder in a wide sweep below the highest level and is designed to provide the best views of the surrounding area. Most surprising and beneficial of all, however, is the fact that walking is now only restricted on the few days when shooting is taking place and then only in selected areas. Details of these limited restrictions can be obtained from the National Park Information Centre in Edale or from the notices which are posted at access points in the shooting season. These notices almost apologise for inconveniencing those who wish to walk on Kinder. What a change from 1932!

The complete circuit of Kinder takes in Edale Cross, Kinder Downfall, The Edge above Black Ashop Moor, Fairbrook Naze and Seal Stones above the Ashop valley, Madwoman's Stones above Jaggers Clough, Ringing Roger above Edale and Crowden Tower above Crowden Brook. Access can be gained from many points, the more obvious being from:

(I) Upper Booth (102854) either by the alternative Pennine Way route up Jacob's Ladder or up Crowden Brook;
(ii) Edale (122856) either by the main Pennine Way up Grinds Brook, by the path up Grindslow Knoll, or the path up The Nab to Ringing Roger;
(iii) the Ashop Valley at 115902 almost due west of Fairbrook Naze; or
(iv) near Hayfield 050870 either past the Kinder reservoir up William Clough or to Edale Cross on the route to Edale.

The only route which presents a problem to the average walker is that from Upper Booth up Crowden Brook, which is not to be recommended for anyone with a heavy rucksack unless they are very agile. For those who have a free choice Edale is perhaps the best starting point as there are ample parking facilities outside the village at 124853 and there is the choice of three routes up or down the plateau. Probably the best route, if enough time is available, is to take the Pennine Way up Grinds Brook and to make the complete circuit in a clockwise direction, making diversions to the main summit from Pyms Chair, called by some the Pagoda Rock, near 085873 and to the subsidiary summit from 075893, and descending from Ringing Roger down The Nab. This would take about eight hours and could be reduced by cutting across from 085873 over the main summit to Red Brook at 083880 or from above Blackden Brook direct to Ringing Roger. Either of these short cuts would save about an hour and, without detracting too much from the walk, would afford a total reduction of two hours on the day—a very useful margin to those travelling some distance to the starting point.

Walkers should make a generous allowance for the walking conditions when planning an expedition on Kinder. Strict adherence to the Naesmith formula is impossible because of the host of minor deviations from a straight path.

KIRK FELL

183. *Sheet 82.* Reference 195105. Cumberland. 2630 feet.*
184. *Subsidiary summit at 199108. 2550 feet.*

This is said to be one of the most neglected of English mountains, lying almost due west and within a mile of Great Gable. Therein probably lies the reason, since it is not on one of the popular routes to Gable.

There is a direct route of ascent from Wasdale Head, which looks to be a hard and uninteresting grind, and there is another route from near the tarn which lies above the dip between Kirk Fell and Great Gable. An easier route is from the highest point of Black Sail Pass. That point can be reached from Wasdale Head by the recognised route up Mosedale Beck in an hour and twenty minutes; from Buttermere over Scarth Gap and then up from Ennerdale in two hours; or from the top of Honister Pass over Grey Knotts into Ennerdale and then up the northern side in 2¼ hours. From the top of Black Sail Pass the main Kirk Fell summit can be reached in about thirty-five minutes by following the line of the fence which runs due south up the crags.

The subsidiary summit is less than half a mile away to the north-east past the tarns which lie in the shallow dip and, from that point, there is an easy descent to the tarn which lies due east above the dip between Kirk Fell and Great Gable. Routes run from here to Honister Pass, either over Great Gable, as described under that entry, or across its northern slopes and over Brandreth and Grey Knotts. Other routes go to the Ennerdale side of Black Sail Pass or direct to Wasdale Head below the southern slopes of Kirk Fell.

Times for the round trip would be 4½ hours from Buttermere, three hours from Wasdale Head or four hours from Honister Pass (five hours if Great Gable and Green Gable are included).

Kirk Fell is a magnificent viewpoint, particularly of the western side of Great Gable, and is only neglected because there are so many other attractions in this area.

KNOCK FELL

185. *Sheets 83 and 84. Reference 722303. Westmorland. 2604 feet.*

Knock Fell lies 3½ miles south-east of Cross Fell and is on the Pennine Way on its ascent from Dufton to Great Dun Fell on the way to Cross Fell and Garrigill. High Cup Nick lies three miles to the south, and it is convenient to include Knock Fell in a round trip which takes in High Cup Nick, as already mentioned under the entry for Backstone Edge.

To allow as much time as possible on the summits it is convenient to travel by car up the road from Knock to the point where the road to the radar station on Great Dun Fell reaches the top of the ridge, east of Green Castle (717315). From that point the summit of Knock Fell can be reached in about twenty minutes. There are a number of cairns on the summit and the remains of mining activity, and the summit provides a good view over the Eden valley to Lakeland. To the east and south, however, the outlook is one of desolation.

By proceeding in an easterly direction for 1½ miles and then turning south-east for a further 1¾ miles, keeping on the higher ground all the way, one reaches Meldon Hill (772291), marked by a trig point and cairns at an altitude of 2518 feet. The going is very wet, even at the best of times, and could well be impossible in wet weather. Moreover, as Meldon Hill is not sufficiently outstanding to be readily recognised when seen from the north, care is necessary in following the route. However, there is not likely to be any competition from other walkers and the area provides a feeling of freedom and independence, such as is cherished by walkers of the Pennines.

From Meldon Hill a descent a little west of south brings one to the Pennine Way along Maize Beck, which leads to High Cup Nick. From this point the route is by Narrowgate Beacon to Backstone Edge, continuing over High Scald Fell and back on to Knock Fell up its southern slope. The route to the summit from the south is marked by a prominent cairn on the skyline and the only problem after leaving High Scald Fell is the patch of wet ground at the source of Swindale Beck (723293).

The round trip takes rather more than five hours but more time should be allowed, if possible, to permit extended exploration of the High Cup Nick area.

Those who object to using a car to get to the main Pennine ridge can reach Knock Fell by following the Pennine Way from Dufton or can take the track from Dufton to the old mines at 719281 in the dip between High Scald Fell and Backstone Edge. Use of the latter route involves a walk over High Scald Fell to get to Knock Fell. Thereafter the walk can be continued to Meldon Hill and High Cup Nick, the return to Dufton being achieved by continuing along the Pennine Way downhill all the way from High Cup Nick. Six hours should suffice for the round trip using the old mine track and rather less if the Pennine Way is used for the ascent as well as the descent.

KNOTT

186. *Sheet 82.* Reference 296330. Cumberland. 2329 feet.*

Knott lies 3½ miles north-east of Skiddaw and about one mile along the ridge running east from Coomb Height, and should not be confused with The Knott in Westmorland in the High Street group, which is covered in the next entry. It forms an obvious extension to the walk to Coomb Height from Mosedale, already described under that entry, and the walk can be continued to Great Sca Fell and then back over Great Lingy Hill and Carrock Fell in a round trip of about five hours.

Alternatively, Knott can be included in the walk from Orthwaite which is also included in the entry for Coomb Height. Its highest point is marked by a cairn and the most interesting ascents are those undertaken in winter or early spring when the face exposed to the north may have a covering which is more ice than snow.

THE KNOTT

187. *Sheet 83.* Reference 437127. Westmorland. 2423 feet.*

The Knott lies due west of Kidsty Pike to the north of High Street. To the walker who has reached High Street by the fine walk over Riggindale Crag from Haweswater the summit of The Knott may be of little interest as it is merely a small cairn on a grassy mound and easily reached along the High Street ridge. However, it is a peaceful spot just off the line of the ridge and leads on to Rest Dod about a mile to the north-west.

KNOUTBERRY HAW

188. *Sheet 90. Reference 731919. Yorkshire (W.R.). 2216 feet.*

Baugh Fell, the big hump between Garsdale and the Westmorland border, has two summits, the higher one bearing the trig point being

Knoutberry Haw. From Garsdale there are lovely lines of walls which run from the valley to the top of the slope, but there is nevertheless an impression of vast size.

A car may be taken down the minor road which leaves the A.684 Hawes to Kendal road at 719907 and parked near Keld. From there, a walk up the line of Dry Gill, and a gradual drift to the east around the level of the 1750-foot contour, through convenient openings in the walls, leads to an ascent up a steep slope which brings one over the crest just south of the summit. A wall runs across the fell from east to west just south of the summit and hides the trig point and the summit cairn.

There are magnificent views of the Howgill Fells and the Garsdale valley but the flat top north of the summit is largely wild and desolate bog. Despite the name, one may not see any knoutberries. These are berries of the strawberry type such as one finds in large quantities on Outberry Plain between Stanhope in Weardale and Newbiggin in Teesdale, their appearance being preceded by a small white flower. Perhaps the needs of the sheep and cattle of Garsdale have been responsible for discouraging their growth on Baugh Fell. They have not, however, been able to discourage the bog cotton which, at the appropriate season, provides a welcome decoration to an otherwise bleak landscape.

From the summit, the walk can be continued through patches of bog and past a number of small tarns to Tarn Rigg Hill. There is no cairn to mark the top but the spot can be identified fairly readily. On the way there are fine views of Ingleborough, Whernside and the other summits of West Yorkshire.

The round trip from Keld takes about 2¾ hours.

KNOWE CRAGS

189. *Sheet 82.* Reference 312270. Cumberland. 2600 feet.*

Knowe Crags form a separate summit at the western end of the Saddleback (Blencathra) ridge. No one would be likely to contemplate an excursion to Knowe Crags without including Saddleback and the interesting routes all take in Saddleback first.

From that summit, Knowe Crags can be reached by an easy walk along the ridge across the main saddle to the south-west. There is a small cairn on the ridge above the Crags and just east of Knowe Crags is a steep line of descent which, after running more south than west down the slope reaches a path which runs from west to east just above Blease Farm and then follows the stream which flows down from between Gategill Fell and Knowe Crags to the hospital road on the northern outskirts of Threlkeld. The stream has to be forded just before one leaves the open fell by a gate north-west of the farm, but this should not present any difficulty.

LADYSIDE PIKE

190. *Sheet 82.* Reference 184227. Cumberland. 2300 feet.*
191. *Subsidiary summit at 185224. 2250 feet.*

Ladyside Pike is on the ridge which runs to Hopegill Head from Whinlatter Pass in the north. The smooth contours of the first part of the ridge and the grass-covered main summit are in marked contrast to the craggy outcrop forming the subsidiary summit and the slab of rock which has to be ascended to reach the Hopegill Head summit. Experienced walkers may enjoy the climb up the crack in this rock to reach Hopegill Head but it might prove difficult for young children as a means of descent, particularly in wet or windy conditions. Accordingly, there is really only one safe route up Ladyside Pike and that is by the path from 169242, near Hopebeck, about a mile south of High Lorton, in a south-easterly direction up the slopes of Swinside and then along the ridge. For those able to continue the ascent to Hopegill Head the most convenient return routes will be due west down the ridge and over the Whiteside summit or down Gasgale Gill. Either route leads to the footpath which runs east of the road to High Lorton back to the starting point. However, since there are good parking facilities at Lanthwaite Green there is something to be said for starting the round trip there, walking the two miles north to Hopebeck before ascending the ridge.

LAMBGREEN HILLS

192. *Sheet 83. Reference 712360. Cumberland. 2280 feet.*

Lambgreen Hills have already been referred to under the entry for Cross Fell. They lie on the Pennine Way route from Cross Fell to Garrigill about $1\frac{3}{4}$ miles north-east of Cross Fell as the crow flies. They are probably hardly noticed by the walkers of the Pennine Way but if one goes a little way to the north—say as far as Bullman Hills about one mile away—one gets a view of pleasant, rounded, green hills which seem somewhat out of place in the Cross Fell landscape. Their name seems very appropriate.

LINGMELL CRAG

193. *Sheet 82.* Reference 209082. Cumberland. 2649 feet.*

Lingmell Crag lies less than a mile to the north of Mickledore, the dip between Sca Fell and Scafell Pikes, and those who reach the area are normally heading for one of the Sca Fells. Thus, despite its central position, it tends to be ignored.

Lingmell is readily accessible from 211078, its ascent from that point being a gentle stroll of a quarter of a mile or so with good views to Great Gable and other summits to the north and magnificent views of Piers Gill below the crags to the east. Accordingly, those who use the Piers Gill route from Wasdale or the Guides Route from Esk Hause for an ascent of one of the Sca Fells can readily get to Lingmell at little expense in either effort or time. If the weather is good, the views will more than repay them. If it is poor, they may be content to settle for Lingmell and feel that their journey has not been wasted.

The summit is marked by a tall cairn.

LITTLE CARRS

194. *Sheet 88.* Reference 271015. Lancashire. 2250 feet.*

Close examination of the 1-inch Ordnance Survey reveals a mark within the 2200-foot contour and a spot height of 2250 feet which establishes Little Carrs, lying less than half a mile north of Great Carrs on the ridge north of the Old Man of Coniston, as a separate summit.

Little Carrs means the little rocks—presumably by comparison with Great Carrs and the other crags to the south—and they just scrape within the definition of a summit by providing a sufficient bump on the gradual slope down from Great Carrs to the Wrynose Pass. No one would think of going to Little Carrs for itself alone but it is a pleasant spot on the Coniston Fell ridge and is crossed by all who reach or leave the Coniston Fells by way of Wrynose Pass.

LITTLE DUN FELL

195. *Sheet 83. Reference 705330. Westmorland. 2761 feet.*

Little Dun Fell lies between Great Dun Fell, with its radar mast, and Cross Fell. A route to it is described under the entry for the latter. Although it appears to be dwarfed by the mast on Great Dun

Fell it is in fact only twenty feet lower than Great Dun Fell at ground level.

'Dun' means 'pasture' and it is a round green hump of no particular significance. It is, however, a welcome stretch of solid ground to anyone who has traversed the swamp between it and Cross Fell and it provides a grandstand view of Cross Fell. Those who have to contend with the swamp in wet weather will take more kindly to it if they remember that it is the source of the Tees and thus responsible, in some measure, for the beauty of High Force.

LITTLE FELL

196. *Sheet 84. Reference 785217. Westmorland. 2446 feet.*
197. *Subsidiary summits at 789238 (Arnside Rake). 2252 feet.*
198. *798218 (Scot Hill). 2150 feet.*

This name is a joke very much in the style of Little John. Anyone who studies Little Fell from the trig point on Mickle Fell or tries to locate its highest point on a misty day will know that it is not to be taken literally.

The obvious route to Little Fell is as an extension of the walk described under the entry for Hilton Fell and it is important to realise that Little Fell also lies with the Warcop Artillery Range and that the comments on the range made in respect of Hilton Fell also apply. The subsidiary summit near Mickle Fell (named Arnside Rake on larger-scale maps) presents no problem as long as one contours round from Hilton Fell rather than attempting a direct approach over Coal Sike. The top is marked by a few rocks and nearby is a well built stone shelter which, although not providing full shelter from strong winds, has at least a fairly sound roof.

There is some dispute about the location of the main summit. On editions of the 1-inch Ordnance Survey prior to 1970 the highest point was given as 2446 feet at reference 782226, the trig point altitude then being shown at 2445 feet. However, the 1970 edition corrects the trig point altitude to 2446 feet—perhaps a tribute to the meticulous accuracy of the Ordnance Survey—and, while one might favour the northern summit on grounds of seniority, posterity will undoubtedly regard the more southerly summit with the trig point at reference 785217 as the true summit. Moreover, as the precise location of the northerly summit is in doubt, there is something to be said for accepting a summit which can be identified. A trig point pillar, although man-made, is never regarded as a blot on the landscape, particularly in the Pennine wastes, and there is no difficulty about the location of the trig point on Little Fell as long as one does not expect to see it from a distance. It is enclosed in a substantial circular stone wall which effectively obscures the traditional pillar from view until one reaches it, a peculiarity which seems to be reserved for Little Fell and Wild Boar Fell.

Athough the northern end of Little Fell is a rounded grassy hill without any notable landmark, the southern end has many rock outcrops and a dry valley which is readily identifiable from some distance on either side. There is also a boundary stone about 400 yards south-east of the trig point bearing the mark W 1857 on one side and B 3 on the other, obviously a companion to that on Tinside Rigg. Do they perhaps mark the limits of Burton and Warcop Fells?

Location of the subsidiary summit on the eastern side (Scot Hill on larger-scale maps) presents some difficulty. It is not readily identifiable from the upper slopes of Little Fell but, from the trig point, it lies directly in line with Selset Reservoir and can be approached along the northern side of Goat Sike. Unfortunately, although the source of Goat Sike on the eastern slope of Little Fell is easily recognisable, it is not easy to trace its course among the boggy wastes. However, the bog is not nearly so bad as appears from the upper slopes of Little Fell. There is a solid layer of stone in places and no really deep gullies. If, therefore, one pursues a course in the general direction of Selset Reservoir a patch of rock, in which is situated a block of stone sheep pens, will be encountered at a distance of about half a mile from the Little Fell trig point and rather less than this distance further on is the bump on these moorland wastes which is Scot Hill. A small cairn marks the highest point but it does not look anything like a summit. To see it looking like a hill rather than just a patch of peat bog one must go to the trig point on Mickle Fell. From there it appears as a very small pimple on the long south-eastern slope of Little Fell.

Those who see the sheep pens may wonder whether the sheep population is sufficient to justify them. In autumn one may see a flock of sheep near the gate leading to the village of Hilton but, in general, encounters with sheep in this area are few and far between. The reader may be surprised to learn, therefore, that the autumn round-up will normally result in about 4000 sheep being driven down to the village of Hilton. That, of course, is only about 100 per square mile, so the sheep are not short of pasture and have a fair chance to escape the shells.

LITTLE GOWDER CRAG

199. *Sheet 82.* Reference 142109. Cumberland. 2500 feet.*

This has no connexion with the Gowder Crag by the Lodore Falls in Borrowdale but is about 400 yards north-west of the summit of Haycock, which has Gowder Crag on its southern side. Little

Gowder Crag overlooks Ennerdale and there is a direct ascent to it from that valley as described under the entry for Haycock.

It can also be conveniently fitted in as an extension of the walk to Caw Fell from Ennerdale or the walk to Haycock from Wasdale.

LITTLE HART CRAG

200. *Sheet 83.* Reference 388100. Westmorland. 2091 feet.*
201. *Subsidiary summit at 385102. 2000 feet.*

Little Hart Crag lies at the head of the Scandale valley, about one mile east-south-east of Dove Crag. It is an easy walk from Ambleside, either directly up Scandale Beck or by way of the ridge over Snarker Pike and Red Screes but the shortest route from a road is from 404118 on the A.592 (Patterdale-Kirkstone) road, up Caiston Beck and then due north from the head of the pass. However, as parking is not easy on the A.592, those with cars may prefer to walk from 403134, just north of Brothers Water, where there are facilities for parking.

The main summit is a rocky hump with cairns at the western and north-eastern extremities, the highest point being that on the west. The subsidiary summit is a rocky outcrop to the north-west and bears no identifying mark.

LITTLE KNAPSIDE HILL

202. *Sheet 83. Reference 645393. Cumberland. 2153 feet.*

Little Knapside Hill is a small bump on the ridge which runs north from Cross Fell to Hartside Cross on the Alston–Penrith road. The route is described under the entry for Cross Fell.

Knapside Hill, although a little higher, is really only an outlying shoulder of Memerby Fell and is not a separate summit.

LITTLE MAN

203. *Sheet 82.* Reference 267278. Cumberland. 2837 feet.*

Little Man is the summit on the ridge running south-east from Skiddaw. The path starting from the Underscar road at 282253, which is the popular and well worn route up Skiddaw, passes to the east of it but there is no difficulty in diverging from the path to the large cairn which marks the summit of Little Man.

The diversion to Little Man can be made whether one is ascending or descending Skiddaw and, since the route to Skiddaw over Carl Side is far more interesting than the broad path up the ridge from the Underscar road, the Carl Side route should preferably be used for the ascent and Little Man taken in on the descent. This arrangement, besides giving an alternative route for the descent, brings the walker down on an easy track which enables him to take full advantage of the views to the south which, from Little Man, are better than those from the Skiddaw summit.

LOADPOT HILL

204. *Sheet 83.* Reference 457181. Westmorland. 2201 feet.*

Loadpot Hill, the most northerly of the summits on the High Street ridge, can conveniently be included in the return walk to Howtown from High Raise as described under that entry. The approach from Wether Hill is marked by the stone chimney of Lowther House, a former shooting lodge, which seems very out of place in this area of high rolling grassland. There is a cairn and a trig point on the summit.

LONG CRAG

205. *Sheet 84. Reference 843253. Yorkshire (N.R.). 2250 feet.*

Long Crag lies above Arngill Head, about 2¼ miles to the east of Mickle Fell. The most convenient route of ascent is by the footpath which runs from 882214 on the Brough–Middleton-in-Teesdale road to Langdon Beck by way of Hagworm Hill. At Hagworm Hill (865245) the footpath is left behind and a walk of 1½ miles in a north-westerly direction brings one to the summit above the line of crags, well over a mile long, which lies to the north-east.

'Crags' is perhaps an exaggeration but there are at least patches of rock and stones on the steep north-eastern slopes which have provided material for a number of cairns along the edge. The summit is not marked but is about a quarter of a mile south on a small grass covered mound in a wide expanse of heather with a patch of bog to the east. From the summit there are views of Teesdale, the trig point on Mickle Fell and the radar masts on Great Dun Fell, while there is a grandstand view of the Cow Green reservoir from the line of so called crags.

It should be noted that the summit lies just inside the boundaries of the Warcop Artillery Range. This is not apparent from the 1-inch Ordnance Survey Map and, although there is probably little risk of trouble, it is as well to ensure that the range is not in use before entering the area and to observe the usual precautions in regard to any metal objects there may be on the ground.

Long Crag can also be approached from the northern end of the footpath. There is convenient parking space just below Langdon Beck in the lay-by at 867298 and from there a path leads over the river to Cronkley Farm and on to the footpath which runs to Cronkley Fell from Holwick. From that point on (861280), unless there have been some radical changes since 1970, there is no trace of a track until the northern slopes of Hagworm Hill are reached some 2½ miles to the south. In fact, the going is so rough that the line of least resistance is to follow the streams which flow down from the Long Crag area. In this way, without too much difficulty, it is possible to reach the line of the crags and then follow a convenient track from about reference 855255 to the top. The round trip from Langdon Beck takes about 3½ hours and can be extended, by those who are interested in the flora of the area, subject to permission from the Nature Conservancy, by a diversion to Cronkley Fell.

When the attention of the Ramblers' Association was drawn to the difficulty in locating the footpath to Hagworm Hill from the north, one of their members made a detailed investigation. He concluded that the only effective way of marking the route would be by a line of cairns, a solution unlikely to be acceptable to the landowner; that only experienced walkers would be likely to venture in the area and they would be skilled map readers and able to find the route without it being marked on the ground; and that there was little or no risk of the right of way over this area being lost through failure to mark the route. No doubt the North Riding authorities ought to see that the route is marked, but there is a lot to be said for leaving this area to those who can read the map.

LONG FELL

206. *Sheet 84. Reference 769198. Westmorland. 2000 feet.*

Long Fell forms part of the south-western rim of the vast, high moorland which forms the Warcop Artillery Range (see the entry for Hilton Fell) and has Mickle Fell as its highest point. It is not a prominent summit. Few will notice it from the Brough–Appleby road, which runs about two miles distant to the south-west, and it will not be noticed by those who walk the bridle-way from Hilton along Hilton Beck because its western slopes are obscured by the more imposing Roman Fell. However, it has been a mining centre of some importance, as evidenced by the tracks from Hilton and Great Musgrave, and its green summit, contoured with limestone on its eastern slope, a feature repeated on the west slope of Mickle

Fell, is an attractive variation from some of the other high land in this area.

Being one of the most accessible of the fells in the Warcop Range, Long Fell, in addition to the standard notices, has the benefit of red flags on its approach routes as a warning when the range is in use. But it is doubtful if anything can be done to see that no one has gone on to the range before the flags are raised and it is accordingly a wise precaution to check that the range is not in use before crossing the boundary line.

Long Fell can be approached from the village of Hilton or by the old roads from 749164 or 772153 on the A.66 Appleby–Brough road. A round trip starting from 749164, following the path up Hayber Beck and continuing above the escarpment to the summit before returning down the old mining road over Middle Fell to the A.66 at 772153, would be quite interesting and would involve a round trip of about 3¾ hours. Hilton, however, is a much better starting point as it provides a round trip with a greater variety of view and without the need to touch a main road. The starting point is from the W.D. flag-pole at 735207 at the north-east end of the village and the circuit can best be tackled by taking the bridleway along Hilton Beck, turning after about 1½ miles to follow the path which goes to the east under Swindale Edge. This path is easy to follow for nearly 1½ miles but tends to disappear as the wetter ground is encountered, although a wooden post at about 770207 marks the crossing of the tributary which runs down from Christy Bank. Up to that point it is a pleasant walk along a sheltered valley with views restricted to the slopes of Roman Fell and Long Fell. From then on, as one contours to the south over the rocky outcrops on the north-western slopes of Long Fell, the views open out on to typical Pennine moorland with the added attraction of the limestone scars on Long Fell. A more direct approach from lower down the valley up the dip between Roman and Long Fells looks attractive, but it is probably best to take the wider sweep because of the Danger Area due north of Long Fell.

Long Fell is dry and the going firm but there is the odd shell case on its upper western slopes. The summit is marked by a very small cairn, an indication, in view of the plentiful supply of building material, that it is not visited very frequently.

For the direct return to Hilton, a short drop down the south-west slope brings one to the old mining road which zig-zags down the steep section and then strikes north-west and continues back to the starting point. This round trip requires about three hours, but those willing to tackle a seven-hour round trip could continue from Long Fell due east to the twin summits of Tinside Rigg, on over Warcop and Burton Fells to Little Fell, then to Mickle Fell, returning over Hilton Fell and down by Hilton Beck to the village. On such a walk one would be unlikely to encounter another human being.

LONG MAN HILL

207. *Sheet 83. Reference 724374. Cumberland. 2160 feet.*

Long Man Hill lies about half-way between Cross Fell and Garrigill, a little to the east of the Pennine Way. It can be ascended, therefore, on the way down from Cross Fell towards Garrigill, as described under the entry for Cross Fell, or it can be reached directly by following the Pennine Way from Garrigill. Pikeman Hill, which also adjoins the Pennine Way and lies on the same ridge about half a mile to the north, can be included in the same walk. The round trip from Garrigill would take about three hours.

The summit of Long Man Hill is not easy to find as the top is flat and boggy. There are not the problems of deep gullies as on Kinder but a roundabout route is necessary if one is to avoid getting wet. However, the highest point is properly marked by a sizeable stone cairn and no one need be in any doubt when they reach it that the summit has been achieved.

LONGSIDE EDGE

208. *Sheet 82.* Reference 248285. Cumberland. 2405 feet.*

Longside Edge is the line of crags which runs north-east from Carl Side to the west of Skiddaw. Ullock Pike is the name of the northern end but it does not qualify as a separate summit, the highest point of the Edge, marked by a cairn, being about the mid-way point. The Edge can readily be reached from Carl Side, the route to which is described under that entry. It makes a very pleasant interlude in the ascent of Skiddaw and gives a close view of the steep western slopes of Skiddaw and fine views of Bassenthwaite.

Carl Side is the best approach for those who wish to continue up Skiddaw because this provides the most convenient starting place for those who wish to make a round trip and return by the pony track. Those who have no such interest would be well advised to get to Longside Edge by the path which starts from 236310 on the minor road which leaves the Keswick–Carlisle (A.591) road to go to Orthwaite and Caldbeck, former home of John Peel at the back of Skiddaw. This avoids the steepness of the Carl Side ascent.

LONSCALE FELL

209. *Sheet 82.* Reference 285272. Cumberland. 2344 feet.*

Lonscale Fell forms the south-east part of the Skiddaw range, its steep eastern crest being easily recognisable from either north or south, particularly when the hills are covered with snow. It involves a diversion from the direct route up or down Skiddaw but it is a pleasant walk and the summit provides good views of the Glenderaterra valley to the east and Derwentwater and the Lakeland hills to the south. Views from Lonscale could be better than those from Skiddaw itself.

Those ascending Skiddaw by the pony track are unlikely to allow any diversion to delay their approach to the main summit and it is much more acceptable to tackle Lonscale Fell on the way down. This can be done by simply striking off due east from about 274273 on the southern slopes of Jenkin Hill or by descending from the main summit to Sale How, about one mile to the east, walking in a south-westerly direction to cross the head of Sale Beck at the 2000-foot level and the contouring round at that level to a point north of Lonscale Fell. A small cairn marks the summit.

To obtain views of the Glenderaterra valley it is necessary to go on to the peak at the east. Glenderaterra can be a ribbon of white water and a welcome contrast to the barren slopes of Skiddaw.

From that point it is convenient to drop down across the southern slope to cross Whit Beck at 282260, following the path from there to Underscar. On such a diversion, particularly if one strikes off over Sale How, one may well be able to descend the southern slopes of Skiddaw without encountering any competition for space. That will be sufficient recommendation to many walkers for an ascent of Lonscale Fell.

LOOKING STEAD

210. *Sheet 82.* Reference 186118. Cumberland. 2508 feet.*

Looking Stead is the summit to the north-west of Black Sail Pass which is crossed on the way to Pillar. It provides good views of Ennerdale, one of the most remote and beautiful of Lakeland valleys, and is memorable to the writer because of the large boulder which crashed 700 feet from the crags on its south-west side to come to rest fifty yards ahead of him during his last ascent of Black Sail from Wasdale. Such an event is fortunately rare, but it is a terrifying experience to hear a large boulder grind its way down the slope. The sound reverberates from the surrounding hills and one has no idea where the blow will fall.

No one would be likely to ascend Looking Stead for itself alone, but it provides a convenient resting place with good views for those who are travelling to or from Pillar, whether they take the direct route or elect to take the route via Pillar Rock recommended by H. H. Symonds. In his book *Walking in the Lake District*, the Rev. Symonds says the walk by the path from the cairn west of Looking

Stead to Pillar Rock is the grandest half hour in the Lake District. This should be sufficient recommendation for anyone to go to Looking Stead.

LOVELY SEAT

211. *Sheet 90. Reference 879950. Yorkshire (N.R.). 2213 feet.*
212. *Subsidiary summits at 878944. 2100 feet.*
213. *889956. 2050 feet.*

Another of the spring pastures! It lies less than a mile from Butter Tubs, those deep round holes eroded in the limestone which give their name to the pass between Hawes and Thwaite, a tough road for the motorist in bad weather but a wild and pleasant road which the motorist or the walker will enjoy.

The easiest line of ascent is from near the highest point on the road (866956) past the beacon at 874955 and along the wire fence to the top. There is a substantial cairn on the main summit. One subsidiary summit is about half a mile away to the south and the other three-quarters of a mile to the north-east. The latter are much more difficult to locate than one would expect from a study of the map. It is not simply a question of looking around for two obvious humps. Heights can be very deceptive in this rolling country and careful compass readings are necessary to identify on the ground the two points which look so obvious on the map.

That lying in an east-north-easterly direction involves a surprisingly steep descent from the main summit followed by a walk across a patch of marshy ground with bog and several gullies. It could be very difficult in wet weather unless the easiest route, a direct approach to the more northerly of the two humps, is taken. There is no indication from a distance as to which of the two is the higher point but, on close examination, a small cairn will be found on the more southerly one. It was almost covered by grass on a visit in 1970 and could not be seen until one was almost on top of it. A surprising feature of the area is the difference in the quality of the grassland, the more northerly part of this elevated area being very much better in appearance than the southern part.

To reach the third summit it is necessary to return to the main summit and then head due south. The going is good but there is nothing to identify the actual summit although, a little beyond it, a patch of rock provides a seat for a view over the boggy waste below. From that point one can return directly to the Butter Tubs road.

The round trip from the road can be accomplished in just under two hours but, when visibility is good, this will not allow enough time to take advantage of the view from the main summit. Until one has looked down on it from Lovely Seat one may not realise what a central point Hawes is with fine routes to Langstrothdale, Ribblesdale, Wensleydale and the Eden Valley as well as the Butter Tubs route to Thwaite and Swaledale.

Finally, while Lovely Seat is in many ways an appropriate name, perhaps it should be mentioned for the benefit of those who do not understand how such a name can roll off a Yorkshire tongue, that the local name is Lunnerset. This goes well with Butter Tubs and is the name to remember.

MALLERSTANG EDGE

214. *Sheet 90. Reference 803003. Westmorland/Yorkshire (N.R.).* 2250 feet.

Mallerstang means boundary mark and Mallerstang Edge is the line of cliffs which marks the eastern side of the upper Eden valley in the south-east corner of Westmorland. The name has been used to identify the summit which lies nearest to the cliffs as the other summits on the ridge have separate names, i.e. High Pike Hill and High Seat.

The boundary referred to is obviously the county boundary which passes through the three summits following the line of the watershed above and to the east of the cliffs. It is marked by a number of substantial cairns, including one six feet in height on the Mallerstang Edge summit. That on Hugh Seat, the next summit to the south, is dated 1664. Why should so much importance be attached to this particular boundary? Was there perhaps a feud between the local officials who marked it out? Or did someone set up an elaborate set of marks for his own glorification? Perhaps the explanation is that the boundary was marked out by the agents of that formidable woman Lady Anne Clifford, Baroness Clifford and Westmorland, Countess of Dorset, Pembroke and Montgomery, who was tough and powerful enough to defy King James I and Oliver Cromwell. Her tomb is in Appleby church and Pendragon Castle at the northern end of the Mallerstang valley (779027) was one of her homes. Her agents would be capable of seeing that the Westmorland boundary was pushed far enough to the east and was properly marked.

While it would be possible to take the footpath from Outhgill, 783015, in the Eden valley, running east up the lower slopes of the ridge, and continue its line through a convenient gap in the crags, it is much more sensible for those who have transport to take the Kirkby Stephen–Keld road (B.6270) to the parking space at 812042 and tackle the ridge from that point. A little way to the west is a green patch leading to a sheep track across the bog at the bottom of the slope. Once beyond the bog, there is a fairly steep 350-foot rise to the northern end of the ridge and a two-mile walk to the south over High Pike Hill and High Seat brings one to the high cairn of the summit. There is no convenient alternative route for the return but, on a ridge such as this, it is no hardship to retrace one's steps.

The Mallerstang Edge summit provides the best viewpoint in this area as it is close to the line of cliffs and affords views down the Eden valley as well as across to Wild Boar Fell.

MARDALE ILL BELL

215. *Sheet 83.* Reference 448102. Westmorland. 2450 feet.*
216. *Subsidiary summit at 448098. 2400 feet.*

Mardale Ill Bell, lying immediately south-east of High Street and due south of Blea Water, is to be distinguished from the Ill Bell which forms the main summit of the ridge between Kentmere and the Kirkstone Pass. The latter requires no prefix and cannot be overlooked, while the former is scarcely noticed as a summit, although its crags form an impressive frame to the southern shore of Blea Water.

The shortest and easiest ascent is by the path which continues the line of the road at the south-west corner of Haweswater, proceeding past Small Water to the head of the Nan Bield Pass. From this point a path strikes north-west to the Mardale Ill Bell summit and High Street.

Mardale Ill Bell is not the sort of summit which attracts the walker and is probably only used as a stepping stone to the more interesting summits which surround it. The direct ascent from Haweswater takes about 1¼ hours but there are a number of possible variations to the route, e.g. via Harter Fell or Riggindale Crag. Walkers based in Patterdale could, of course, approach it over High Street or Thornthwaite Beacon, but would be unlikely to think such an excursion worth-while.

MELDON HILL

217. *Sheet 84. Reference 772291. Westmorland. 2518 feet.*

Meldon Hill lies west of the main Pennine ridge and looks north over the collecting area for the upper Tees which provides the water which comes down at Caldron Snout and High Force. Its ascent from Langdon Beck in Teesdale would involve a round trip of over fifteen miles and is not to be recommended to anyone who can tackle it from the west. A circuit including Knock Fell and High Cup Nick can conveniently be arranged from Dufton or from the road to the radar station on Great Dun Fell and is described under the entry for Knock Fell.

The summit bears a number of cairns and a trig point and looks down on the Cow Green reservoir.

MELMERBY FELL

218. *Sheet 83. Reference 653380. Cumberland. 2331 feet.*

Melmerby Fell lies about half-way along the ridge between Cross Fell and Hartside Cross on the Alston–Penrith road. Maiden Way, the old Roman road which runs from the Eden valley to Alston and then on to Hadrian's Wall, crosses the ridge immediately south of it.

By far the easiest route to Melmerby Fell is the walk along the ridge from Hartside Cross (647418), the starting point being at a height of 1903 feet and the route being dry and mostly grassy. For those who cannot, or prefer not, to start from Hartside Cross, the alternatives are to start from Townhead (635340), the southern end of Maiden Way, or from its northern end, 680425 on the Alston–Penrith road, A.686. The northern section of Maiden Way is not really an attractive proposition as a round trip can only be achieved by a 2½ mile walk along the A.686 road. From the south, however, after reaching Melmerby Fell by the Maiden Way route, there is the attraction of a walk south along the high ground in a south-easterly direction to the Cross Fell summit, returning thence down the path which runs from 683352, north of Cross Fell, in a westerly direction to Townhead. This round trip, embracing Melmerby and Cross Fells, would take about five hours as compared with 2½ hours for the walk from Hartside Cross to Melmerby Fell, returning by the same route.

MICKLE FELL

219. *Sheet 84. Reference 805245. Yorkshire (N.R.). 2591 feet.*

No Lancastrian is likely to be in any doubt about the highest summit in Lancashire, but Yorkshiremen are not unanimous about the highest point in Yorkshire. One guide book gives Wild Boar Fell as the highest point and Yorkshiremen have been known to accept this. Possibly they are still reluctant to recognise the demarcation of the boundary along Mallerstang Edge, across the Eden valley from Wild Boar Fell, and the substantial cairns there, instead of representing an encroachment by Yorkshiremen into Westmorland, perhaps originate from the determination of Westmorland to assert its rights.

The other old claim which has confused the issue in the past is that which gave Whernside a height in excess of 5000 feet and asserted that it was the highest summit in England.

For the benefit of those who have not studied the matter in detail, the following list may be of interest:

Pen-y-ghent (W.R.)	2273 feet
Great Whernside (W.R.)	2310 feet
Wild Boar Fell (Westmorland)	2324 feet
Great Shunner Fell (N.R.)	2340 feet
Ingleborough (W.R.)	2373 feet
Whernside (W.R.)	2419 feet
Mickle Fell (N.R.)	2591 feet

Whernside is thus the highest summit in the West Riding while Mickle Fell, in the North Riding, is the highest in Yorkshire. There are no mountain summits in the East Riding.

However, it is easier to establish that Mickle Fell is the highest summit in Yorkshire than it is to get permission to climb it. Not only does it lie within the area of the Warcop Artillery Range, with all the access problems this entails (as described under the entry, HILTON FELL), but it also lies within the Upper Teesdale National Nature Reserve. As with the Artillery Range the Reserve is not marked on the 1-inch Ordnance Survey map, one reason apparently being a wish to avoid publicity, but a fairly complete account is given in *The Natural History of Upper Teesdale* obtainable from the Editor, Botany Department, University of Durham, South Road, Durham City, at the pre-decimalisation price of 5s. 6d.

If one writes to the Nature Conservancy at Belgrave Square, London, S.W.1 for permission to ascend Mickle Fell one eventually receives a reply from their office in Grange-over-Sands, Lancashire. Their position is even simpler than that of the Army. They are concerned with plant life—grouse and other livestock apparently do not count—and it is not their responsibility to give permission to those who wish to walk on Mickle Fell. However, they may well send the request on to the Earl of Strathmore's agent at Chester-le-Street, County Durham, who is likely to reply to the effect that permission cannot be granted because it will disturb the grouse.

Better results are obtained if one is a botanist and asks the Grange-over-Sands office for permission to visit Mickle Fell for the purpose of studying the erosion of the blanket bog, the high level grassland, and the vegetation of the bryophite flushes. This will probably produce a very helpful reply from the Conservancy office in Newcastle-upon-Tyne indicating that the Teesdale staff will give what help they can and suggesting that contact be made with the Warden's office in Middleton-in-Teesdale.

The Warden's Office is indeed helpful to botanists, and can readily differentiate between botanists and walkers. They are very keen to send one on to Cronkley Fell by the right of way marked in red on the 1-inch Ordnance Survey and are quite emphatic that the track to Silverband Shop (Reference 837271) is not a right of way and that anyone attempting to approach Mickle Fell from the east is likely to meet with difficulties.

Accordingly, the determined walker will plan his ascent of Mickle Fell from the west on a day when the Warcop range is not in use. It is really an extension of the walks to Hilton Fell and Little Fell which have already been described, the Mickle Fell summit being only two miles east of Hilton Fell and little more than a mile beyond Arnside Rake, the northern subsidiary of Little Fell.

From Hilton Fell it is important to walk in an arc along the slopes of Little Fell so as to avoid the swamp at the head of Coal Sike. Those who approach from the southern end of Little Fell, if they contour round the eastern slopes, should take care to see the old stone bridge which spans Force Beck near 790228. Whichever approach is adopted the best line of ascent up the steep end of the Mickle Fell ridge—300 feet in all at this point—is by the grassy western corner which avoids the steeper limestone escarpment. Then after reaching the tall thin cairn at the spot height of 2547 feet, a gentle stroll over the round grassy summit brings one to the big summit cairn. This is one of the biggest in England and represents a considerable amount of labour as there is not an abundance of cairn building material at this point.

The summit is rather disappointing. There are a few slabs of rock above the limestone escarpment and a few old pits which are presumably relics of mining activity, but one is unlikely to see any grouse, unlikely to notice anything exceptional about the grass and even less likely to be able to see the North and the Irish Seas, both of which are said to be visible from the top. There is a better view if one continues along the ridge to the trig point at 827246, a distance of about 1½ miles from the summit. On the way one may see the remains of a substantial stone shelter and the wreckage of an aeroplane on the southern slopes near 813246. The trig point itself looks out over a vast area of waste bog stretching clockwise in a big arc from Meldon Hill in the north-west to Little Fell in the west. It is also the point from which one can see the outline of Scot Hill as a small pimple on the southern slope of Little Fell.

This then is the great Mickle Fell, a summit which derives more interest from the obstacles encountered when one wishes to walk it than from its intrinsic merits. Perhaps Yorkshiremen are right to ignore it. They have acknowledged its existence by building a massive cairn but, having done so, they are apparently content to allow the problem of access to be handled in London, Lancashire, Westmorland, or Durham—in fact anywhere except in Yorkshire. Who will blame them?

MURTON FELL

220. *Sheet 84. Reference 758240. Westmorland. 2207 feet.*
221. *Subsidiary summit at 750257. 2206 feet.*

Murton Fell lies 4½ miles north-east of Appleby in the north-western part of the Warcop Artillery Range.

In May 1968 one could approach the subsidiary summit from Maize Beck without encountering any of the usual range warning signs. It was, therefore, somewhat surprising to see a Danger Area centred on grid reference 764264 marked on the 1970 edition of the 1-inch Ordnance Survey. However, a check as recently as April 1973 revealed that there were still no warning signs on the northern side of Murton Fell. There are signs on the western side facing towards Hilton Beck, so that one has the odd situation that one can enter the range area over Murton Fell without passing a warning sign and can then pass another set of signs which imply that one is passing out of the range when one is, in fact, getting even further in. A very odd situation when one thinks of the meticulous care with which the range authorities are supposed to check the marking of the range. Let us hope it is a sign that the range is becoming redundant! Nevertheless, walkers will be well advised to check with the range authorities that firing is not taking place before they venture on Murton Fell.

Being just north of the Pennine Way on the route from Langdon Beck in Teesdale to Dufton, Murton Fell can be reached from the Teesdale area and can be tackled in conjunction with a visit to High Cup Nick. However, it would involve a round trip of about 7½ hours, with much of the return over the outward route. Accordingly, anyone who can conveniently make the ascent from the west would be well advised to do so.

There are two obvious routes from the west, the first being along the Pennine Way from Dufton heading in the direction of Langdon Beck. This is an easy walk providing fine views of High Cup Nick on the ascent and the subsidiary summit is a little over half a mile south of High Cup Nick, with the main summit about 1½ miles away to the south-east. The going as far as the subsidiary summit is not too bad but beyond that point there is a patch of difficult bog. The subsidiary summit at 750257 is marked by a prominent cairn constructed of turf and stone with a small stone shelter close by. They are not on the actual summit, the shelter being the nearer of the two, but they are visible and readily recognisable for some miles to the north-east—a very useful landmark in this wild open country. They also provide a magnificent view-point for the summits to the north and east.

Although the main summit at 758240 is a foot higher it is not visible from the subsidiary, but it can be identified from the prominent cairn at 744250. It is not such a good viewpoint as that overlooking High Cup Nick and bears a much smaller cairn. However, it is on firm ground and the going from there to the Hilton Beck path is easy, as also is the route down Hilton Beck to the village of Hilton, from which point it is a four-mile walk along a minor road to the starting point at Dufton. The round trip takes about five hours, unless some delay is imposed by the attractions of the High Cup Nick area.

As an alternative to starting from Dufton one can begin at Hilton and walk in the reverse direction to that already described. Hilton has the advantage of a red flag at the entrance to the range which is hoisted when the range is in use, so that it is probably the best choice for a starting point. This approach also has the advantage of giving one the dramatic view of High Cup Nick one gets on approaching from the east. From the west there is a gradual build-up of the view but, from the east, one plods through the flat marshy land along Maize Beck and then suddenly finds it disappear into the great hollow of High Cup Nick. A most impressive sight, particularly if one has walked from Teesdale.

Those who object to the bog on Murton Fell can readily avoid it by following the Hilton Beck path to its junction with that along Maize Beck at 783258 and then following the Maize Beck path to High Cup Nick. It involves a detour of a few miles but the country is magnificent and well worth the extra mileage.

NAG'S HEAD

222. *Sheet 84. Reference 794413. Cumberland/Durham. 2207 feet.*

233. *Subsidiary summit at 796416. 2200 feet.*

Nag's Head is the most northerly summit on the watershed between Weardale and the South Tyne. Knoutberry Hill, north-east of it on the same ridge, although marked with a spot height of 2195 feet, does not qualify as a separate summit.

The summit lies little more than a mile north of Dead Stones and on the same ridge and could accordingly be included in the round trip embracing Burnhope Seat, Scaud Hill and Great Stony

Hill as described under the latter entry. Alternatively, Nag's Head could be reached in a two-mile walk from Killhope Cross (799433), the highest point on the St. John's Chapel–Nenthead road (B.6293).

The summits of Nag's Head are not marked, but the county boundary is marked by a boundary stone bearing the letters A and P and a figure 10.

NETHERMOST PIKE

224. *Sheet 83.* Reference 343142. Westmorland. 2900 feet.*

Nethermost Pike is on the Helvellyn ridge about three-quarters of a mile south of the main summit. Those who ascend Helvellyn, from whatever direction, can readily reach it along the ridge. It affords fine views of Striding Edge, but its main attraction is that, being ignored by the vast majority of those heading for Helvellyn, it provides a much better resting place than the Helvellyn summit.

A direct ascent, from the Patterdale side, recommended for scramblers only, is described in A. Wainwright's book *The Eastern Fells.*

NINE STANDARDS RIGG

225. *Sheet 84. Reference 826061. Westmorland. 2171 feet feet.*

This summit lies about three miles south-east of Kirkby Stephen and is most readily reached from the Kirkby Stephen–Muker road (B.6270) either over Coldbergh Edge or, if a drier route is desired, by the path starting from reference 809043. A walk embacing the two summits takes just under two hours and it does not make sense to treat them separately. Accordingly, the route to Nine Standards Rigg is given under the entry for Coldbergh Edge.

Nine Standards Rigg will be memorable to all those who go there because of the imposing sight of its 'standards' on the north-western skyline giving the impression of a line of Daleks on the march as one approaches from the south. The standards are on the northern slope of the summit and are not visible as one approaches from the south until the trig point marking the summit is reached, but they are readily visible from near Nateby on the B.6259 road.

The standards had unfortunately suffered some damage when seen in the summer of 1972 and it is perhaps doubtful whether they will be able to survive for long once their outer walls have collapsed. 'Nine Standards' was then still a fair description, even though two smaller cairns had been set up close by. Originally, they were massive well-built stone cairns up to twelve feet in height. They were not identical, the middle one being much larger than the others and the last one being square whereas the others were rounded. Altogether they represented a very considerable amount of work. Were they perhaps a legacy of the old mining community which formerly operated on the summit? Whatever their origin, it is to be hoped that they will be allowed to grace the northern slopes of the Nine Standards Rigg summit for a long time to come.

OLD MAN OF CONISTON

226. *Sheet 88.* Reference 272978. Lancashire. 2631 feet.*

This summit is listed under *O* in deference to the 1-inch Ordnance Survey, although there are no doubt many who would prefer to see it under *C*. When in the Coniston area the reference to Coniston is in any event superfluous.

As befits one of the better known summits, and the highest in Lancashire, there are several possible routes of ascent, many of them making use of the ridge which runs north from the summit of the Old Man over Brim Fell, Swirl How and Carrs to the Wrynose Pass. Seven routes to this ridge are given under the Brim Fell entry. The present entry will therefore deal only with routes which go directly to the summit. There are two, the first being the popular route by the well-worn path up the eastern face and the other a little-known route up the southern end. The former can be approached by the Walna Scar Road, parking for a few cars being available at 289971 where the quarry road which forms the path at this point strikes off to the north. After almost a mile the road turns west towards the Old Man and heads for the summit. The point where this turn is made (285981) can also be reached on foot from Coniston by the delightful route along Church Beck. Youth Hostellers will naturally use the latter route since it passes near the Copper Mines Youth Hostel; car owners may prefer the former because it saves them 600 feet of ascent. The Youth Hostellers have the better bargain as anyone who has walked along Church Beck will testify. Beyond the point where the two paths join it is merely a question of slogging along the broad track until the summit is reached.

The alternative route up the southern end is quite different. One continues along the Walna Scar Road to 283968 and follows the quarry road to the right at that point. When the quarry road ends it is a matter of heading for the summit, making use of the grassy terraces to manoeuvre round the steeper rocks. It is a route for the experienced walker and care is necessary when the rock is wet. As a route for the descent it would not be very attractive, but it provides the quickest ascent of the Old Man and avoids the crowds who use the east face route.

While the route up the southern end has its uses for those who are in a hurry, it is not to be compared with the ascent via Goat's Water and Brim Fell which is described under the Brim Fell entry. This must be recommended as the first choice, even for the relatively inexperienced walker.

A trig point and a tall, thin cairn are usually to be seen on the summit, which has an excellent viewpoint. But the chief attraction of an ascent of the Old Man is the possibility of walking the high ridge towards the Wrynose Pass and returning to Coniston by one of the alternative routes described under the Brim Fell entry.

OUTBERRY PLAIN

227. *Sheet 84. Reference 923326. Durham. 2216 feet.*
228. *Subsidiary summit at 939331. 2144 feet.*

This summit, lying almost due north and about five miles distant from Middleton-in-Teesdale, is readily accessible from Swinhope Head on the minor road which runs from Newbiggin in Teesdale to Westgate in Weardale. Swinhope Head is at an altitude of 1992 feet and just over half a mile to the east is the summit of Westernhope Moor. Shortly after one leaves the road the ruins of a wall appear on the skyline and there is a good path along it towards the summit. There is, however, nothing to indicate the highest point of Westernhope Moor. On the crest, a little way to the north of it, are three cairns looking over into Weardale and they are the best guide to its general location.

From this point the going is rougher, consisting of tussocky grass and patches of bog. In 1¼ miles, keeping to the highest ground in a south-easterly direction, one reaches the trig point at 923326, which, as it is not named on the 1-inch Ordnance Survey, has been given the same name as the summit a mile to the north-east.

The going from the trig point to the summit marked Outberry Plain on the map is distinctly worse than the ground further west, consisting of large areas of bog with deep gullies. Fortunately many of them are reasonably dry and it is possible to walk in them. The summit is not readily identifiable and is not marked, but is just south of the line of double posts. The whole area is covered by a flowering plant somewhat similar to a strawberry which is the Knoutberry or Outberry from which the summit takes its name. It is apparently a semi-alpine flower with the botanical name *Rubus chameomorus.*

The round trip to the unmarked summit and back to Swinhope Head takes just over two hours and one is not likely to encounter anyone on the way. A compass is essential.

PAVEY ARK

229. *Sheet 82. Reference 285079. Westmorland. 2288 feet.*

Pavey Ark forms part of the Langdales but because it lies further back from the valley and is not readily visible from the valley bottom it is not so well known to tourists as Harrison Stickle and Pike O'Stickle. The two Stickles are a very impressive sight when seen from across the valley, particularly from the top of Pike of Blisco, but they are not nearly so impressive at close quarters as the view of Pavey Ark across Stickle Tarn.

The ascent of Pavey Ark from a north-westerly direction is no problem. Once one gets to Harrison Stickle by any of the routes outlined against that entry, it is merely a question of walking about half a mile to the north-east. For scramblers—and only for experienced scramblers—there is a direct assault from Stickle Tarn by Jakes Rake across the southern face of the crag.

There is something for everyone at Pavey Ark and anyone ascending the Langdale Pikes should not fail to visit it. If they propose to descend by Mill Gill they will have no problem as Pavey Ark is on the route down.

PEN-Y-GHENT

230. *Sheet 90. Reference 838734. Yorkshire (W.R.). 2273 feet.*
231. *Subsidiary summit at 839743. 2050 feet.*

Pen-y-ghent lies two miles north-east of Horton in Ribblesdale, brooding over it like a crouching lion. Together with Ingleborough and Whernside it forms the subject of the well-known 'Three Peaks' walk, a walk which involves three distinct ascents as these southern summits of the Pennines are not in a pronounced ridge such as is found in the Cross Fell range. They stand alone and the summits of Pen-y-ghent and Ingleborough, the former presenting a sharp nose to the south-west and the latter flat-topped, are readily recognisable and can be identified from a range of about twenty miles. Of the two, Pen-y-ghent, with its pronounced rock strata of millstone grit and limestone, is by far the better known.

Apart from its natural attractions, and featuring in the Three Peaks walk, Pen-y-ghent has the advantage of being one of the few summits on the Pennine Way and, after Scafell Pikes and Helvellyn, is now perhaps the best known of English summits. Fortunately for the walkers of the Pennine Way, the approved route from Malham to Horton in Ribblesdale uses the best ascent of Pen-y-ghent. Walkers who are solely interested in Pen-y-ghent can pick up the route at 843715 on the road from Stainforth in Ribblesdale to Halton Gill in Littondale. It runs past the isolated, but very attractive Dale Head farm and Churn Milk Pot Hole and then up the sharp southern end of Pen-y-ghent, thus providing walkers with first-hand experience of the interesting rock strata.

The summit is marked by a trig point and cairn and there is some doubt whether the former is quite vertical—perhaps a tribute to the wind which can be particularly strong at this point.

About mid-way along the ridge to the north which leads to Plover Hill is the subsidiary summit. It is not marked and not easy to identify. However, the ridge provides a very peaceful walk, away from the crowds which are to be encountered at the main summit, and from anywhere along its northern end those who prefer an alternative route for the return journey can head directly for the road. The going is rough because of the tussocky grass, but, if one heads for the stream of 857735 and the weather is sunny, the journey will not be wasted.

The round trip from the road over Pen-y-ghent to Plover Hill, returning by the same route, takes about three hours. Alternatively, one could ascend from Horton in Ribblesdale by the Pennine Way on its southern course. This is less interesting than the route in the other direction and the round trip would take a little longer. Those who wish to walk from Horton in Ribblesdale would find it preferable to take the minor road to Dub Cote Farm (820716) and then go through the farm on the footpath to Long Lane (827711), striking the Pennine Way at Churn Milk Pot Hole. From this point the Pennine Way could be followed up the Pen-y-ghent ridge and then down the north-west slope back to Horton in Ribblesdale, a round trip of about 3½ hours.

PIKE OF BLISCO

232. *Sheet 88.* Reference 272043. Westmorland. 2304 feet.*

Commonly known as Pike o' Blisco, Pike of Blisco, to give it the Ordnance Survey name, lies about a mile east of the Crinkle Crag–Bowfell ridge between Wrynose Pass and Langdale. Cumberland seems to have made a determined attempt to embrace the summit within its borders but, according to the 1-inch map, did not succeed. This is surprising, as the cairn on the summit is a prominent landmark such as might well be a boundary mark.

The summit could be included in an ascent of Crinkle Crags and Bowfell from either Langdale or Wrynose, but this would involve a diversion which the average walker would prefer not to make. It is preferable to make a separate excursion and the walk is well-suited to one of those Lakeland days when the weather prevents a longer expedition. From the Three Shire Stone on Wrynose Pass one can take the path which leads to Red Tarn and then head a little north of north-east to the summit, the return trip being of achievement in little more than one hour. With clear weather, however, the views of the Langdale Pikes, the Crinkles and Bowfell from the summit and the cairn and rocks of Pike of Blisco will ensure that one hour is inadequate.

A better walk would be the approach from Langdale, taking the Oxendale route to Red Tarn and ascending Pike of Blisco from there. From the summit a descent down the eastern slope leads to the path which runs over Wrynose Fell to join the road from Little Langdale below Blea Tarn. This round trip would require about 2¾ hours.

PIKE OF STICKLE

233. *Sheet 82.* Reference 274074. Cumberland. 2323 feet.*

This is the lower and more westerly of the Langdale Pikes. The most direct ascent is by the path from the Langdale valley on the left side of Dungeon Ghyll, but the summit can also be reached from Grasmere by way of Easedale Tarn and Sergeant Man or from Langstrath by way of Greenup Gill and High Raise. The direct route from the Langdale Valley, taking in Harrison Stickle and Pavey Ark and returning down Mill Gill can be done in as little as three hours, but those who have the good fortune to be there on a clear day would obviously delay their descent in order to enjoy the views. For those with time to spare, an extension along the plateau over Thurnacar Knott and High Raise, the centre of the Lake District, can be recommended.

PIKEMAN HILL

234. *Sheet 83. Reference 724383. Cumberland. 2050 feet.*

Pikeman Hill lies a little over three miles north-east of Cross Fell, just east of the Pennine Way on its course from Cross Fell to Garrigill. The distance from Garrigill is just over three miles and the 2½-hour return trip from that point to Pikeman Hill would provide a pleasant sample of what the Pennine Way has to offer. Although the summit appears from the map to be only a minute hump on the ridge, it is readily recognisable and is marked by a cairn.

PILLAR

235. *Sheet 82.* Reference 171121. Cumberland. 2927 feet.*

Pillar does not have the crowds one associates with Great Gable or Helvellyn but, being part of a magnificent ridge close to the heart of Lakeland, it provides a much more interesting walk and better views. Wasdale is by far the best starting point, the route from Wasdale Head being by the Black Sail Pass route, striking north-west from the top of the Pass over Looking Stead and along the ridge to the summit. There are magnificent views into Ennerdale, including Pillar Rock to the north of the summit, and to the Buttermere Fells across the valley, while there are most impressive views of the Sca Fell group to the south-east. The summit itself is flat but the highest point is not in doubt as it is marked by a trig point.

From the summit the ridge continues south-west across Wind Gap to Steeple and then south-east over Red Pike and Dore Head to Yewbarrow. In the early 1940s Dore Head was a magnificent scree run which brought one down to the Mosedale valley with an exhilarating run in what appeared to be a few seconds. Descent by this route is no longer so exciting or so easy and it is preferable to continue over Yewbarrow to get the fine views from its crags down into Wasdale. Care is however necessary in attempting the descent from its southern end and many will find it preferable to descend by the western slopes or to return to Dore Head to take the footpath down the Over Beck valley back to Wasdale. Five and a quarter hours will be required for the route described, but additional time will be necessary for those who make a diversion along the ridge to Steeple or retrace their steps on Yewbarrow. Extensions are possible to include Scoat Fell, Haycock and Seatallan, but the Red Pike–Yewbarrow ridge is the more interesting route.

Pillar can also be reached from Ennerdale. Anyone staying at the Black Sail Youth Hostel can readily walk the circuit already described by ascending Black Sail Pass from the Ennerdale side and continuing from that point, the only disadvantage being the need to ascend Black Sail Pass again from the Wasdale side at the end of the day. Alternatively, one could include an exploration of the Ennerdale valley by walking from the parking site at 109155 as described under the entry for Haycock, a round trip of 7½ hours.

An ascent from Borrowdale is also a possibility and used to be the climax to a week of walking at the C.H.A. Glaramara centre. The route followed was to the top of Honister Pass, then south-west over Grey Knotts and Brandreth, contouring from there under the crags of Great Gable and Kirk Fell to the head of Black Sail Pass. From that point the ridge over Looking Stead, Pillar, Steeple and Red Pike was followed to the scree run down Dore Head and tea at Middle Row Farm in Wasdale Head, after which came a walk over Sty Head back to Borrowdale. Eight and a half hours would be a fair time for this route. A long, hard but never to be forgotten day which was calculated to establish Pillar as a favourite Lakeland summit—not so much for the summit itself but for what one saw and experienced on the way to and from it.

There remains, for the more experienced walker, the route to Pillar from Looking Stead by way of Pillar Rock. The Rev. Symonds refers to the route from Looking Stead to Pillar Rock as the finest half hour in Lakeland and those who get to Looking Stead with time to spare will surely wish to walk as far as Pillar Rock, even if they return to ascend by the ridge rather than scramble up the direct ascent from Pillar Rock.

PLACE FELL

236. *Sheet 83.* Reference 405169. Westmorland. 2154 feet.*

Place Fell lies at the southern end of Ullswater across the valley from Patterdale and is perhaps best known from the colour photograph of Ullswater taken from Gowbarrow Park. It tends to be ignored by the more energetic walkers but provides a delightful half-day excursion.

There is an easy ascent by the path which runs from Patterdale to Boredale, the main path being left at its highest point in favour of another which runs more or less due north to the summit. The summit, embellished with a trig point and cairn, provides very good views of the eastern slopes and ridges of the Helvellyn range and of the Patterdale valley.

To get the best out of this excursion the walker should walk in a north-westerly direction across the summit between Hart and Black Crags to join at, or near, reference 414179 the path which runs on the west side of High Dod down to the south shore of Ullswater. From that point there is a lovely and most interesting walk along the shore of Ullswater back to Patterdale. To those whose basic memories of Ullswater are of a placid sheet of water between gently sloping hills the crags of the southern shore between Long Crag and Silver Point will come as a big surprise.

PLOVER HILL

237. *Sheet 90. Reference 849753. Yorkshire (W.R.). 2231 feet.*

Plover Hill is the summit at the northern end of the Pen-y-ghent ridge and is ignored by the vast majority of those who climb

Pen-y-ghent. The Pennine Way takes the majority away to the west before Plover Hill is reached so that the few who continue to Plover Hill have the place very much to themselves. The wall along the ridge provides shelter from the prevailing wind and seems to have been built from outcrops of rock which formerly broke the smooth appearance of the hill. A lot of stone has gone into the building of the stone walls of the Pennines and the evidence of the removal of rocky outcrops from Plover Hill suggests that the smooth lines of many summits are probably to some extent artificial. Obviously no one would cart stone from a quarry if supplies could be made available on the spot.

Plover Hill, being only two miles away from the main Pen-y-ghent summit and forty feet lower, can readily be included in any of the walks to the Pen-y-ghent summit.

RAISE

238. *Sheet 83.* Reference 343174. Cumberland/Westmorland. 2889 feet.*

Raise is on that great ridge which runs north from Dollywaggon Pike over Helvellyn and the Dods to Clough Head, just south of the Keswick–Penrith road. It is about 1½ miles along the ridge to the north of Helvellyn and is traversed by those who ascend or descend the ridge by Sticks Pass en route to or from Helvellyn. Those who ascend it with no further objective in view are probably confined to skiers, who find good facilities on its eastern slopes.

A high point on the ridge, marked by a cairn, it commands good views of Catstye Cam and Helvellyn but is not otherwise of particular interest to the walker.

RAMSGILL HEAD

239. *Sheet 83.* Reference 443128. Westmorland. 2581 feet.*

Ramsgill Head is on the main High Street ridge where it makes a slight bend to the east and pushes out a subsidiary line over The Knott to Rest Dod on the west of Ramsgill Beck.

It is a little more than a mile north of the main High Street summit and has two cairns, one to mark the summit and one near the crags above Ramsgill Beck. It is best ascended as part of an excursion to High Street as described under that entry.

KNOWE CRAGS (Lakes)

NINE STANDARDS RIGG (Pennines)

SADDLEBACK (Lakes). Sharp Edge

RANDYGILL TOP

240. *Sheets 89 and 90. Reference 687001. Westmorland. 2047 feet.*

Randygill Top is one of the Howgill Fells, lying north-east of Sedbergh. Its name is perhaps connected with the many streams which have their origins on its flanks.

From the walker's point of view it is somewhat inconveniently located near the eastern edge of Ordnance Survey Sheet 89 and reference to the adjacent Sheet 90 is necessary for the most direct route of access. This is by way of the minor road to Narthwaite which leads off from the Sedbergh–Kirkby Stephen road (A.683) at 700971. There is a convenient parking space on the Sedbergh side of the junction or beside the Cross Keys Hotel. The latter is perhaps the best parking place as there is a bridge there across Cautley Beck leading to a footpath going north-east to Narthwaite.

From Narthwaite a track diverges to the left along the west side of Windale Hill and proceeds up the valley of Backside Beck round to Adamsthwaite, whence a road runs down the east side of the hill back to Narthwaite. The track is left at a point north-west of Windale Hill near reference 698997 and a route can be taken in a north-westerly direction to the col between Randygill Top and Spengill Head, a gentle walk from that point bringing one to the summit.

The cairn marking the top is very small but Randygill Top, in common with the other Howgill Fells, has a nice rounded shape which makes easy the identification of the highest point. One is in fact surprised to see a cairn on this grassy dome and its small size is not necessarily an indication that the summit is not well known or of little importance, the nearest cairn building material being a rocky outcrop a little way down the southern slope. How different is the situation on a summit such as Brim Fell where every casual walker can readily make a contribution to the mound of stones.

One can return by descending in a south-easterly direction, proceeding over Kensgriff and Yarlside to descend to Cautley Spout, a lovely streak of water which flows down from the eastern slopes of The Calf to join the River Rawthey near the starting point. Spring is perhaps the best time for the walk, the blossom on the hawthorn trees along Backside Beck being a sight to remember. Three hours ought to be sufficient for the round trip, but it is a pity to hurry a walk in such country as this when the weather is fine.

Alternatively, Randygill Top can be included in the ascent of The Calf by way of Bowderdale as described under the entry for The Calf.

RAVEN HOWE

241. *Sheet 83.* Reference 450144. Westmorland. 2358 feet.*

Raven Howe is on the High Street ridge about three-quarters of a mile north of High Raise. Two routes which cover it are given under the entry for High Raise, one being by the footpath up Fusedale and the other a slightly longer route up Bannerdale and over Heck Crag near Angle Tarn. The former is a safe and pleasant excursion when High Street is covered in snow. Under such conditions, if the snow is not too deep, the course of the Roman Road over Raven Howe is clearly visible.

RED CRAG

242. *Sheet 83.* Reference 451153. Westmorland. 2328 feet.*

Red Crag is the summit immediately north of Raven Howe on the High Street ridge. It is traversed twice in the walk to Raven Howe by way of Fusedale and once if the Bannerdale route is taken.

RED HOWE

243. *Sheet 88.* Reference 250034. Cumberland. 2426 feet.*

That great arc of summits which extends from Slight Side in the west past the Sca Fells, Esk Pike, Bowfell and the Crinkles divides at its south-eastern extremity into Cold Pike on the east and a nameless summit further west which is sometimes confused with Stonesty Pike. However, Stonesty Pike is further north and the summit which is a mile south of the highest Crinkle and lies above the slopes of Red Howe can probably most conveniently be called Red Howe. It is too far from the Three Shire Stone route to the Crinkles for anyone on that route to be willing to contemplate the diversion necessary to reach it but it can be included as part of the ridge by those starting from the Duddon side of the Pass at 247018 or 256020. These starting points involve a long, steep and uninteresting climb up the southern face and there is a lot to be said for tackling Red Howe as a separate excursion from the top of Hardknott Pass (231015). From this point the route goes up the hill to the north and then contours round it to the head of Mosedale. A number of rocky outcrops and two large pools are encountered on the way but there is an easy walk down the grassy slope to the head of the valley once these are passed. From here the route goes to the right of the substantial cairn, which provides a viewpoint for Scafell Pikes, round and above Black Crag and then up the grassy slope inclining to the left of the crags. Near the crags is a convenient gap opening to the right and leading to the first, or most southerly, of the Crinkle Crags. From here it is a question of descending down the rock across the dip and up to the Red Howe summit, a point easily recognisable once Pike of Blisco and Cold Pike are located on the eastern side.

The summit is located in a wilderness of stone and masses of rock interspersed with patches of marsh. Despite the masses of building material close by, the cairn is quite small, a clear indication that visitors are comparatively rare.

For the return journey, having had the benefit of the views into Langdale on reaching the Crinkle, one can take a lower and more westerly route past the top of the stream which flows between Red Howe and Stonesty Pike, then under the crags by a little used path to the original line of ascent and thus back to Hardknott. The round trip takes three hours and the views obtained on the way, and the more interesting and easier walking, amply repay one for extra time as compared with a frontal ascent from the south.

RED PIKE (BUTTERMERE)

244. *Sheet 82.* Reference 16115. Cumberland. 2479 feet.*

This Red Pike lies at the western end of the ridge which divides Buttermere and Ennerdale, one of the finest ridge walks in the Lake District. Routes are described under the entry for High Crag.

The summit lies at the top of a very steep slope but the ascent is well worth while because of the views it gives, not only of many Lakeland mountains but also of the many stretches of water ranging from Derwentwater to Bleaberry Tarn. Red Pike is an apt name for this sharp peak, its namesake above Wasdale being grey and green, except perhaps in the setting sun.

RED PIKE (WASWATER)

245. *Sheet 82.* Reference 167102. Cumberland. 2629 feet.*

This Red Pike, the higher of the two, lies on the ridge which runs from Black Sail Pass over Pillar to Yewbarrow. It can be walked from Wasdale, from the head of Ennerdale, or from Borrowdale as described under the entry for Pillar. One could arrange a smaller circuit by walking up the Nether Beck valley past Scoat Tarn to strike the ridge at a point between Steeple and Red Pike, but this would hardly be worth while since the Pillar end of the ridge provides most of the best views, much more rugged than the Buttermere ridge walk, nearer to the heart of Lakeland and more savage.

RED SCREES

246. *Sheet 83.* Reference 397088. Westmorland. 2541 feet.*

Red Screes is less than half a mile west of the Kirkstone on Kirkstone Pass and was presumably its original home. Seen from the Kirkstone Pass or from the hills to the east of it there is no doubt about the origin of the name, but some confusion arises on the Ordnance Survey maps. The 1-inch Lake District map of 1960 places the name Kilnshaw Chimney across the summit, while Red Screes is reserved for the crags a little further north. On the 1964 Sheet 83 (Penrith) edition, however, the name Kilnshaw is omitted and the name Red Screes extends north from the summit. Accordingly, Red Screes is regarded as the proper name.

The best ascent of Red Screes is from Ambleside as part of a ridge walk over Fairfield, starting by the footpath which runs from 386053 on the Ambleside–Kirkstone road and reaching Red Screes by way of Snarker Pike and Raven Crag. Those who prefer a valley walk to the long drag up Snarker Pike could ascend by the Scandale valley track which leaves Ambleside at 377051 and then strike back to Red Screes in a south-easterly direction from Scandale Pass. The latter route is, of course, appreciably longer but the valley is quiet and secluded and some may think the extra distance well worth while.

From the trig point at the summit there is a magnificent view in all directions, but particularly of High Street and Windermere. The crags and the view down into Kirkstone Pass are also of interest. There is little of interest in proceeding from the summit to Middle Dod, which does not rank as a separate summit. For those who ascend by Snarker Pike, the direct route to Scandale Pass and then over Little Hart, Dove and Hart Crags to Fairfield, returning thence due south down the Rydal Fell ridge to Ambleside can be recommended.

REST DOD

247. *Sheet 83.* Reference 433137. Westmorland. 2278 feet.*

Rest Dod is an off-shoot from the main High Street ridge and its chief interest is as a viewpoint over the Martindale deer sanctuary. It can conveniently be included in the walk to High Street via Riggindale Crag, returning by Kidsty Pike as described under the entry for High Street. Alternatively, at little expense in effort, it can be included in the walk from Howtown by way of Bannerdale as part of the excursion to High Raise. A minor deviation from the direct route is necessary at 427136 but the extra distance involved is less than half a mile. The summit is marked by a cairn.

ROBINSON

248. *Sheet 82.* Reference 203168. Cumberland. 2417 feet.*

Robinson is one of the Newlands Fells and, although a well-known sight to those who have visited the Newlands valley, is probably unfamiliar to many experienced Lakeland walkers. Certainly many of those young enthusiasts who concentrate their attention on Great Gable, Scafell Pikes and Blencathra will not have visited Robinson.

They need not neglect it until they have a car to get them round Derwentwater and into the Newlands valley as it is readily accessible from Newlands Hause on the road from Buttermere to Keswick, or from the top of Honister by way of Dale Head. However, the best way to walk it is as part of a circular tour from the northern end of the Cat Bells ridge below Keswick. Usually this is tackled in a clockwise direction up Cat Bells and along over Maiden Moor to Dale Head and then round to Robinson, but there is a lot to be said for the reverse direction, proceeding up the Newlands valley to High Snab (223189) and then by the footpath above Scope Beck to Robinson. This route gives one the benefit of the views to the south and east when on the high ground between Robinson and Dale Head and views ahead over Derwentwater on the long ridge walk from Dale Head to Cat Bells.

Robinson, and particularly the use of the single word, is an unusual name for a summit. There are two separate theories about its origin, one from historians and one from the inhabitants of Lakeland. The former attribute the name to the man who purchased it at the time of the dissolution of the monasteries in the sixteenth century, while the latter attribute it to the Robinson family of Lorton. Perhaps the Robinson of the historians was one of the Robinsons of Lorton!

ROGAN'S SEAT

249. *Sheets 84 and 90. Reference 919031. Yorkshire (N.R.). 2203 feet.*

Not a lofty eminence where Rogan surveyed the landscape, but Rogan's spring pastures. It is a wild remote area, located somewhat inconveniently near the edge of the map, and it has the attraction of being situated near the inn at Tan Hill (897067 on Sheet 84). Tan Hill has a long history, being a meeting place for shepherds and having been an ancient source of coal from open cast workings. It must be a very desolate spot in the winter months, but in summer, motorists and walkers help to make up what the landlord has lost in custom from the miners and shepherds of earlier times.

From near Tan Hill inn a bridle-way goes off in a south-easterly direction in what appears to be a continuation of the line of the road from Brough to Tan Hill and there are occasional boundary stones marked with a letter 'B' marking its course across Mirk Fell Gill at 905063 to the old pits in William Gill. About half a mile beyond the old mine workings it is necessary to leave the path and head for the cairn on Water Crag (928047). From Water Crag the line of the high ground should be followed in a direction slightly west of south over Wham Bottom to Rogan's Seat.

The summit is rather flat, except for a few peat hags, but the highest point can be found without too much difficulty and is marked by a small cairn of ten stones. There are two stone shelters nearby. The view is limited because of the flat nature of the top but consists of some of the wildest moors of the Pennines which, despite the crowd there may be at Tan Hill, will probably be completely deserted.

Alternatively, Rogan's Seat can be approached from Gunnerside (950982) in Swaledale, taking the path which runs up the west side of Gunnerside Gill. This crosses the gill at 938022 and continues on the east bank past the old mines on Gunnerside Moor to 935030, from which point Rogan's Seat is about one mile due west.

The round trip from Tan Hill, returning by the same route, should take about three hours while that from Gunnerside requires four.

ROSSETT PIKE

250. *Sheet 82.* Reference 248076. Cumberland/Westmorland 2106 feet.*

Rossett Pike is a little over a mile south-east of Esk Hause, the central hub of Lakeland, and the best views of its graceful summit are obtained by walkers proceeding up Mickleden from Langdale. But, of the many thousands who continue from Mickleden up the Rossett Gill route to Esk Hause, very few are interested in making the short diversion necessary to reach the summit. Their minds are set on more distant objectives and the same considerations apply to those who pass on the other side of Rossett Pike by way of Langstrath or the Stake Pass route, even when using the latter as an indirect approach to Angle Tarn. This is fortunate as Rossett Pike is thus left to those who are prepared to make it the subject of a leisurely visit.

Stonethwaite (264137) at the bottom of Langstrath provides an interesting starting point for such a walk, the route being by way of Greenup Gill, High Raise, across the Stake Pass at 264087 and then along the ridge which runs above the crags to Rossett Pike, descending from there to Angle Tarn and returning down Langstrath. Apart from some short sections of Greenup Gill the gradients are easy and, although there is not an identifiable path for most of the section between High Raise and Stake Pass, the going is good and the direction obvious. Six hours should be adequate for the round trip.

The ridge between Stake Pass and the summit provides good views of the Langdale Pikes, Mickleden and Bow Fell, the best viewpoint being marked by a substantial cairn. A smaller cairn is on the rocks close to the summit overlooking Angle Tarn.

ROUGH CRAG

251. *Sheet 83.* Reference 454113. Westmorland. 2062 feet.*

Rough Crag is the summit which lies between Riggindale Crag and Haweswater on the ridge running up to High Street. As previously mentioned, this is the most interesting approach to High Street and Rough Crag marks the end of the grassy slope. It is a fine halting place for lunch, giving good views of Haweswater, Kidsty Pike and the Mardale Ill Bell crags.

ROUND HILL

252. *Sheet 84. Reference 744362. Cumberland. 2249 feet.*
253. *Subsidiary summit at 748380. 2054 feet.*

Round Hill is an accurate description of the main summit which lies immediately west of Tyne Head, three miles south of Garrigill. The subsidiary summit is $1\frac{1}{4}$ miles farther north, connected to the main summit by a broad ridge.

The obvious line of approach is by the Tyne Head road from Garrigill. One may park a car just beyond Hill House where the public road ends, and then strike up the hillside just past the stone structure which is presumably a relic of the old lead mining industry. There is a convenient gate in the first wall and a hole in the second in line with the subsidiary summit, and the going is quite good.

There are two cairns on the subsidiary summit, one east and one west of the high wall which runs along the ridge, located at the best viewpoints towards Garrigill rather than the highest point. From this point a walk due south on the east side of the wall brings one to the main summit. There are a number of marshy patches and a small tarn extending on both sides of the wall just before the summit is reached. This summit does not carry a cairn but its location seems to be at the angle of the wall just north of the wire fence which runs almost due east to the Tyne Head road. There is a boundary stone at that point with the letter 'A' on its face and the letter 'P' on the top and on the northern face.

RYDAL FELL

254. *Sheet 83.* Reference 356092. Westmorland. 2022 feet.*
255. *Subsidiary summits at 356093. 2000 feet.*
256. *355096. 2000 feet.*

Rydal Fell is on the ridge which runs from Fairfield over Greatrigg Man and Heron Pike to Rydal village just north of Ambleside. It lies between Greatrigg Man and Heron Pike and there are footpaths from Grasmere to the two latter summits from which it can readily be reached. However, as described under the entry for Fairfield, Rydal Fell can best be included in one of the Fairfield circuits, preferably ascending from Ambleside by way of Snarker Pike, Red Screes and Hart Crag and then descending from Fairfield by the ridge over Rydal Fell to Rydal village. This circuit takes about six hours.

THE SADDLE

257. *Sheet 82.* Reference 165158. Cumberland. 2050 feet.*

The Saddle is one of the Buttermere Fells, being the bump north-east of Red Pike to the north of the path which runs from the top of Red Pike north of Bleaberry Tarn to Sour-milk Gill and Burtness Wood. It can readily be ascended on the way to or from Red Pike but it is doubtful if anyone would wish to go there for itself alone, even though it provides a fine viewpoint over *the* Buttermere valley.

SADDLEBACK

258. *Sheets 82 and 83.* Reference 323278. Cumberland. 2847 feet.*

Many Lakeland enthusiasts will object to finding this mountain under *S* rather than under *B* by its alternative name of Blencathra. Blencathra, hill of the devils, sounds so much better and somehow one could not envisage Saddleback as the name for the Blencathra Hounds. However, the Ordnance Survey is the authority and it gives preference to Saddleback.

Saddleback lies about four miles north-west of Keswick, due north of Threlkeld village on the Keswick–Penrith road. It is a familiar sight to those who travel north from Grasmere over Dunmail Raise, a magnificent view presenting itself as one commences the descent on the northern side, particularly if the slopes are covered in snow. Apart from Skiddaw, which dominates the scene from many places in and around Keswick, Saddleback is perhaps the most viewable of Lakeland summits. Its somewhat isolated position, the familiar 'saddle' skyline, its varied sloping ridges and the proximity of a number of roads all help to attract attention to it. Moreover, although it has easy routes of ascent, some of which only require half a day for the return trip, it also has in Sharp Edge and the ridge up Hallsfell some of the best rock scrambles in the country. Incidentally, it has two saddles, one visible from the south and another which can be seen from the east on the Mungrisdale road.

The easiest ascent is by the well-worn path from Scales (343268), turning off to the left over Scales Fell from 345276 or continuing up the river valley to 333282 before turning left to Scales Tarn and thence up the grassy slope on the left to the summit. Those who wish to tackle the scramble up Sharp Edge need to continue beyond 333282 to the right of Scales Tarn.

Hallsfell Top, however, is preferable as the route for the ascent. Directions to the start can be confusing, particularly to those who are using old maps, because of the construction of the Threlkeld by-pass. The best course is to turn off the Keswick–Penrith road at the more easterly of the road junctions to Threlkeld and then turn almost immediately to the right and park by the old quarry. Follow the road on the west side of the quarry to the farm. From that point a path is marked going almost due north past the farm buildings and then across the stream which comes down from Middle Tongue. From there a well marked path proceeds directly on to Hallsfell Top, the main summit of Saddleback. At least it is well marked at the lower levels, and experienced walkers should find no difficulty in following the ridge when a few patches of rock are encountered nearer the summit. Beginners should not tackle it on their own and even experienced walkers will have difficulty in snow or in strong winds.

Those who wish to try Sharp Edge and still use the Hellsfell Top route can do so by proceeding from the summit down the grassy slope for about 1000 feet to Scales Tarn and then re-ascending by Sharp Edge.

From the summit, which has an untidy heap of stones as a cairn, walkers who do not tackle Sharp Edge should at least walk past the tarn and the quartzite crosses over the more northerly of the saddles to the top of Foule Crag and then return and proceed south-west across the saddle which is seen from south of the Keswick–Penrith road to Knowe Crags. On a clear day the views are quite outstanding. From that point, the most obvious return route is more or less due south down the slope to the west of Knowe Crags, although it would be quicker, and perhaps more enjoyable, to return to the main summit and descend by the Hallsfell ridge.

The round trip to the summit by Hallsfell Top, returning via Knowe Crags, takes about three hours. Rather more than a further hour should be allowed for the Sharp Edge extension. Those who want a longer walk could consider starting their ascent from Mungrisdale, as described under the entry for Bannerdale Crags, and proceeding over Bannerdale Crags to ascend by Sharp Edge.

As far as is known, Hallsfell has no special connexion with the Hall family, the name being Hallsfell and not Hall's Fell. One suggestion is that the name is a corruption of hause. Certainly it is a narrow neck of land, but not in the same sense as the well-known hauses of Lakeland.

SAIL

259. *Sheet 82.* Reference 198203. Cumberland. 2500 feet.*

Sail, on its ridge west of the Newlands valley, is rather better known than the Pennine Sails but has probably not been heard of by many addicts of the Gable–Sca Fell area. It lies on the long ridge due west of Keswick which runs in an arc from Rowling End above Newlands to Grisedale Pike above Braithwaite. This ridge walk has already been referred to under the entry for Causey Pike. It provides plenty of variety and Sail is the rounded summit which lies between the sheer drops provided by Scar Crags to the east and Scar Crag leading to Crag Hill on the west.

SAILS

260. *Sheet 90. Reference 808965. Yorkshire (N.R.). 2186 feet.*

Sails, on Abbotside Common, is the last summit on the ridge which starts just south of the Kirkby Stephen–Muker Road and forms the eastern boundary of the Eden valley in its upper reaches. For some reason the summit carries a very substantial cairn on its western side whose construction involved appreciable effort, its base being five feet square and its height about six feet. Unlike the substantial cairns to the north of it, it is not on the county boundary.

Walkers who are keen on ridge walks can be recommended to approach Sails from the parking space at 812042 on the Kirkby Stephen–Keld road (B.6270), as described under the entry for Hugh Seat. The only difficulty is the bog immediately south of Hugh Seat where, if the accepted method of walking in the gullies is adopted, there is the problem of keeping on course, particularly if visibility is poor. This walk entails the retracing of one's steps back along the ridge in a round trip of 5½ hours.

Those who prefer to have a different route for the return journey can readily do so by starting their walk from 843922 on the A.684 Hawes–Kendal road, proceeding up Cotterdale as far as 821973 and then walking south-west to the Sails summit. This avoids the bog below Hugh Seat, the return being effected by walking due south down the ridge to 823931, from which point the path from the Malerstang valley to a point just west of the entrance to Cotterdale can be joined.

Views from Sails are very extensive, particularly in the direction of Wensleydale where much of the upper basin of the Ure lies in full view.

ST. SUNDAY CRAG

261. *Sheet 83.* Reference 369135. Westmorland. 2756 feet.*

St. Sunday Crag, the great crag which overlooks Grisedale on the side opposite Striding Edge, is perhaps best known to many from that beautiful coloured photograph of Ullswater taken from Gowbarrow Fell. Because of the proximity of Fairfield and Helvellyn it is doubtful if it is ever ascended for itself alone, but many must know it as the finest route between Fairfield and Patterdale. Even if one does not wish to descend to Patterdale there is a lot to be said for a walk from Fairfield over the stony summit of Cofa Pike to St. Sunday Crag for the views one gets over Ullswater.

However, it is as a ridge route to or from Patterdale that St. Sunday Crag can best be used. The route from Patterdale is from 386157 on the Grisedale road, through Glenamara Park on the north side of Black Crag and Birks to the St. Sunday Crag ridge. From the cairn at the summit it is worth while making a diversion a short distance due east to Gavel Pike before continuing over Cofa Pike to Fairfield.

Fairfield offers a choice of several routes for the return to Patterdale. One can go east to Hart Crag and then descend by the ridge which goes down to Bridgend, a mile or so south of Patterdale, and gives views of St. Sunday Crag from the south. Or one can go west to Grisedale Hause and then return by the Grisedale path to Patterdale or head north and ascend Dollywaggon Pike and Helvellyn, returning to Patterdale by Striding or Swirral Edge, the Keppel Cove path or the Sticks Pass. There is enough choice here to satisfy the taste and capacity of everyone.

SALE HOW

262. *Sheet 82.* Reference 276286. Cumberland. 2200 feet.*

Sale How lies due east of the southern end of the Skiddaw summit about mid-way between that point and Skiddaw House. It makes a pleasant diversion for anyone descending Skiddaw by the pony track and the going is very easy except for a marshy patch in the dip between it and Skiddaw. This is the most sensible approach to Sale How, a grass covered dome of little interest to other than the sheep. However, for those who want a round trip without an ascent of Skiddaw, the path to Skiddaw House from 281253 can be taken and a westerly course steered to the cairn which marks the summit of Sale How. From there, as an alternative to a descent by the pony track, it is possible to contour around Sale How Beck to Lonscale Fell and descend directly to the starting point.

SCA FELL

263. *Sheet 82.* Reference 206065. Cumberland. 3162 feet.*
264. *Subsidiary summit at 209059. 2850 feet.*

Sca means sharp or abrupt and anyone who has stood below Mickledore at the foot of the 600-foot crag, said to be the highest in England, will know how Sca Fell got its name. At the foot of the crag, just before the start of Lord's Rake, is a memorial in the form of an engraved cross to a roped party of four climbers who fell to their deaths in 1903. The letters beside the cross are their initials. This is believed to be the first fatal rock-climbing accident in England.

There are straightforward walking routes to the summit from

Eskdale over Slight Side, from Burnmoor Tarn, or from Wasdale by Green How, but all experienced walkers will wish to make the ascent by Lord's Rake from below Mickledore. Lord's Rake cuts across the north face of Sca Fell, at first a steep path between rock faces and then two sections involving a gentle descent followed by a steeper rise on a path along a rock face with a sheer drop on the outside. It can be a nasty experience in snow and ice or early spring when there is loose rock about, but in normal times should not present any difficulty. Wasdale and Eskdale are probably the best starting points. From the former one can ascend by Lingmell Gill on the direct route to Mickledore or one can follow Lingmell Beck past Burnthwaite farm, bearing right at 213092 and ascending by Piers Gill. At the crossing of Piers Gill at 213078 the Corridor Route from Sty Head is joined and can be followed to the summit of Scafell Pikes, the Mickledore ridge then being taken to descend to the start of Lord's Rake. Alternatively, the ascent of Scafell Pikes can be omitted by walking below the crags to Lord's Rake. The Piers Gill route is very much more impressive than the direct route up Lingmell Gill, but it is essential to have clear weather if it is to be tackled in safety.

Following the ascent of Lord's Rake, an easy walk to the left up the final slope brings one to the main summit. It is a mass of rock but the highest point, a large rock with a cairn on the top, is not in doubt. A cairned track leads to the subsidiary summit about half a mile to the south. In sharp contrast to the main summit it has more grass than rock and has two cairns. From this point one can contour round the slope in a north-westerly direction to pick up the Green How path back to Wasdale. Four and a half hours should suffice for the round trip by the Piers Gill route, with an extra half hour if the main summit of Scafell Pikes is included.

For the Eskdale route, one can take a car to the Eskdale side of Hardknott Pass and then walk up the valley to ascend to Mickledore, directly by Cam Spout or by way of Dow Crag as described under that entry, dropping down to Lord's Rake on the far side. After ascending by Lord's Rake to the two summits of Sca Fell, the return to Eskdale can be accomplished by continuing down the ridge to the south over Slight Side and on to the Eskdale road about a mile below Hardknott Pass. Six hours should suffice for the direct route but at least seven are required for the ascent by Dow Crag.

The crossing of Mickledore is, of course, only necessary for those ascending from Eskdale if they wish to ascend by Lord's Rake. They can shorten their route to Sca Fell if they are prepared to miss some of the best scenery by turning left off the Cam Spout path a little way short of the crags and following the gully and the slope above it to the summit. They may save an hour, but few will think it worth while.

SCAFELL PIKES

265. *Sheet 82.* Reference 216072. Cumberland. 3206 feet.*
266. *Subsidiary summits at 220069. 2500 feet.*
267. *221068. 2500 feet.*

Charles Lamb, when writing of his visit to the Lake District early in the nineteenth century, did not mention Scafell or Scafell Pikes and was more impressed by Ingleborough, Pen-y-ghent and Skiddaw. Others at that time were of the opinion that

> Pendle, Ingleborough and Pen-y-ghent
> Are the highest peaks between Tweed and Trent.

Since the advent of the 1-inch Ordnance Survey, however, no one can have any doubt that the main peak of Scafell Pikes is the highest summit in England.

In common with other major English summits there are several routes of ascent and it is fitting that Scafell Pikes should have the best selection of such routes. No one would recommend the Thirlspot route to Helvellyn to someone who had already ascended by Striding Edge but, no matter what route is used for a first ascent of Scafell Pikes, there are three others—or perhaps two combinations of three other routes—which need to be attempted before one gets a true appreciation of this most magnificent of English mountains.

Perhaps the best arrangement is to tackle the ascent in three separate walks from Eskdale, Wasdale and either Borrowdale or Langdale. From Eskdale, leaving a car at the beginning of Hardknott Pass, one may walk up the pleasant Eskdale valley past the waterfalls and through the gorge until the Sca Fell range comes into view. Then comes the steep climb up Cam Spout and Mickledore and then the rough rocky summit. The return journey can be made by way of Little Narrowcove, this route being picked up from the main ridge at the dip before the rise to Broad Crag. The round trip would require at least six hours.

From Wasdale the recommended route is that up Piers Gill, as described under the Sca Fell entry, the return being by way of Sca Fell or by the Brown Tongue–Lingmell Gill path. Five hours should suffice if the Brown Tongue–Lingmell Gill route is used and 5½ if Sca Fell is included.

From Borrowdale the recommended route is Sty Head by way of Taylorgill, then the Guides or Corridor Route across the north-west slopes to the summit, a walk along the main ridge over Broad Crag and Ill Crag to Great End and Esk Hause, and a return to Borrowdale by Grains Gill. Six hours should suffice.

The Longdale starting point would necessitate a walk up Rossett Gill to Esk Hause and Sty Head, the Guides or Corridor Route to the summit, and a walk along the main ridge back to Esk Hause, followed by the retracing of one's steps down Rossett Gill. Obviously this is less satisfactory than the Borrowdale route, although it may appeal to those based in that area if they can face up to the seven hours walking involved.

The summit itself is a mass of sharp edged rocks bearing a trig point and a solid stocky cairn in which is placed a slab recording the gift by Baron Leconfield, 'subject to any commoners rights' of the Scafell summit as a memorial to men of the Lake District who were killed in the 1914–18 war. Tracks to it from the Corridor Route, Mickledore and Esk Hause are well-worn and walkable without much discomfort and there is no difficulty in deviating from the main ridge to get to Broad Crag, Ill Crag and Great End, but anyone who wanders farther afield may be in for a rough passage. A rough scramble is certainly necessary for anyone wishing to explore the two subsidiary summits at an altitude of 2500 feet on the high ground which runs south-east towards Dow Crag above Eskdale. They are separated by a distance of about 100 yards and are rather less than half a mile from the main summit of Scafell Pikes. There is no recognised path but, if one proceeds on a compass bearing to the south-east, after a reasonably level, though rough and rocky, walk for 100 yards away from the summit a steep descent involving some rough scrambling over huge sharp-edged rocks is encountered. From the bottom of that steep drop the slope eases and farther on one is agreeably surprised to come across a small area of grass on which there may well be a few sheep, which suggests that there is a possibility of access from Eskdale.

There is nothing to mark the first of the two summits but a small cairn of three stones, delicately balanced on an outcrop of rock above Little Narrowcove, is near the location of the second. It is not placed on the highest of the rocky outcrops and may indicate a route down into Little Narrowcove or perhaps the best viewpoint from which to see Ill Crag whose bleak western face dominates the scene.

Rather than return to the main summit it may be preferable to make a direct approach from the more northerly of the subsidiary summits at 220069 to the west of the col, reference 217075, at the head of Little Narrowcove to the west of Broad Crag. From this point one can descend to Eskdale, continue along the ridge to Esk Hause or take a short cut back to Borrowdale by descending the northern slope of the Corridor Route.

What other summit can offer the grim ravine of Piers Gill, the grandstand views of Gable as one follows the Corridor Route under the north-western face, the green and peaceful scenes as one walks beside the rushing waters of the Esk followed by the wild bowl of upper Eskdale under its arc of crags and the steep rise up Cam Spout and, finally, the high walk on the ridge of shattered rocks and the evil-looking face of Ill Crag? This is indeed a summit worthy to be the highest in England.

SCANDALE HEAD

268. *Sheet 83.* Reference 381097. Westmorland. 2050 feet.*

Scandale is a well-known name because of the delightful valley of Scandale Beck which runs down to Ambleside between the High Pike and Snarker Pike ridges and also because of the pass which joins the Scandale valley to that of Caiston Beck in a route from Ambleside to Patterdale which was no doubt of more importance before the days of the motor car and the main road down Kirkstone Pass. But those who have walked the Scandale area may not have noticed the summit of Scandale Head or have any recollection of it. However, a careful search of the map will reveal, immediately above the *d* in Scandale Head, a 2050 foot contour line which encloses an area of perhaps 10,000 square yards. It is convenient to use the name Scandale Head to identify the summit although it obviously refers primarily to the collecting area for water which flows into Scandale Beck.

A visit to the Scandale Head summit involves a minor deviation from the recognised routes in this area, but there should be no difficulty in finding it, lying as it does on the ridge running south from Black Brow, the summit between Dove Crag and Little Hart Crag. The prominent cairn to the north-west at 378099 is also a useful guide.

It will come as a surprise to those who have walked this area to find that Scandale Head carries a cairn. This is not readily apparent as there are three grassy humps on the summit ridge and the cairn is located in the hollow between the central hump and that to the south.

SCAR CRAGS

269. *Sheet 82.* Reference 207207. Cumberland. 2205 feet.*

Scar Crags stretch for a distance of half a mile along the ridge just west of Causey Pike. The summit is at the western end and only just over 200 feet higher than Causey, so that the gradient is quite gentle. These crags should not be confused with Scar Crag which forms the southern face of Crag Hill beyond Sail along the same ridge.

SCA FELL (Lakes). 1903 Memorial Cross near foot of Lord's Rake

SCAFELL PIKES (Lakes). (*above*) Sca Fell and Lord's Rake from Mickledore. (*below*) Scafell Pike Cairn with Sca Fell in background

Scar Crags are normally walked as part of the ridge between Causey and Grisedale Pikes but they can be approached directly by the footpath which runs from 175172 at Buttermere via Sail Beck, crosses the ridge at 205206, and then descends by Stile End to Braithwaite. As an ascent from Braithwaite, which is conveniently located for an ascent of the ridge by Grisedale Pike or Rowling End this path has little to recommend it but, as a route from Buttermere, it is excellent. When used in conjunction with a return to Buttermere by the path down Wanlope and Whiteless Pike it offers a round trip which can be extended along the ridge as far as the individual walker requires.

The best view of the tremendous slabs of rock which form Scar Crags is obtained by stepping to the left off the ridge track just west of the Causey summit. A head for heights is necessary.

SCAUD HILL

270. *Sheet 84. Reference 795363. Durham. 2342 feet.*

This is the highest summit in Durham, although few natives of Durham seem to be aware of the fact. It is a desolate spot, lying north-west of an old mining area about mid-way between Alston and Middleton-in-Teesdale. An old mine road runs from 814351 on the main road, through Grass Hill Farm, to the upper western slopes of Scaud Hill. A high cairn crowns the slope above that point but it is not the main summit. This lies about half a mile to the south-west across a wilderness of bog somewhat reminiscent of The Cheviot.

The cairn on the main summit, although it can be seen clearly on the sky-line from the eastern slopes, is a very small affair of nine stones. It is not, in fact, the highest point in Durham. This is the trig point on Burnhope Seat with an altitude of 2449 feet, the main summit of Burnhope Seat being in Cumberland at a height of 2452 feet.

From Scaud Hill one may follow the low ridge which forms the watershed between Weardale and the South Tyne over Burnhope Seat to Knoutberry Hill and return by way of the ridge running east from Dead Stones to the road at 842397, then over the dam at the eastern end of Burnhope Reservoir and the road which crosses from Weardale to Grass Hill Farm and Teesdale. The high land is a very desolate and windswept area, but one where there is peace and solitude.

The walk by the old road to Scaud Hill and return would take little more than 1½ hours. A further three hours would be required for the round trip by Dead Stones and Burnhope Reservoir.

SCOAT FELL

271. *Sheet 82.* Reference 159114. Cumberland. 2760 feet.*
272. *Subsidiary summits at 157114. 2750 feet.*
273. *154112. 2750 feet.*

Scoat Fell is one of the cross-roads of Lakeland. Not so central, important or well known as Esk Hause, but a cross-roads nevertheless and situated on one of the finest ridge walks in the country. One of the summits of Scoat Fell is the second highest point on the ridge from Looking Stead over Pillar to Red Pike and Yewbarrow, the other ridges running from Scoat Fell being that to Steeple in the north and that to Haycock and Little Gowder Crag in the west. Apart from the high level routes along these ridges, which cross at Scoat Fell, there is a route up Nether Beck from Wasdale across the col between Haycock and Scoat Fell and down into Ennerdale.

Fortunately, the area west and north of the Pillar ridge is not so frequented as other parts of Lakeland so that Scoat Fell is not a well-known name even to some of those who have walked the ridge. No one would visit the area simply to see Scoat Fell but it is the essential link between the summits in this area and deserves to be better known.

SEATALLAN

274. *Sheet 82.* Reference 140084. Cumberland. 2266 feet.*

Seatallan forms a convenient extension to the walk from Wasdale Head to Haycock and Little Gowder Crag, whether this is via Black Sail Pass and Pillar or Red Pike and Scoat Fell. From Little Gowder Crag the route lies almost due south below the crags south of Haycock and then over a marshy area until the grassy slope leading to the summit is reached. The summit is marked with a trig point and cairn and provides a good viewpoint over lower Wasdale and the sea coast.

The return to Wasdale can best be achieved by proceeding due east, through the gap in the crags north of Middle Fell, down to the path along Nether Beck which reaches the Wastwater road near the middle of the lake.

Alternatively, Seatallan can be ascended in as little as two hours by walking up Nether Beck from Wasdale as far as 150088 and then proceeding due west to the summit. The return may be varied by descending south-east to Greendale Tarn and taking the footpath along the stream running south, reaching the road at Greendale Farm (144056), from which point the road can be followed back to the starting point in Wasdale.

SEAT SANDAL

275. *Sheet 83.* Reference 344115. Westmorland. 2415 feet.*

Seat Sandal lies between Grasmere and Helvellyn and routes to Helvellyn pass on either side of it. A diversion to its summit would take less than half an hour, but those going to Helvellyn normally are not interested, and those returning too tired, to make the ascent. This is perhaps unfortunate since it is a fine viewpoint. However, there is compensation in that those who desire a short walk with a worth while view and little competition from the crowds can readily obtain it. For such, the best route is by the stream which runs below the northern slope of Seat Sandal to reach the Dunmail Raise road at 327117. By ascending this attractive valley to its highest point and then ascending due south up the north slope of Seat Sandal, the summit cairn is reached in about 1¼ hours.

SEATHWAITE FELL

276. *Sheet 82.* Reference 228096. Cumberland. 2000 feet.*
277. *Subsidiary summit at 229093. 2000 feet.*

Seathwaite Fell lies at the head of Borrowdale with the Grains Gill route to the east, Sty Head to the west and Sprinkling Tarn and the crags of Great End to the south. It looks like a minor version of Glaramara, particularly when seen from the top of Sty Head.

One could take an easy line of ascent to Seathwaite Fell by following either the Sty Head or the Grains Gill path from the Seathwaite hamlet in Borrowdale. The Sty Head route is the longer of the two and can be rough going, so those who want the easiest route should opt for Grains Gill. Leaving this route at 231091, due east of Sprinkling Tarn, there is an easy but interesting approach down the east side of the tarn to the lower summit, followed by the negotiation of a few wet patches of waterlogged ground and a scramble to the cairn at the main summit just north of the tarn which lies near the centre of the 2000-foot contour line. Just south of the cairn is a thin streak of white quartz in the rocks which form the summit. The outcrops of rock spread around the high ground here encourage one to scramble over them to get the different views, the tarn itself being in a very delightful location which will surely invite swimmers who are fortunate enough to be there on a sunny day.

However, those who prefer a little variety to their walk and are prepared to tackle a reasonably steep ascent, may prefer to attack the fell from the north. The crags marked on the map are not really so fearsome as they appear on the map and there is a walkable route up the line of the stream which runs down to the Sty Head track a little way short of its junction with the route up Taylor Gill about twenty minutes walk from Stockley Bridge. Those who are prepared to cope with some wet walking at the start of the day may prefer to ascend by Taylorgill, taking the path towards Sour Milk Gill through the farm buildings at Seathwaite and turning left along the far side of the stream. The path is difficult to follow in places but the general direction is obvious and from the point where the path rejoins the line of the stream it becomes a most delightful walk. It involves the odd bit of scrambling in the steeper parts but will present no difficulty to seasoned fell walkers, who will probably enjoy this alternative to Sty Head and should not experience any difficulty in picking up the Sty Head route from the bridge over Taylorgill or, in dry weather, a little lower down.

From the point where the Sty Head route is left a fairly steep ascent over grass and rocky outcrops brings one, in the space of about half an hour, to the best viewpoint over the Borrowdale valley. This is marked by a substantial cairn at the spot height of 1970 feet. From this point the main summit is reached by a gentle walk and a short scramble to the cairn to the north of the tarn which lies near the centre of the 2000-foot contour line. Another cairn marks a high point to the south of the tarn but the subsidiary summit is within the other 2000-foot contour line just east of Sprinkling Tarn. As it appears to be lower than the other cairned points and bears no distinguishing mark, walkers may well be tempted to wonder whether the 1-inch Ordnance Survey is completely accurate.

From the summit one is quite close to Esk Hause, the central cross-roads of Lakeland, and the choice of walks is quite embarrassing. An easy walk would be to strike south from Esk Hause over Allen Crags and Glaramara, thus permitting a first-hand comparison of Seathwaite Fell and Glaramara and completing a round trip in about 4½ hours.

SELSIDE PIKE

278. *Sheet 83.* Reference 491112. Westmorland. 2142 feet.*
279. *Subsidiary summit at 487104. 2200 feet.*

The more southerly summit is the higher of the two but the northerly one is the more prominent and is the one named on the 1-inch Ordnance Survey map. There is a easy and pleasant ascent from Mardale by the old Corpse Road which leaves the road along the reservoir near 479118 and runs in a north-easterly direction towards Swindale. Near the highest point of this road a deviation to the south should be made up Selside End and the ridge then followed to the two summits. The going is good, apart from a marshy patch below Selside End, and the first summit, which has a large cairn, gives a fine view of the secluded Swindale valley.

This is a very quiet area and one is not likely to encounter anyone else on the way. The walk can be extended farther west past Artle Crag to Branstree—named on the Bartholomew's map but not on the Ordnance Survey—and then south-west to the Gatesgarth Pass leading back to the southern end of Haweswater or south-east to the path at 485089. From this latter point the path runs north-east up Mosedale Beck to Swindale Head, from which point the Old Corpse Road can be taken back to the starting point.

SERGEANT MAN

280. *Sheet 82.* Reference 287089. Westmorland. 2414 feet.*

Sergeant Man is on the high ground about a mile north of the Langdale Pikes and half a mile south-east of High Raise, the centre of Lakeland. The best approach is from Grasmere by way of Easedale Tarn and the footpath which runs south-west from there to Blea Rigg. The walk can be continued to High Raise and Ullscarf as described under the entry for High Raise.

Sergeant Man has a prominent cairn but, as a viewpoint, does not compare with High Raise.

SHEFFIELD PIKE

281. *Sheet 83.* Reference 370182. Westmorland. 2232 feet.*

Sheffield Pike, a mile due west of Ullswater between Glencoyndale and Glenridding Beck, is not mentioned in the Baddeley Guide and is probably not visited too frequently because walkers in that area are more likely to be heading to or from the Helvellyn ridge by a more direct route. However, there is no reason why it should not be used as an alternative to the Sticks Pass for the ascent to, or descent from, the Helvellyn ridge. On the descent this is a simple matter of continuing due east from 357183 over almost level ground instead of turning to the south. Otherwise, the ascent of Sheffield Pike can probably best be undertaken in conjunction with an excursion to Green Side, starting from Glenridding, Dockray or Dowthwaitehead as described under the Green Side entry. Sheffield Pike gives particularly good views of Ullswater and is well worth a visit.

SHELTER CRAGS

282. *Sheet 82.* Reference 249054. Cumberland/Westmorland. 2650 feet.*

Shelter Crags are just north of the Crinkles on that magnificent ridge which separates Langdale and Eskdale. There are routes to the Three Tarns, just to the north of Shelter Crags, from Eskdale and Langdale. From Eskdale it is a question of following the main valley as far as 227036, then taking the Lingcove Beck path to 238052 and then heading north-east in a direct line to Three Tarns. From Langdale there is a choice of the rather monotonous ascent by The Band from Stool End or the more interesting route up Oxendale and Hell Gill. On reaching Three Tarns, whichever of the three routes is used, a walk of half a mile due south brings one to the summit above Shelter Crags.

However, those who can do so will be well advised to visit Shelter Crags on a walk of the ridge from the Wrynose Pass over Cold Pike and Crinkle Crags, and then on to Bow Fell as described under the entry for Bow Fell.

SIMON FELL

283. *Sheet 90. Reference 754752. Yorkshire (W.R.). 2100 feet.*
284. *Subsidiary summits at 755751. 2100 feet.*
285. *755758. 2050 feet.*

Simon Fell is the high land to the north and east of Ingleborough. It can readily be included in a walk up Ingleborough, those who start from Clapham having the advantage of a circular route from Gaping Gill up Ingleborough, across to Simon Fell and then down its southern slopes through somewhat wet ground back to Gaping Gill.

From the flat summit of Ingleborough there is a steep drop of about 300 feet to the wet and boggy area in the dip between Ingleborough and Simon Fell and the wall, which appears to follow the line of the parish boundary, can then be followed to the two highest summits, one being south of the wall and one about ten yards to the north of it. The other summit is about half a mile to the north of the wall and near the wall which runs north to south just above the eastern escarpment. The central summit is the only one which has a cairn, consisting of a few small stones, barely visible above the grass.

It is important to use the latest 1-inch Ordnance Survey Map for this walk as the older edition marks the spot height at 759748 as the main summit. This is certainly the most prominent point on the landscape and is marked by a tall post. Those who approach Ingleborough from Clapham and return by way of Simon Fell can readily take in the viewpoint at 759748 and make their descent to Gaping Gill from there.

As an alternative to the ascents of Ingleborough from Ingleton or Clapham, an approach by way of Simon Fell from Ribblehead can be recommended, particularly to those who wish to keep the walking to a minimum. The start is from the minor road which leaves the Ribblehead–Horton-in-Ribblesdale road at 775786, signed to Colt Park, and giving access to Park Fell. From the Park Fell summit a walk of 1¼ miles to the south-west along the high ground brings one to the most northerly of the Simon Fell summits. After continuing to the main summit just north of the parish boundary the wall can be crossed by a stile at 748748 to reach the southerly summit. The walk can then be continued to the Ingleborough summit.

Distances for the round trip, including Ingleborough, are seven miles by the Ribblehead route, nine miles by the Ingleton route and eleven miles from Clapham. The latter is easily the best as it has a shady walk in woodland, includes Trow Gill and Gaping Gill, and involves the least retracing of steps.

It is to be hoped that all who visit Simon Fell will take particular care to avoid damaging the stone walls which follow the parish boundaries across the summit. They were intact and in good condition in the summer of 1971.

SKIDDAW

286. *Sheet 82.* Reference 260291. Cumberland. 3054 feet.*

'A long uninteresting slog up a wide pony track' is the usual description, and probably a fair description, of the ascent which starts from the end of the road at 281253 and heads north-west up the slope to the summit. However, there are other routes. They rely on an ascent by the south-western slope of the summit ridge from 257283. This point can be reached by way of Carl Side from Mill Beck as described under the Carl Side entry, by way of Longside Edge from 236310 on the minor road from the A.591 to Orthwaite, or from Mill Beck (257262) by the valley between Carl Side and Little Man. Of these the Carl Side route is the shortest, while the Longside Edge route is the easiest and also the most interesting. It is, however, possible for those who ascend by Carl Side to make a diversion of half an hour or so to Longside Edge to get the views over Bassenthwaite and to Skiddaw.

From Carl Side Tarn, near 257283, there is a well-marked path which, apart from a steep middle section, brings one to the summit ridge of Skiddaw with little difficulty. The actual summit is marked by a cairn and trig point.

For the descent, for those ascending from Mill Beck, it is convenient to use the pony track back to 281253, while those starting from Longside Edge will probably find it best to retrace their steps on the route used for the ascent. As an alternative to the pony track, however, it is possible for those who desire solitude, to go east to Sale How immediately after dropping down from the summit ridge. The walk can then be continued round to Lonscale Fell and 281253 reached by a direct descent from Lonscale Fell.

The round trip from Mill Beck, ascending by Carl Side and returning by the pony track would take about four hours, with an additional hour for the extension to Sale How and Lonscale Fell and a further half an hour if the diversion to Longside Edge is included. A round trip from 236310 by way of Longside Edge would take 3½ hours.

SLIGHT SIDE

287. *Sheets 82 and 88.* Reference 210050. Cumberland. 2499 feet.*

Slight Side is the southern extremity of the Sca Fell summit and provides an easy line of ascent or descent from, or to, Eskdale. There are two routes from Eskdale, one starting near the Woolpack Inn nearly a mile east of Boot and one starting a mile farther east, and they meet for the steep rise up the southern slope of Slight Side. From Slight Side one can continue along the ridge to Sca Fell. The average walker, however, will probably prefer to ascend Sca Fell by Lord's Rake and get to Slight Side by following the ridge to the south. If his starting point was Eskdale, reaching Lord's Rake up the lonely Esk Valley and then by way of Mickledore, the descent to Boot will complete his circuit while, if it was Wasdale, the return can be made preferably by the ridge back to the main summit of Sca Fell and then down the slope of Green How direct to Wasdale or by contouring round the summit to Green How and then going down the slope. The walk from the Woolpack directly to Slight Side should take little more than 2¼ hours with a further forty-five minutes to reach Sca Fell summit, while the return from Sca Fell would require about 1¾ hours. Going by way of Mickledore and Lord's Rake would involve a walk of about six or seven hours for the round trip according to the route chosen.

Slight Side has a steep southern face and a huge rock for its summit with a path through a cleft in its centre. There are small cairns on each side and, although that on the east is probably the higher of the two, there is little to choose between them.

STAPLE MOSS

288. *Sheet 84. Reference 857237. Yorkshire (N.R.). 2000 feet.*

Staple Moss is among the high rolling moors north of the Brough–Middleton-in-Teesdale road, about three miles east-south-east of Mickle Fell. This country requires careful map and compass reading but Staple Moss, lying on the ridge between Arngill and Hargill Becks, can be located quite easily if one follows the footpath which runs from 882214 along the Hargill Beck up to 864238 where the path turns due north to Hagworm Hill. From that point it is merely a question of walking due west up the slope for about half a mile. There are a few marshy patches at the beginning but on the whole, the path provides very good going, as does the summit. This is surprising, as the name Staple Moss means the posts in the moss.

The summit is not marked but there are several high sections of wall—possibly a form of shooting butt—near the top. When reading the map in this area it may be useful to remember that there is a prominent cairn on Low Bink Moss to the east and on the spot height above the crags at 836237 to the west.

The summit ridge continues in a north-westerly direction to Long Crag, the going being quite firm and the slope scarcely noticeable. Unfortunately, those who proceed in this direction will encounter a line of W.D. Danger signs marking the limit of the Warcop Artillery Range and reading :

> Danger W. D. Range, Shelled Area.
> Beyond this point you proceed at
> your own risk.

There is said to be no risk to those who avoid tampering with stray bits of metal and provided the range is not in use. Red flags flying at selected points on the western boundaries of the range indicate when it is in use but they would not be visible from the Staple Moss direction. To proceed past the line with confidence it is first necessary to make contact with the Warcop Training Centre to ascertain whether or not firing can be expected. They usually have an off-day on Monday.

STARLING DODD

289. *Sheet 82.* Reference 143157. Cumberland. 2085 feet.*

On the broad ridge which runs up to Buttermere Red Pike from a point just east of the lower end of Ennerdale Water, Starling Dodd is a gentle contrast to the Red Pike–High Crag ridge. The walk to it from lower Ennerdale, as described under the entry for

Great Borne, makes a pleasant afternoon excursion and, for those with more time to spare, could readily be extended to include the Red Pike–High Crag ridge, returning by the same route or, for the more energetic, by way of Scarth Gap and the shores of Buttermere and Crummock Water to the Scale Beck route to Floutern Tarn. The walk to and from High Crag would take nearly six hours, while that returning by Buttermere would take 6½.

STEEPLE

290. *Sheet 82.* Reference 157117. Cumberland. 2687 feet.*

This northern spur off the Pillar–Haycock ridge is well worthy of attention as a diversion from the main ridge walk described under the entry for Pillar because of the magnificent views it gives of Ennerdale and of the crags on the north of the main ridge. It is a jumble of broken rock and a sharp contrast to Scoat Fell and the country farther west.

Steeple also provides a ridge route into Ennerdale, which can be used for a round trip from the parking site at 108154 as described under the entry for Haycock.

STONY COVE PIKE

291. *Sheet 83.* Reference 418099. Westmorland. 2502 feet.*

Stony Cove Pike is the rocky summit which marks a route from the Kirkstone Inn by Threshthwaite Mouth to High Street. The route beyond Stony Cove Pike involves a steep drop, which will deter those who have to return to Kirkstone and have only limited time available. Views from the top of the rise into the Trout Beck valley and over to Thornthwaite Beacon are well worth while, however, and warrant the walk of a little more than quarter of a mile to the east of the Stony Cove Pike summit. In winter conditions when snow is on the ground, Stony Cove Pike seems very wild and very remote from civilisation and this could well be the best time to see it. A cairn marks the highest point.

STRIDING RIDGE

292. *Sheet 83.* Reference 350149. Westmorland. 2600 feet.*

Such is the popularity of the famous ridge leading from Patterdale to Helvellyn that regular visitors to Lakeland will find it difficult to believe that there are people who have not heard of Striding Edge. Photographs, postcards, calendars and guide books have done more to publicise it than those who have walked along it, and there are no doubt some who have been deterred from attempting it on seeing photographs of the narrow ridge with the steep slopes on either side. In some ways these slopes are more impressive than the sheer drop on one side of other ridge walks, since the sheer drop is only in view occasionally while the Striding Edge slopes are in view all the time.

The ridge is no longer so forbidding as it was in the 1930s. Many thousands have made their way along it since that time and seem to have trampled the path into a broad highway in comparison with the narrow track which existed previously. It is still an impressive route, however, and no one who attempts it in reasonable weather should have any cause to regret it.

The obvious route for the ascent is that from the road which runs into Grisedale from Patterdale. It is signed to Helvellyn and there is a sizeable car park where the road deteriorates to a track near the bridge at 383156. From that point it is only a question of following the crowd up the well-worn path, which is something of a grind for nearly two miles, after which the ridge is reached. Alternatively, for those who prefer to walk alone, the route described under the Birkhouse Moor entry can be used as far as the beginning of the ridge.

Those who think that Striding Edge will lead them to the top of Helvellyn in a gentle progression are in for a shock. Helvellyn involves a drop along the ridge from the highest point of Striding Edge and then a very steep scramble—worse than anything on Striding Edge—to the summit. This steep section can be avoided on the return journey by descending down the somewhat less steep Swirral Edge, about 500 yards north of Striding Edge on the other side of Red Tarn. The round trip from the car park at the bottom of Grisedale over Striding Edge to Helvellyn, returning over Swirral Edge, should take just under four hours, but it would be a mistake to confine the walk within these limits on a fine day. An extension along the Helvellyn ridge or to Catstye Cam should certainly be considered.

STY BARROW DOD

293. *Sheet 83.* Reference 341187. Cumberland/Westmorland. 2756 feet.*

294. *Subsidiary summit at 343189. 2750 feet.*

These are the first summits north of the Sticks Pass on the Helvellyn ridge. This ridge, which starts with Clough Head just south of the

Keswick–Penrith road, is gentle, rolling and usually deserted country on the section north of the Sticks Pass whereas the Helvellyn section is usually crowded. No lover of the wide open spaces will wish to miss this walk despite the problem, for those who wish to get back to their starting point, of having a choice of returning by the same route or by the road along St. John's Vale. This can be avoided by taking the area in two parts, the first starting from 316231 at St. John's in the Vale to Clough Head and Great Dod, returning by Groove Beck and the Old Coach Road, and the other starting from Glenridding up Sticks Pass to Stybarrow Dod, Green Side, Hart Side and Sheffield Pike. Those who do not object to returning by the same route can be recommended to ascend by Clough Head and, after walking south to Stybarrow Dod, to retrace their steps, thus enjoying the solitude of the high rolling ridge to the full. Four and a half hours should suffice for the round trip. The main summit is marked by a cairn.

SWARTH FELL

295. *Sheet 90. Reference 755967. Westmorland. 2235 feet.*

Aisgill on the railway between Settle and Appleby is one of the most famous places on the British railway network but for walkers it is more important as the starting point for an excursion to Swarth Fell. It is a quiet spot, about one mile east of Swarth Fell, and three miles north of the Moorcock Inn on the B.6259 road to Kirkby Stephen, yet anyone who remains there for any length of time may be surprised at the number of railway employees who walk to or from the signal box on the railway there.

The best approach to Swarth Fell is to follow the line of the stream which runs from 777966 almost directly in line for the Swarth Fell Pike summit. It is a pleasant walk across the rough moorland pasture, after which comes the short ascent to the summit and then the ridge to Swarth Fell. There are five cairns on the route, probably marking the boundary between the West Riding and Westmorland, and the going is good. Magnificent views to Morecambe Bay, Lakeland and the Pennines unfold on the way and there are few signs of pedestrians.

There is an obvious extension of the walk to the north to Wild Boar Fell, the only problem being a small patch of bog in the dip between.

SWARTH FELL PIKE

296. *Sheet 90. Reference 763957. Westmorland/Yorkshire (N.R./W.R.). 2100 feet.*

Swarth Fell Pike is on the western skyline at the southern end of the Mallerstang valley and is the meeting point of Westmorland and the North and West Ridings of Yorkshire. Its ascent is described under the previous entry.

The summit is marked by what appears to be an unusual trig point, a circle of concrete level with the ground.

SWIRL HOW

297. *Sheet 88.* Reference 273006. Lancashire. 2630 feet.*

Only one foot lower than the Old Man of Coniston, Swirl How lies nearly two miles to the north, on the same ridge and beyond Brim Fell. It is one of the cross-roads of the Lake District, the north-south ridge continuing over Carrs to the Wrynose Pass while Black Sails and Wetherlam go off to the east and Grey Friar to the west. Swirl How is thus the best viewpoint of the Coniston ridge and has the added advantage of being less frequented than the Old Man.

There is a direct ascent from Coniston by way of Church Beck and Levers Water to the col between Swirl How and Black Sails, but the preferable route is the ascent from the Walna Scar road by way of Brim Fell and then along the ridge north to the cairn which marks the summit of Swirl How.

TARN CRAG

298. *Sheet 83.* Reference 488078. Westmorland. 2176 feet.*

Tarn Crag lies due south of the Haweswater Hotel, over-looking the upper part of Long Sleddale. Besides its cairn it carries a survey post, presumably to line up with that below Artle Crag, a relic of the construction of the pipeline for Manchester's water. It could obviously be reached from Long Sleddale but it is best tackled as an extension of the walk to Branstree (the summit above Artle Crag) from Haweswater, whether this is done by Gatescarth Pass from the southern end of the lake or by the Old Corpse Road and Selside Pike.

From Branstree the direction lies south-south-east down a gentle slope to the path which runs from Long Sleddale to Mosedale and then, after crossing that path, up a similar slope to Tarn Crag. The going is very good, apart from a wet patch in the dip, and there are good views of Mosedale and Long Sleddale from the top.

Mosedale is a very lovely valley and an alternative approach to Tarn Crag would be to follow the Old Corpse Road to Swindale Head and then to take the footpath which runs from Swindale up Mosedale towards Long Sleddale, leaving it at the highest point on the ridge between the two latter valleys and following the line of the route from Branstree to Tarn Crag. The round trip from the start of the Old Corpse Road along Haweswater via Swindale Head to Tarn Crag, returning over Branstree, Selside Pike and Selside End would only take 4½ hours.

From Tarn Crag it would be convenient to continue to Grey Crag, the most easterly of Lakeland summits, which should not be confused with Gray Crag above Hayeswater about five miles to the north-west. It lies three-quaraters of a mile to the south-east of Tarn Crag, the only difficulty on the way being the patch of wet ground between the two on the north-east side of Greycrag Tarn.

TARN RIGG HILL

299. *Sheet 90. Reference 744917. Yorkshire (W.R.). 2200 feet.*

Tarn Rigg Hill is one of the summits of Baugh Fell, the great mound which lies between Garsdale and Wild Boar Fell. Knoutberry Haw is the other summit and the entry under that heading gives a route to the two. The summit, although not far from the pleasant Garsdale, is a wild and desolate spot. North of the summit is a deserted area of bog which does not tempt one to go farther and it is probably best to return more or less directly to the starting point in Carsdale.

There is no cairn to mark the summit but there is no difficulty in identifying its location.

THORNTHWAITE CRAG

300. *Sheet 83.* Reference 431100. Westmorland. 2569 feet.*

Topped by its magnificent fourteen-foot beacon, a landmark for miles around, Thornthwaite Crag stands at a meeting of routes just west of the course of the Roman Road's final ascent on to High Street. Gray Crag goes off to the north, High Street to the north-east and the Froswick–Ill Bell ridge to the south, while

Mardale Ill Bell and Mardale Harter Fell lie just due east and Stony Cove Pike due west.

The best route to the Crag is probably that from the Garburn Pass between Kentmere and Troutbeck up the Yoke, Ill Bell, Froswick ridge as described under the entry for Froswick, but there is a direct ascent by way of the old Roman Road up Hagg Gill from Troutbeck, three miles north of Windermere. It is also accessible from the Kirkstone Inn by way of Stony Cove Pike or from Haweswater by way of Mardale Ill Bell.

THREE PIKES

301. *Sheet 84. Reference 834344. Durham. 2133 feet.*

Three Pikes is in that wild and desolate area, much scarred by mine-workings, which lies between Teesdale and Weardale. There is little more to be said about it, except, perhaps, that it is a place where one can probably walk without fear of competition.

From just south of Rough Rigg farm at 822342 a badly defined path leaves the Middleton-in-Teesdale–Alston road in a northerly direction just left of a small stream and there is easy, though somewhat rough, access to Three Pikes from the point where this path crosses the 2000-foot contour. At first sight it is difficult to see the reason for the name but this becomes obvious if a more distant view is taken from Great Stony Hill to the north-west.

It would be less than fair to Three Pikes to omit mention of the Ski Hoist marked on the south-eastern slopes. Allenheads, nearly eight miles to the north, is a popular skiing centre and it will be interesting to see if Langdon Beck can offer any serious competition.

THURNACAR KNOTT

302. *Sheet 82.* Reference 279080. Cumberland/Westmorland. 2351 feet.*

Thurnacar Knott, slightly higher than Pike of Stickle but lower than Harrison Stickle, is the first summit on the broad ridge which runs north from the Langdale Pikes over High Raise, the centre of Lakeland, to Ullscarf. It is perhaps seen to best advantage when the ridge is covered in snow.

No one would climb to Thurnacar Knott for itself alone but the summit, which is marked by a cairn, can readily be included in the walk along the ridge as described under the High Raise entry.

TINSIDE RIGG

303. *Sheet 84. Reference 777199. Westmorland. 2000 feet.*
304. *Subsidiary summit at 774198. 2000 feet.*

Tinside Rigg lies within the boundaries of the Warcop Artillery Range, about which some details are given in the entry for Hilton Fell. Access to the two summits of Tinside Rigg is therefore restricted to the days when firing is not in progress.

Although the main footpath from the village of Hilton runs up Hilton Beck past the disused mines and so on to Maize Beck west of High Cup Nick, a subsidiary path diverges up the valley to the right about 1¼ miles from the village and continues under Swindale Edge to reach a height of nearly 2000 feet between Tinside Rigg and Warcop Fell. The Tinside Rigg summits are within quarter of a mile of the path at this point. Little more than a quarter of a mile farther on is the summit of Long Fell.

The round trip to the three summits from Hilton village should not take more than 2½ hours. Those who take exception to returning by the same route, could return to Hilton by the old mining track down the north-western slope of Long Fell.

Anyone with the time available would be well advised to proceed a little farther to the east and then strike due north to Little Fell, about 1½ miles distant, returning to the Hilton Beck bridleway after traversing the Little Fell summit. Unfortunately, the walking between Tinside Rigg and Little Fell is over somewhat marshy ground and a few shell cases remind one that this is the Warcop Artillery Range.

The Tinside Rigg summits are not of particular interest. They are reasonably dry and, although there is plenty of rock at hand, they are not marked with cairns. That on the west has a substantial boundary stone on its northern edge bearing the marking W. 1857 on one side and B. 2 on the other. A similar stone with the markings W. 1857 and B. 3 is on the eastern extremity of Little Fell.

The eastern summit has a shelter of stone walls at the top, which seems designed for use as a shooting box, although there are no signs of grouse in the area.

TOM SMITH'S STONE

305. *Sheet 83. Reference 654465. Cumberland/Northumberland. 2071 feet.*
306. *Subsidiary summit at 656467. 2050 feet.*

Tom Smith no doubt had something to do with the placing of the stone to mark the Cumberland/Northumberland boundary on this rounded bump just north of Woldgill Tarn at the point where

SCAUD HILL (Pennines) from Burnhope Seat

WILD BOAR FELL (Pennines) from Ais Gill

WILD BOAR FELL (Pennines). Pendragon Castle

the Pennine range devides into two arms at its northern extremity, one going north-east to Grey Nag and one north-west to Cold Fell. The stone also marks the meeting of three parishes, which may have been more important to Tom Smith then the location of the county boundary.

It would be interesting to know more about the origin of the name and it is a pity it does not have a Cumbrian or Northumbrian flavour. Is it just a local joke at the expense of some stranger to the area who went to a lot of trouble to mark a boundary in which no one else was interested? Or did Tom Smith have so much trouble in getting his stone across the Woldgill Tarn Bog that it was indelibly engraved on local memory? Certainly it is a desolate spot which might well fail to get a name on its own merits.

Provided one can pick a route across the boggy area near Woldgill Tarn the summit can be reached from Hartside Cross on the Alston–Penrith road, traversing Black Fell on the way. A preferable route is to strike up to Great Heaplow along the Pennine Way from about 696490 on the Alston–Brampton road and continue over Whitley Common round to Grey Nag, and then down the ridge to Tom Smith's Stone.

The stone itself is hidden by a fence post as one approaches from the south but its identification presents no difficulty as there are no competing features in this wild spot. Nothing marks the subsidiary summit on the low hump to the north-east.

TONGUE HEAD

307. *Sheet 82.* Reference 241080 Cumberland. 2250 feet.*

Tongue Head marks the head of the Langstrath valley which runs up from Borrowdale between Glaramara to the west and the High Raise ridge to the east. It is also on the Rossett Gill route from Langdale to Esk Hause, lying between Allen Crags and Angle Tarn. It must be well known to the many thousands who have used the latter route as well as to the fewer number who have walked the secluded Langstrath valley, but one does not hear it mentioned in conversation. Those who travel those routes have their minds on higher places.

TOR MERE TOP

308. *Sheet 90. Reference 969765. Yorkshire (N.R./W.R.). 2050 feet.*
309. *Subsidiary summit at 968767. 2050 feet.*

Tor Mere Top is about 1½ miles south-east of Buckden Pike above Buckden at the head of Wharfedale. Its wet and boggy nature may come as a surprise to those who know the graceful outline of Buckden Pike as seen from the north or west, but it is not the only wet and boggy spot in this area, Yockenthwaite Moor, 3½ miles north-west of Buckden Pike, being one of the worst patches in this country.

There is an easy ascent from 986757 on the Kettlewell–Wensley road and the walk can conveniently be continued to the summit of Buckden Pike. Those who prefer a longer walk can take the road from Starbotton (953748) two miles south of Buckden, up the south-west slope, continuing up the path at the end and diverging to the summit from about 966760. This route offers the advantage of an alternative path for the return to Starbotton from 962771.

TYNEHEAD FELL

310. *Sheet 84. Reference 765356. Cumberland. 2000 feet.*
311. *Subsidiary summits at 765355. 2000 feet.*
312. *766353. 2000 feet.*
313. *766352. 2000 feet.*
314. *767351. 2000 feet.*

This is precisely the example to demonstrate that the system adopted in this book for identifying the mountain summits of England is nonsense. Not only that; Tynehead Fell has a most irritating set of summits because the general level is so near the 2000 foot mark that they are extremely difficult to identify. Those who go there would be well advised to regard them as a challenge to their map reading ability. If they doubt whether the small rings on the 1-inch map do in fact indicate separate 2000-foot contours they may well check on them by acquiring a 6-inch map—1953 edition, originally issued at a price of 4s. but now sold for 60p. This shows eight such rings, the largest being little more than one-tenth of an inch in diameter, and the smallest little bigger than those on the 1-inch map. With a scale of 1 : 10560 this suggests that the smallest of these areas is about forty feet across. It should be visible and the only problem is one of identification.

There is no difficulty in getting to these summits. From milestone 12 on the road from Middleton-in-Teesdale to Alston it is merely a question of a walk of three-quarters of a mile in a south-westerly direction, over rough moorland with a few wet patches, to the tall cairn which marks the northern summit. Alternatively, the Tyne Head road can be taken from Garrigill as far as 754356, from which point a walk of one mile due east brings one to the northern summit. The remaining summits, according to the Ordnance Survey, lie to the south and south-south-east from that cairn. However, there is a broken cairn on a hump somewhat nearer the road than is expected from the map reading and a collection of other humps west of the wire fence which crosses the fell.

If the map is not strictly correct the Ordnance Survey can be forgiven any minor inaccuracy, the levelling having last been revised in 1896! This is certainly a remote area. However, it is not without its admirers. According to some reports the secluded house below the northern slopes was once occupied by a pre-war star of London's West End.

ULLSCARF

315. *Sheet 82* Reference 292122. Cumberland. 2370 feet.*

Ullscarf, which means the cave where the wolves played, lies towards the end of the broad ridge which runs north from the Langdale Pikes. The route from Grasmere to High Raise is described under the entry for High Raise and from there it is only necessary to continue north across the depression of Greenup Edge for a distance of about two miles to reach the Ullscarf summit. It is bare open country with a few rocks but no obvious cave.

The best route back to Grasmere, if time permits, is to return to the Greenup Edge Pass and take the easterly route, forking left after about three-quarters of a mile to follow the ridge round to Helm Crag via Gibson Knott. This gives fine views of the Grasmere area in all directions. If the alternative fork to the right is taken one has a gradual descent down Far Easdale Gill to Grasmere. A pleasant walk, but one which only offers a saving of less than half an hour as compared with the more exciting Helm Crag route.

Alternatively, Ullscarf may be approached from Stonethwaite in Borrowdale (263137) by the path up Greenup Gill. The walking distance to Ullscarf is about four miles with a total rise of 2055 feet—say 2¼ hours in all—and there is an attractive alternative route for the return by way of Blea Tarn to Watendlath and then back to Rosthwaite by the pony track. The return by this route involves about six miles of walking with a rise of little more than 200 feet, so that the round trip would make a very pleasant afternoon walk—with tea in Watendlath as an added attraction. But Watendlath teas are not what they were in the 1930s when one of the Mrs. Tysons offered twenty-seven types of cake.

VIEWING HILL

316. *Sheet 84. Reference 790335. Durham. 2100 feet.*

Viewing Hill lies almost at the head of Teesdale. It can readily be reached from the mining track which leaves the Middleton-in-Teesdale–Alston road at 783354. Those who wish to locate the small summit cairn without too much effort will find it easier to follow the track to a point south of the hill rather than leave it at a point to the north-west.

Preferably the walk should be combined with a visit to Herdship Fell as described under that entry.

WALNA SCAR

317. *Sheet 88.* Reference 254957. Lancashire. 2000 feet.*
318. *Subsidiary summit at 257964. 2000 feet.*

Walna Scar, which has the southernmost summit of Lakeland, runs south from Dow Crag and separates Dunnerdale from the Coniston valley. The Walna Scar road joins the town of Coniston with Seathwaite in Dunnerdale and crosses the ridge at a point close to the 2000-foot level. Fortunately, in its higher reaches, it is not fit for four-wheeled vehicles. Cars cannot easily proceed beyond 288971 on the road out from Coniston and, in the short stretch to that point, are forced to compete with the occasional heavy lorry running to the quarries in the side of the Old Man. For this reason the ascent from Seathwaite is probably the better route, but the choice will largely depend on one's starting point. Those staying in the Coniston area would hardly find it worth while to motor round to Seathwaite before starting their walk.

Those walking from Coniston need to take care to avoid the tracks which go off to the quarries and to Goat's Water. Just before the head of the pass and on the right-hand side is a well constructed small stone shelter which is worthy of examination. A little way past this point the grassy Walna Scar ridge goes off to the south. There is no path but the small cairn which marks the first summit is within 200 yards of the main track. About half a mile further on is a cairn of moderate size on a rocky outcrop which marks the second summit. For a view of the Duddon valley it is worth while walking on slightly south of west to the substantial cairn at White Pike which, although slightly lower than the first two cairns, has a magnificent field of view because of its position directly above the valley.

Those who approach Walna Scar from the Duddon side should turn off the main valley road at 232968 on the minor road which is signed to Long House Farm. It is well surfaced up to 240968, the entrance to Seathwaite Tarn reservoir, and then becomes a pleasant grassy track to the top of the ridge.

Whether one reaches Walna Scar from Coniston or from Seathwaite, the walk can readily be extended over Brown Pike and Dow Crag on to the Old Man–Wrynose ridge. The return to Coniston may be by the Goat's Water path or from Swirl How via Levers

Water or Wetherlam, and that to Seathwaite over Grey Friar or along the ridge to the Three Shire Stone and then down the Wrynose Pass.

WANLOPE

319. *Sheet 82.* Reference 188197. Cumberland. 2533 feet.*

Wanlope is the first part of the ridge which runs south-west from Crag Hill, roughly mid-way along the Causey Pike–Grisedale Pike circuit, over Whiteless Pike and Blake Rigg into Buttermere. There is some confusion over the name. Wanlope is given on the Ordnance Survey but the Baddeley guide map and the Bartholomews map show Wandope, and the only mention in the Baddeley text is to Wandhope.

Those who walk the Causey Pike–Grisedale circuit are more likely to choose Grasmoor or Hopegill as a diversion, but they would find an extension to Whiteless Pike and Wanlope equally rewarding. Wanlope merely involves a walk of half a mile from the shoulder of Crag Hill, round the end of Scar Crag, while Whiteless Pike involves a drop to the west for about 100 feet from the summit of Wanlope and then a walk south of less than one mile along the path which runs from Coledale Hause between Grasmoor and Crag Hill.

However, Wanlope can also be approached as a separate excursion from Buttermere, starting from 175172 and proceeding by way of Blake's Rigg and Whiteless Pike. Anyone using this route, however, should remember that the path from Whiteless Pike does not continue to Wanlope. Wanlope's western slopes are a broad grassy expanse over which the walker can ramble at will to make his own way to the top. Once there, one has a choice of a walk over Craig Hill and Sail to descend by Sail Beck back to Buttermere, or a walk over Crag Hill, Eel Crag, Coledale Hause and Hopegill Head to Whiteside. From the latter summit, those who prefer the high ground will probably elect to retrace their steps back to Buttermere instead of making a round circuit by descending to Lanthwaite Green and taking a combination of road and footpaths back to Buttermere. The lower route gives a round trip of five hours while retracing ones steps by way of Hopegill Head requires 6½ hours.

WATER CRAG

320. *Sheet 90. Reference 928046. Yorkshire (N.R.). 2188 feet.*

Water Crag lies at the head of Arkengarthdale, 2½ miles south-east of the Tan Hill inn. It forms the northern end of the high ground which has its southern extremity in Rogan's Seat and access routes are described under the entry for Rogan's Seat.

Water Crag is much drier than Rogan's Seat, being stony in parts and having patches of heather and whinberries. The prominent cairn seen on the approach route from Tan Hill is not the summit but marks the 2176 spot height at 924047, the trig point and summit cairn being about 600 yards further east. Looking east across the desolate waste which stretches below the summit one may be surprised to see what, at first sight, appears to be the figure of a man. Closer inspection will show it to be the high cairn of Standard Man at 956047.

WESTEND MOOR

321. *Sheet 84. Reference 842437. Northumberland/Durham. 2075 feet.*

322. *Subsidiary summit at 833442. 2050 feet.*

Westend Moor is the high ground extending south-east from Killhope Law to the north of the Weardale Forest. Although a somewhat flat ridge it seems to be kept reasonably dry by the shallow ditch which runs along its length. There is easy access from 853433 near the highest point of the B.6295 road between Cowshill and Allenheads. The wall running slightly north of west from that point has a gate near the corner of the field which brings one to the far side of the wall running in a north-westerly direction and leading on to the ridge. The first and main summit is not marked but the second—at least in July 1969—was marked by a single pole. Killhope Law is just over a mile further along the same ridge.

A much better route, particularly for those who object to retracing their steps and those who are interested in relics of the old lead mining industry, is the bridle-way from 825433 on the B.6293 road between Alston and Stanhope. A little lower down the valley, at about 827429, is a 34-foot water wheel and remains of mine buildings which are preserved by the Durham County Council in conjunction with a picnic area. There are good parking facilities there and a circular tour with a minimum of road walking is possible by taking the bridle-way to its highest point at 829445, following the line of the two Westend Moor summits from that point to 851433 whence a path runs almost due west to Clevison Currick and then south to the B.6293 road. From a little lower down the road at 844415 a path runs on the north side of the Killhope Burn and then through the Weardale Forest to rejoin the road at 819433 just west of the starting point. The round trip should not take more than about 2¾ hours.

Allenheads is said to be a thriving ski-centre in the winter season and Westend Moor is no doubt a popular area for the sport. Ski enthusiasts, in suitable conditions, will no doubt be able to devise their own routes to the two summits.

WESTERNHOPE MOOR

323. *Sheet 84. Reference 907335. Durham. 2115 feet.*

Westernhope Moor is part of the high ground between Teesdale and Weardale, east of the minor road which joins Newbiggin and Westgate. There is easy access from 898332 on that road near Swinhope Head at an altitude of 1992 feet. Just east of this point there are the ruins of a wall and a good path runs along its northern side to the summit. This is only half a mile from the road. There is nothing to mark it, but its location is just south of the three cairns which mark the crest of the rise from Weardale.

From this point the walk can be continued over somewhat rough country to Outberry Plain.

WETHER FELL

See DRUMALDRACE.

WETHER HILL

324. *Sheet 83.* Reference 456168. Westmorland. 2200 feet.*
325. *Subsidiary summit at 455163. 2200 feet.*

Wether Hill, the hill where wethers were kept, is on the High Street ridge about 3½ miles north of the main summit. No one would wish to ascend Wether Hill for itself alone and it needs to be tackled as part of a walk along the ridge. An ascent as part of a walk from Howtown, either up Fusedale to High Raise and back via Loadpot Hill, or by way of Bannerdale, is described under the entry for High Raise.

Up to 1966 the main summit was marked by a substantial post sticking out of the summit cairn, but in April of that year it was broken off at the level of the cairn.

WETHERLAM

326. *Sheet 88.* Reference 288011. Lancashire. 2502 feet.*
327. *Subsidiary summit at 289008. 2350 feet.*

Wetherlam is one of the Coniston fells and can readily be reached from the ridge running north from the Old Man of Coniston by descending Prison Band from Swirl How, or it can be reached from

Black Sails as described under that entry. For the walker starting from Coniston the High Fell ridge approach via Black Sails is by far the most interesting route, but the direct return by the Lad Stones ridge from Wetherlam is only a half-day excursion. Accordingly, those who want a full days' excursion will probably prefer to ascend Wetherlam by the Lad Stones ridge, reversing the route indicated under the Black Sails entry, and then continue by Prison Band to Swirl How and the main ridge running down to the Old Man of Coniston.

The summit is marked by a substantial cairn and there is a smaller cairn on the subsidiary summit of Hen Crag about a quarter of a mile to the south. Views from the main summit, because they are quite unimpeded to the north and east, are some of the finest in Lakeland. In autumn, apart from embracing a wide range of Lakeland summits and distant views of the Pennines, the view covers a tremendous expanse of woodland in all its autumn glory, green fields and stretches of water ranging from Morecambe Bay, Windermere and Coniston Water to Tarn Hows. Such views compel one to linger on the summit and make nonsense of the Naismith formula.

WHAM BOTTOM

328. *Sheet 90. Reference 923042. Yorkshire (N.R.). 2150 feet.*

This title seems a piece of nonsense. Perhaps the Ordnance Survey have put the name a quarter of an inch to the north-west of its intended position. Certainly it seems to apply more to the bump on the broad ridge which connects Water Crag and Rogan's Seat than to the marshy area to the east of it.

A route to this area is described under the entry for Rogan's Seat, and the hump of Wham Bottom is readily found when approaching Rogan's Seat from the more westerly of the cairns on Water Crag. The summit is marked by a stone building about ten feet square. Considerable skill and effort have gone into its construction but its purpose is not apparent. Perhaps it was built as a shelter for whoever watched over the sheep and cattle on Rogan's spring pastures. He would need solid walls in that exposed location.

WHERNSIDE

329. *Sheet 90. Reference 738815. Yorkshire (W.R.). 2419 feet.*

Whernside, the highest point in the West Riding of Yorkshire, lies two miles north-west of Ribblehead Station and overlooks Blea

Moor, scene of perhaps the most difficult engineering feat in the construction of English railways. The air shafts of the railway tunnel constructed below the moor are clearly visible from the Whernside summit.

Whernside should not be confused with Great Whernside, which is located seventeen miles away in an east-south-easterly direction above Kettlewell in Wharfedale. The appellation 'Great' is not applied in any scientific sense as Great Whernside is probably smaller in extent and is certainly 109 feet lower in height than Whernside. But 'Whernside' means the hill from which millstones were obtained and it is quite possible that Great Whernside produced more and bigger stones than came from Whernside.

Whernside owes its popularity with walkers to the fact that, together with Ingleborough and Pen-y-ghent, it makes up the well-known Three Peaks walk.

The 1-inch Ordnance Survey does not show any path on Whernside but there is a well marked path to the summit from 739791 near the entrance to Bruntscar farm. There is a minor road to Bruntscar farm from 743776 just east of Chapel le Dale on the B.6255 road from Ingleton to Hawes and the path starts in the field from the gate at the right of the farm, proceeding through a gap in the wall on to the ridge east of Coombe Scar. The walk along the ridge to the summit is pleasant and easy going, providing fine views to the south-east with Ingleborough and Pen-y-ghent as outstanding landmarks. The trig point which marks the summit is not obvious from a distance but will be found in a corner of the wall which traverses the ridge. For views to the north, it is necessary to follow the ridge for some distance beyond the highest point.

It is probably best to retrace one's steps back to the starting point, but those who insist on an alternative route for the return can descend from the summit down the south-east slope to 752801 and then follow a more or less level route south-west to Bruntscar Farm.

These routes have the disadvantage of being on the Three Peaks route. Those who prefer to walk alone may like to use the ascent from Kingsdale. A minor road runs from Dent to the B.6255 road just west of Ingleton and from its highest point, 724821 on White Shaw Moss, the Whernside summit is only about a mile distant. The going is rougher than the route from Bruntscar Farm but much shorter.

WHITE FELL

330. *Sheet 89. Reference 662974. Westmorland/Yorkshire (W.R.). 2100 feet.*

White Fell is one of the Howgill Fells north-west of Sedbergh, the summit lying between The Calf and Bush Howe. The walk along this ridge is described under the entry for Bram Rigg Top. White Fell is mainly of interest as a line of descent from the main ridge to the Sedbergh–Howgill road.

WHITE PIKE

See Clough Head.

WHITE SIDE

331. *Sheet 83* Reference 337167. Cumberland. 2832 feet.*

White Side is on the Helvellyn ridge about one mile north of the main summit, and should not be confused with the Loweswater Whiteside which is a more independent summit of much more striking appearance, although over 500 feet lower in altitude.

The Helvellyn White Side is the first summit reached on the well-walked route from Thirlspot. This is one of the old routes to Helvellyn and perhaps the least satisfactory, with little of interest to recommend it. Accordingly, White Side is best tackled as an extension of the walk to Helvellyn by Dollywaggon Pike or Striding Edge, or as a preliminary to Helvellyn on the approach by the ridge from the north.

Although White Side is largely grass covered, its summit is marked by a substantial cairn.

WHITELESS PIKE

332. *Sheet 82.* Reference 180189. Cumberland. 2159 feet.*

Whiteless Pike is three-quarters of a mile south-west of Wanlope on the ridge which runs up to the west of Wanlope from Buttermere. It has a steep slope to Rannerdale Beck on its western side and a line of crags on the east and provides fine views over the Buttermere valley to the High Stile ridge beyond. Access is as described under the entry for Wanlope, the shortest route being by the path which starts from 175172 just north of the village of Buttermere.

It should be noted that there is a slight overlap in the Wanlope and Whiteless Pike ridges on either side of a stream which runs down to Sail Beck, and that the path along the Whiteless Pike ridge does not run to the Wanlope summit but continues straight on in the gap between Grasmoor and Eel Crag to Coledale Hause.

WHITESIDE

333. *Sheet 82.* Reference 171219. Cumberland. 2317 feet.*
334. *Subsidiary summit at 174222. 2250 feet.*

These little-known summits overlook Loweswater and form the western end of the impressive ridge running west from Hopegill Head. The origin of its name will be obvious to anyone who has admired the Gasgale Crags from Grasmoor.

Access can be gained either down the ridge from Hopegill Head, by direct ascent by the path which leaves the Gasgale Gill path at 163211 or by a more roundabout ascent by the path which leaves the Lorton–Buttermere road at 156220. The latter is not recommended as the path is difficult to follow and the route of comparatively little interest.

The summits, neither of which is marked by a cairn, give fine views over Lorton Vale, to Grasmoor and up to Hopegill Head, but the interest here lies not so much in the summit itself as in the ridge above Gasgale Crags and those who ascend by the western slopes should not return without following the ridge to Hopegill Head—that is unless they undertake the walk in a strong wind which might make some parts of the ridge unduly hazardous. Seen from Whiteside on a wild, stormy day the ridge looks more forbidding than Striding Edge, but on a calm, sunny day the only difficult section is no more than a few yards in length.

Although Whiteside is on the outer edge of the Lakes, the area offers many possibilities for extended excursions. Taking the footpath from 168243 on the minor road between Hopebeck and Scales one could ascend the Swinside slope to Ladyside Pike and continue along the ridge to Hopegill Head. There is a scramble up the rock face before Hopegill Head is reached which would present problems for a descent in wet weather, and may well be too much for young children, but the average hill walker will enjoy it. From that point the excursion can be extended to Grisedale Pike, Eel Crag, Wanlope or Grasmoor before turning west along the ridge to Whiteside, descending to the valley just above Lanthwaite Green Farm and then following the footpath running below the western slopes of Whiteside back to the starting point. The round trip, omitting any extension from Hopegill Head, should not take more than 3¼ hours.

Alternatively, one could start from the car park near to Lanthwaite Green Farm and walk to Coledale Hause by the Path along Gasgale Gill returning, after any extension from that point, by way of Hopegill Head and the ridge to Whiteside.

Other possibilities are to start from Braithwaite (two miles west of Keswick) and to go to Whiteside by way of Grisedale Pike, to start from Buttermere and reach Whiteside by way of Whiteless Pike and Wanlope, or to start from Stair in Newlands and reach Whiteside by way of Causey Pike, Scar Crags and Eel Crag. What a wonderful area this is, and scarcely known to many of those who frequent the central area of Lakeland.

WIDDALE FELL

335. *Sheet 90. Reference 795880. Yorkshire (W.R./N.R.). 2100 feet.*

336. *Subsidiary summit at 798878. Yorkshire (N.R.). 2100 feet.*

Widdale Fell is bordered by four dales, Dentdale to the south-west, Widdale to the south-east, Mossdale to the north-east and Garsdale to the north-west. The most obvious line of ascent is from Stone House in Dentdale as described under the entry for Great Knoutberry Hill. Its two summits are peat haggs without, as far as one can see under snow conditions—which are probably the best conditions for a visit to this area—any positive marks of identification. However, by alignment with the two tarns, Widdale Great Tarn and Widdale Little Tarn, and the trig point on Great Knoutberry Hill, it is possible to be reasonably sure of their general location, if not of the precise summits.

WILD BOAR FELL

337. *Sheet 90. Reference 758988. Westmorland. 2324 feet.*

One guide book says that this is the highest hill in Yorkshire and there are Yorkshire people who are prepared to accept the statement. However, those who approach down the B.6259 road which runs from the Moorcock Inn at the head of Garsdale down the Mallerstang valley to Kirkby Stephen, will see a Westmorland boundary sign well south of the summit and reference to the 1-inch Ordnance Survey map will reveal that Wild Boar Fell is about a mile inside Westmorland.

Grasmoor in Lakeland, which also owes its name to the wild boar, is similar in having an extensive flat area at high altitude, but it is not apparent why these features should attract wild boars. Helvellyn and Ingleborough ought to have been equally attractive. Perhaps the answer is that they were but, already having names, did not need to be identified by reference to the animals which frequented them. For evidence that the wild boar did in fact frequent Wild Boar Fell one needs only visit the church in Kirkby Stephen where there is the tomb of a member of the Musgrave family who killed the last of them.

An easy ascent of Wild Boar Fell has already been described under the entry for Swarth Fell. This is a fine, pleasant route without any difficulty, the only minor discomfort being a small patch of bog in the dip between Swarth Fell and Wild Boar Fell. Unfortunately this approach does not provide the best views of Wild Boar Fell, which is at its most impressive when seen from the north. It is considered to provide one of the finest views in the Pennines and when seen from near Pendragon Castle (778026) it dominates the Mallerstang valley. An ascent from about 766999 on the route to Ravenstonedale, which starts from 782998 on the B.6259 road, therefore provides a more impressive approach. Anyone taking this route and desiring a round trip can continue over the summit to Swarth Fell Pike, descend from there to 778964 on the B.6259 road, and then take the footpath which runs from there to 782996, almost back to the starting point.

The summit is dry and flat and the trig point, like that on Little Fell, is enclosed in dry stone walls. The walls are the home of a small mouse who is not unduly worried in the presence of visitors.

WINDY GYLE

338. *Sheet 70. Reference 856153. Northumberland. 2036 feet.*

Windy Gyle is one of the Cheviots but in appearance seems more akin to the Pennines. It seems to turn its back on the green, rounded hills rising out of steep valleys, which are the normal Cheviots, and the wild, grim look of the long flat ridge which is the approach from the north-east along the Pennine Way reminds one that it is pointing the way to Cross Fell and High Cup Nick. The contrast reminds one of the difference between the Pennines and the Howgills, the Cheviots of Westmorland.

Windy Gyle is nearly five miles south-west of the summit of The Cheviot and can be approached by way of Cushat Law and Bloody Bush Edge as described under the entry for the latter summit. The Forestry Commission plantations near Cushat Law, the rounded summits of Cushat Law and Bloody Bush Edge and the pleasant valley of the Usway Burn with its isolated farm are in sharp contrast to the bleak and boggy moorland which surrounds Windy Gyle. A substantial cairn—Russell's Cairn—marks the summit and is said to mark the grave of a Russell killed in the sixteenth century. It may well lie in Scotland as it is on the north side of the wire fence which presumably marks the border. Whether it does or not—and the farmer at Uswayford was certainly of the opinion that, although the fence was intended to mark the border, it did not follow the true line, some part of Windy Gyle above the 2000-foot level is within the Northumberland border and accordingly qualifies as an English mountain.

There is nothing very remarkable about the summit except that it is a target for an excursion, and the main interest lies in the approach routes. Apart from the approach by way of Uswayford from Alwinton described under the Bloody Bush Edge entry, it is possible to reach Windy Gyle from the head of the Coquet Valley, or from the Bowmont valley south of Town Yetholm. The shortest route is from 860115, near the head of the Coquet valley, by way of The Street over Hindside Knowe and Black Braes to the Pennine Way at 835150, then north and, later, east to Windy Gyle. For the return journey there are the alternatives of a walk south-east to 864145 then south-west to Trows, Rowhope and the starting point, or a walk north-east to the border crossing at 872160, returning down the ancient Clennell Street to the Uswayford road—or perhaps through Uswayford itself—and then continuing south-west along the road back to the starting point.

The starting point from the Bowmont valley is Mowhaugh (817206), about five miles south of Town Yetholm, and the route follows the track along the Calroust Burn and then along Windy Rig to Windy Gyle, continuing to the border crossing at 872160 and returning north-west along Clennell Street through Cocklawfoot. What attractive names they are!

Times for the round trips would be seven hours starting from Heigh above Alwinton, 3¼ or 4¼ hours from the Coquet valley according to whether the short route or that by way of Uswayford was taken, and 4½ hours from Mowhaugh.

YAD MOSS

339. *Sheet 84. Reference 782378. Cumberland. 2450 feet.*

Yad Moss appears twice on the map in this area; once in the area below Scaud Hill near the Alston–Middleton-in-Teesdale road and again on the high ground to the west of Burnhope Seat. It is the latter which is classed as a summit. There is nothing particularly unusual in having a moss as summit, this name also appearing in Bink Moss and Staple Moss.

There is a direct approach from Darngill Bridge on the B.627 road (reference 774371) north-east up the slope to the Yad Moss summit. The going is quite easy until the marshy area on the top is reached. Even there, deep gullies are not in evidence and the only problem is a number of very wet patches. A tall cairn stands on the south-western slope and a low cairn of larger stones overlooks Garrigill, but the actual summit is not easy to identify and is not marked.

From the summit one can walk over a patch of marshy ground to Burnhope Seat and then return to Darngill Bridge by way of the stream which is the reason for its existence. The whole is a very pleasant walk of less than an hour's duration and well worth the effort.

YARLSIDE

340. *Sheet 89. Reference 685985. Westmorland. 2097 feet.*

Yarlside is one of the Howgill Fells, lying to the north-east of Sedbergh. The best ascent is that described under the entry for Randygill Top, these two summits being in the eastern side of the Howgills and situated to form a convenient excursion independent of the other summits in this area. Alternatively, one could approach Yarlside from the Cross Keys Hotel (697969) by way of Cautley Spout or it can be included in the return journey from The Calf to Bowderdale as described under the entry for The Calf.

Yarlside provides fine views of Cautley Spout to the south-west as well as of the Backside Beck valley to the east and the rolling hills to the south. Its sides are steep and cannot be overcome without a little breathlessness, but the summit ridge with its small cairn is green and gentle.

YES TOR

341. *Sheet 175. Reference 581901. Devon. 2030 feet.*

Yes Tor is a granite outcrop in the Dartmoor National Park, a little way south of Okehampton. It is part of a War Department Artillery Range and it is necessary to check that firing is not taking place before entering the range area. Particulars of firing times on Dartmoor are said to be obtainable from the police or local Post Offices. This seems to be an excellent service and some mitigation of the inconvenience occasioned by the War Department activities. More important, the Dartmoor Range seems to operate on the basis that some part of the week-end shall be preserved for the benefit of walkers rather than the gunners. What a welcome change from the position on the Warcop Range!

A walk to Yes Tor can conveniently be combined with the ascent of High Willhays, as described under that entry. It is a pleasant stroll but those who expect it to look like the summits of northern England will be disappointed. Dartmoor has a charm and character of its own and Yes Tor is a typical sample.

YEWBARROW

342. *Sheet 82.* Reference 173085. Cumberland. 2058 feet.*
343. *Subsidiary summit at 176092. 2009 feet.*

Casual visitors to Wasdale can be forgiven if they mistake Yewbarrow for Great Gable. From the lower end of Waswater it is a much more imposing sight than either Great Gable or Sca Fell and yet it is not nearly so well known as many of the other summits in this area. Partly this is because of the attraction of the higher summits and partly because a direct ascent from Wasdale up the southern end of the ridge is difficult, thus making Dore Head the preferred beginning or end of the walk of the Pillar–Red Pike ridge.

The easiest ascent is by way of Dore Head and it can conveniently be taken in as a continuation of the walk from Wasdale by way of Black Sail Pass, Pillar and Red Pike. Tackled in this way it may come as something of an anti-climax and it is perhaps preferable to ascend as a short separate excursion if one happens to have just over two hours to spare on a fine day at Wasdale Head. For such a day it is best to take the route from 167067 alongside Over Beck to Dore Head and then walk the length of the ridge, first over the subsidiary summit and then over the main summit, descending down the southern end of the ridge by the path which runs to the starting point. Those who are reluctant to try their luck on the route down the southern end can return to Dore Head and either descend to Mosedale Beck on the east or take the path which runs below the west side of Yewbarrow to join the route down the south end of the ridge by Bell Rib.

Yewbarrow provides magnificent views of Wastwater through gaps in the crags on its summit and deserves to be better known. But how many walkers will opt for Yewbarrow if the alternatives are Scafell Pikes or Pillar or Gable?

YOCKENTHWAITE MOOR

344. *Sheet 90. Reference 909811. Yorkshire (N.R./W.R.). 2109 feet.*

Yockenthwaite means Eogan's clearing and is the name of a hamlet in Langstrothdale, the continuation of Wharfedale north of Buckden. Yockenthwaite is one of the pleasantest spots in the country, sheltered in the valley with the Wharfe, a broad, shallow stream, running over a bed of limestone. At week-ends it gets a lot of traffic as it lies on the route to Hawes and is a favourite picnic spot, but there are occasions when it is deserted. The moor, which pre-

WINDY GYLE (Cheviot) from King's Seat

YES TOR (Devon)

WINDY GYLE and BLOODYBUSH EDGE (Cheviot). Uswayford

sents a steep slope to the valley and has a summit two miles to the north, is a vastly different place.

Those who wish to avoid the steep slope from the valley may approach it by way of the old pack horse road which runs from Bishopdale almost due north to Bainbridge in Wensleydale. This road leaves Bishopdale at 944805 at the altitude of 1376 feet and, if one follows the left-hand stone wall to its end near the open moor, a footpath will be seen heading in a westerly direction. It can be followed for about two miles and its smooth turf makes a very pleasant walk compared with the rough grass on the moor. At that distance, however, a gully is reached which runs towards the summit and from that point it is necessary to steer for the summit on a compass bearing. It is not easy to find as there are no landmarks and the trig point is not visible from the south-east until one is close at hand.

However, perseverance and much ploughing through bog eventually leads one to the most decrepit of trig points. Certainly this was its condition in the early summer of 1968. It is in a most desolate spot with bog stretching around in all directions—bog which may well be the worst in England.

Alternatively, the Yockenthwaite Moor summit can be approached from Cragdale Moor, starting from Langstrothdale or from Stalling Busk as described under the Cragdale Moor entry. But there is a lot to be said for sampling the bog one encounters in the ascent from Bishopdale. It is not easy to put bogs in order of merit. Kinder at once comes to mind as a noteworthy specimen, as also does Chapelfell Top, and Murton Fell has some bad patches. However, Yockenthwaite is a keen contender for the distinction of having the worst sample and no student of such matters can afford to ignore it.

The round trip from Bishopdale takes about three hours (more if conditions are very wet) while that from Deepdale via Cragdale Moor would take perhaps 3½.

YOKE

345. *Sheet 83.* Reference 437067. Westmorland. 2309 feet.*

Adam Seat just south of Haweswater was the first summit in this list and Yoke, 2½ miles south-west of Adam Seat, ends it.

Yoke is at the southern end of the ridge which runs slightly east of south from Thornthwaite Crag and has Ill Bell as its most prominent point. It provides a gentle introduction to the crags of Ill Bell and, can be ascended from either Troutbeck or Kentmere by way of the Garburn Pass. Whichever route is adopted, the approach to Yoke is from a point west of the highest point of the Garburn

Pass striking almost due north over ground which is inclined to be wet until the ridge is reached. A cairn at a point about 1¼ miles from the Garburn Pass marks the start of the main ridge and the Yoke summit is about half a mile further north. It is a pleasant spot with rocky outcrops and its cairn stands on a rocky platform.

From Yoke the walk can be continued to Ill Bell, just over half a mile further on and then over Froswick to Thornthwaite Crag with its magnificent beacon. At this point, those who started from Troutbeck may return down the line of the old Roman road along Hagg Gill back to the starting point, while those coming from Kentmere can continue to High Street, just over a mile to the north-east, then south-east to Mardale Ill Bell and the Nan Bield Pass. Here another choice presents itself, there being a gentle descent down the slope back to Kentmere or an ascent to Harter Fell and a walk along the ridge over Kentmere Pike back to Kentmere.

Of these routes the ascent from Kentmere with the return over Harter Fell and Kentmere Pike is obviously the more attractive and it only takes about 6½ hours. That from Troutbeck takes five hours.

It is perhaps unfortunate that the list of summits could not end with something a little more dramatic. Windy Gyle or Whiteless Pike would have made more of a climax. But Yoke wins on a strict alphabetical basis and the round trip to it from Kentmere is a tolerable sample of what English summits have to offer.

APPENDIX I

Summary by Counties

County	Summits: Within the county	Summits: On county boundary	Highest summit: Name	Highest summit: Height in feet
Cumberland	128	22	Scafell Pikes	3206
Derbyshire	5	—	Kinder	2088
Devon	2	—	High Willhays	2038
Durham	10	8	Scaud Hill	2342
Lancashire	14	3	Old Man of Coniston	2631
Northumberland	14	7	Cheviot	2676
Westmorland	85	28	Helvellyn	3113†
Yorkshire (N.R.)	16	12	Mickle Fell	2591
Yorkshire (W.R.)	24	15	Whernside	2419
	298	95*		

* One summit is at the meeting place of three counties.
† On the Cumberland and Westmorland boundary.

See also Appendix V.

APPENDIX II

Summary by Areas

		Highest point	*Height in feet*
Dartmoor	2	High Willhays	2038
Cheviots	11	Cheviot	2676
Howgills	11	The Calf	2219
Lakes	200	Scafell Pikes	3206
Peak	5	Kinder	2088
Pennines	116	Cross Fell	2930
	345		

See also Appendix V.

APPENDIX III

Map Reading

Beginners will gain a lot of useful information by studying a copy of *Map Reading for the Countrygoer* obtainable from the Ramblers Association, 1/4 Crawford Mews, York Street, London, W1H 1PT, but they should not assume that this is all that is required. Practical experience is essential. Moreover, although they will naturally make their first attempts in fine weather, if they are to become successful mountain walkers, they must aim to be able to find their way in adverse conditions. Map reading ability is not really put to the test until one is worn out and battling with wind and rain in conditions of poor visibility. At such times, accurate map reading may be the key to survival.

If anyone thinks this overstates the case, let him visualise a situation in which, at the remotest stage in a walk, the weather changes with comparatively little notice to produce gale force winds, heavy rain and visibility restricted to twenty feet or less. Add to this the fact that much of the terrain is flat or gently rolling and interspersed with patches of bog which becomes more difficult as the rain continues. I had walked the mountains for nearly forty years before I encountered such conditions and only then did I realise how serious a failure in map reading could be. Yet such conditions are a potential hazard for much of the year in the mountains of England.

Apart from the technical points dealt with in the Ramblers Association publication, there are a number of very elementary points which should not be overlooked. First, it is essential for anyone like myself who suffers from poor eyesight to carry their reading glasses or a magnifying glass. I do not expect to have to wear glasses when out of doors but have learned by experience that the map does not yield up its information unless one can read it!

Second, it must be realised that, as daylight fades, a source of light will be necessary before the map can be read and that it will gradually become impossible to recognise distinguishing features in the landscape. While it may be possible to follow a well-worn path by moonlight, the safest course is to get down to a road before there is any risk of darkness descending. And darkness sometimes comes very quickly in the mountains.

Finally, the most elementary point to remember, and one that is apt to be overlooked when one gets lost, is that the map is almost certainly correct and that a failure to recognise the country in view indicates a failure on the part of the map reader. In nearly forty years of map reading I have found only three mistakes in the 1-inch Ordnance Survey—and one of those was corrected in a revised edition before I was able to point it out.

The safest method of proceeding is to keep a close check on time and distance so as to be able to rectify mistakes before they become serious. Careful planning based on a study of the map before setting out is worth while and for this purpose the Naismith formula can be used to assess the time required. It is quite simple. Allow one hour for every three miles as shown on the map and add half an hour for each thousand feet of ascent. This gives the time for any walk extending over three hours or more and includes an allowance for meals en route. Care must be taken, however, to add up all the various sections in which height is gained rather than merely to take the difference between the lowest and highest points. One must also recognise that additional time may be required if the pace of the party is below average or if conditions are abnormal. Additional time should in any event be allowed as a safety margin for any walk in winter conditions. Such adjustments are a matter of experience.

Another useful aid is the National Grid System. Those who did not become familiar with it during their service in the Army can readily pick it up from the notes at the foot of each 1-inch Ordnance Survey map.

Despite all precautions, accidents may happen. In such case assistance may be called by six blasts on a whistle at intervals of ten seconds, which should be repeated every other minute. If one has left details of the intended route and has not deviated from it, the task of a rescue party will be very much easier.

Risks will also be very much reduced if the party consists of at least three persons. Inexperienced walkers should certainly avoid walking alone—and one is inexperienced for a very long time when dealing with mountains.

APPENDIX IV

Clothing and Equipment

Special clothing and equipment is not necessary for a short excursion in fine weather up the easiest of the summits I have listed, but, as soon as one goes beyond that stage, some precautions are necessary.

No one has yet developed a standard outfit to suit all conditions and each person must be guided to some extent by his own experience. All too often it may be found with some of the equipment on offer that one can only keep dry from the rain at the expense of getting wet from perspiration.

It must be appreciated that temperatures may fall considerably as altitude is gained and that weather conditions may change quite quickly with apparently little warning. Despite their low altitude our mountains are a menace to those who underestimate them and inexperienced walkers with inadequate clothing and equipment give a lot of unnecessary trouble to the Mountain Rescue organisations. It may therefore be helpful to note the following advice from the Lakeland Mountain Rescue Organisation :

A CHECK-LIST FOR FELL WALKERS

ARE YOU WEARING

Brightly coloured wind- and rain-proof clothing?
Suitable boots?

DO YOU KNOW

How to use your equipment?
What time it gets dark?
The International Mountain Distress Signal?

HAVE YOU GOT

Map?
Compass?
Whistle?
Torch?
Spare food?
Spare warm clothing?
Watch?
First Aid?
Ice axe (if there is snow on the fells)?

HAVE YOU left information about where you are going with someone who will miss you if you don't come back?

IF THE ANSWER TO ANY OF THE ABOVE IS "NO"
OUR *ADVICE* TO YOU IS

DON'T GO

APPENDIX V

Addendum

Originally, the Black Mountains were omitted from this account on the grounds that they belonged to Wales. This is not entirely correct, four of their eastern summits being on the borders of Herefordshire and Monmouthshire and proper, therefore, to be regarded as English. Relevant details are :

BLACK HILL
Sheet 141. Reference 275348. Herefordshire. 2101 feet.

This summit, marked by a trig point, lies about a mile east of the Offa's Dyke Path and is typical of the flat-topped Black Mountain range. It can readily be reached by a diversion from the Black Mountain summit at 256350.

BLACK MOUNTAIN
Sheet 141. Reference 256350. Herefordshire. 2306 feet.

The name is that used on the Bartholomew's map, the actual summit not being named on the 1-inch Ordnance Survey map. It lies on the Offa's Dyke Path in the section between Pandy (334217 on Sheet 142) and Hay-on-Wye—about 5½ miles from the latter and ten miles from the former. With the opening of the Offa's Dyke Path it may shortly become one of the better known of English summits.

CHWAREL y FAN
Sheet 141. Reference 257295. Monmouthshire. 2228 feet.

This summit lies on the Welsh border to the east of the Vale of Ewyas and the easiest approach is from the path which runs due north from 250287 on the minor road running along the border on the Grwyne Fawr valley to 252315 near to the Capel-y-ffin monastery. The path crosses the ridge at 250303 and from that point the summit is about half a mile to the south-east.

RED DAREN

Sheet 142. Reference 282308. Herefordshire/Monmouthshire. 2003 feet.

Red Daren strictly applies to a feature further down the ridge to the south-east, but is the only convenient name to identify this summit. It lies on the Offa's Dyke Path between Pandy (334217) and Hay-on-Wye, and is marked by a trig point. Black Mountain is three miles further north on the same ridge.

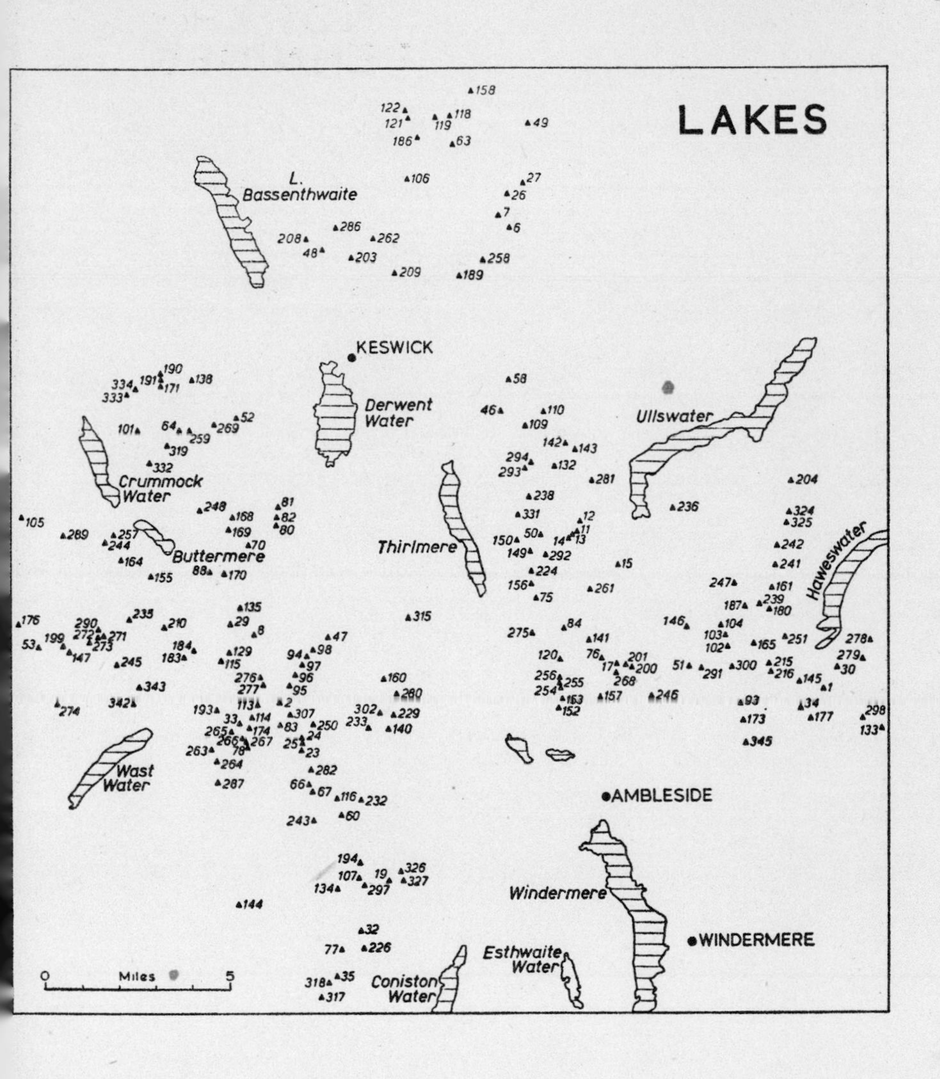
LAKES
158
122
121
118
119
186
63
49
L.
Bassenthwaite
106
27
26
7
6
286
262
208
48
203
258
209
189
KESWICK
Derwent
Water
190
334
191
171
138
333
58
46
110
109
Ullswater
52
101
64
269
259
319
142
143
294
132
293
332
Crummock
Water
281
204
238
248
81
168
82
331
236
324
325
105
289
257
244
169
80
70
12
11
150
50
14
13
242
Buttermere
Thirlmere
149
292
241
164
88
170
155
224
15
Haweswater
156
261
247
161
75
239
187
180
135
176
235
29
210
315
290
272
271
273
53
199
147
8
47
184
183
129
115
94
98
97
96
95
245
343
276
277
160
280
275
84
146
104
103
141
102
165
251
278
120
76
201
17
200
268
51
291
300
215
216
145
279
30
256
255
254
153
152
157
246
1
274
342
113
193
33
114
174
83
2
307
250
302
233
229
140
93
173
34
177
298
133
265
266
267
263
78
264
25
24
23
345
282
Wast
Water
287
66
67
116
232
AMBLESIDE
243
60
194
107
19
326
327
134
297
Windermere
144
32
77
226
WINDERMERE
Esthwaite
Water
0
Miles
5
318
35
317
Coniston
Water

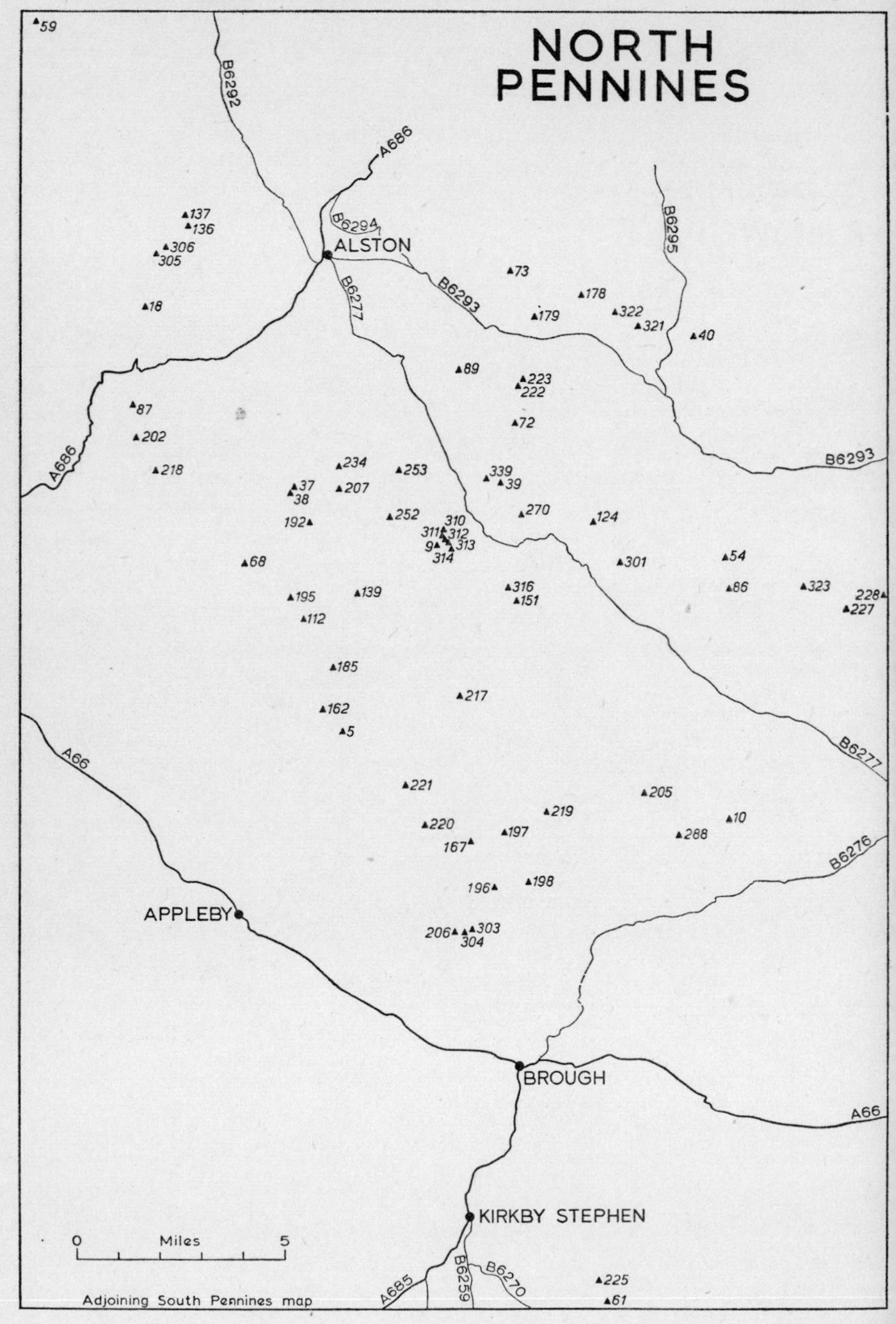
NORTH PENNINES
ALSTON
APPLEBY
BROUGH
KIRKBY STEPHEN
B6292
A686
B6294
B6277
B6293
B6295
A66
B6276
A685
B6259
B6270
0 Miles 5
Adjoining South Pennines map
59
137
136
306
305
18
87
202
218
73
178
179
322
321
40
89
223
222
72
234
253
339
39
37
38
207
192
252
310
311
312
9
313
314
270
124
68
301
54
86
323
228
227
195
139
316
151
112
185
217
162
5
221
205
219
10
220
197
288
167
196
198
206
303
304
225
61

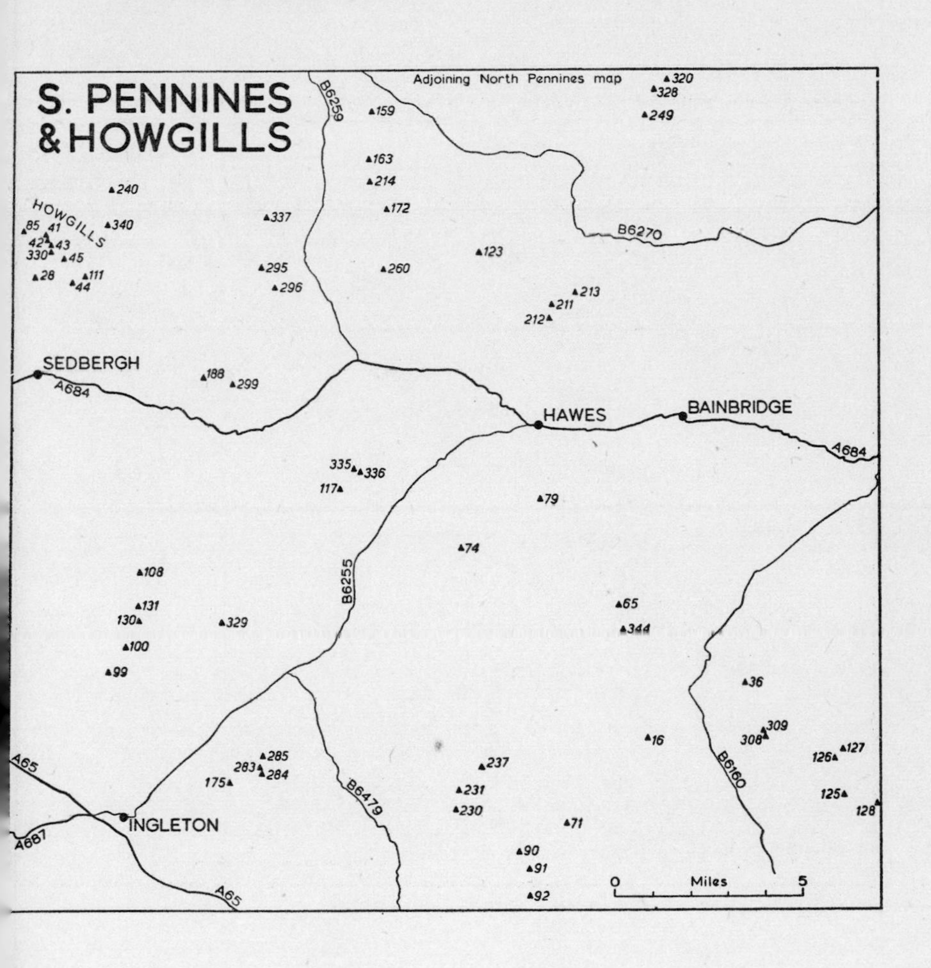
S. PENNINES & HOWGILLS
Adjoining North Pennines map
HOWGILLS
SEDBERGH
HAWES
BAINBRIDGE
INGLETON
B6259
B6270
B6255
B6479
B6160
A684
A65
A687
Miles
0
5

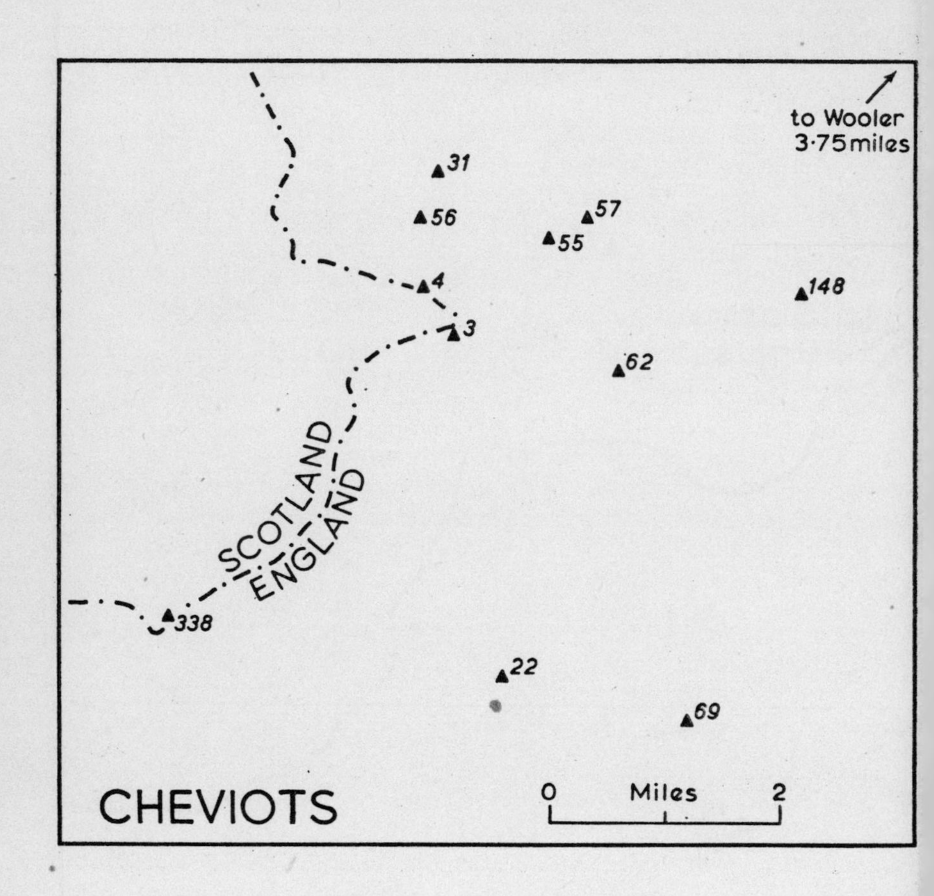
to Wooler
3·75 miles
31
56
57
55
4
148
3
62
SCOTLAND
ENGLAND
338
22
69
CHEVIOTS
0
Miles
2

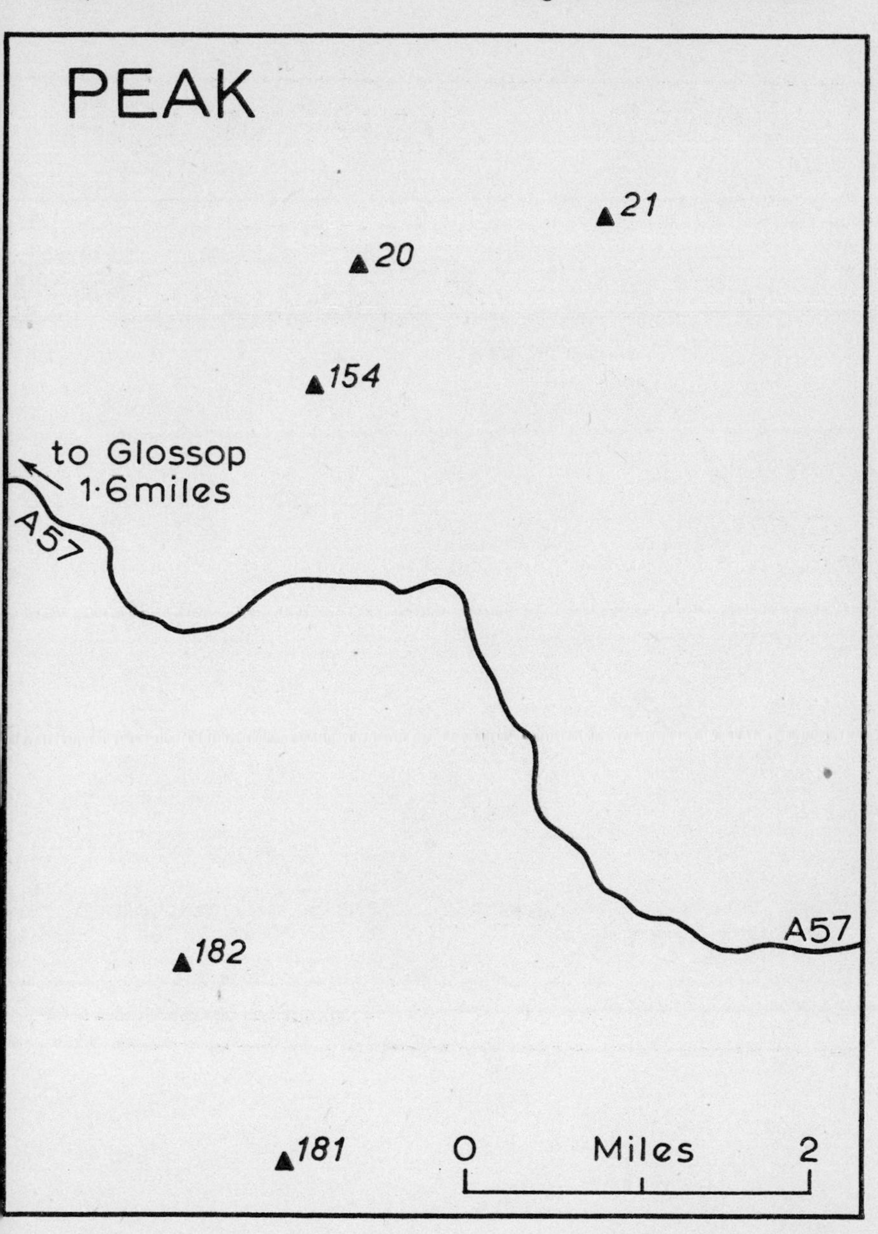
PEAK
21
20
154
to Glossop
1·6 miles
A57
A57
182
181
0
Miles
2

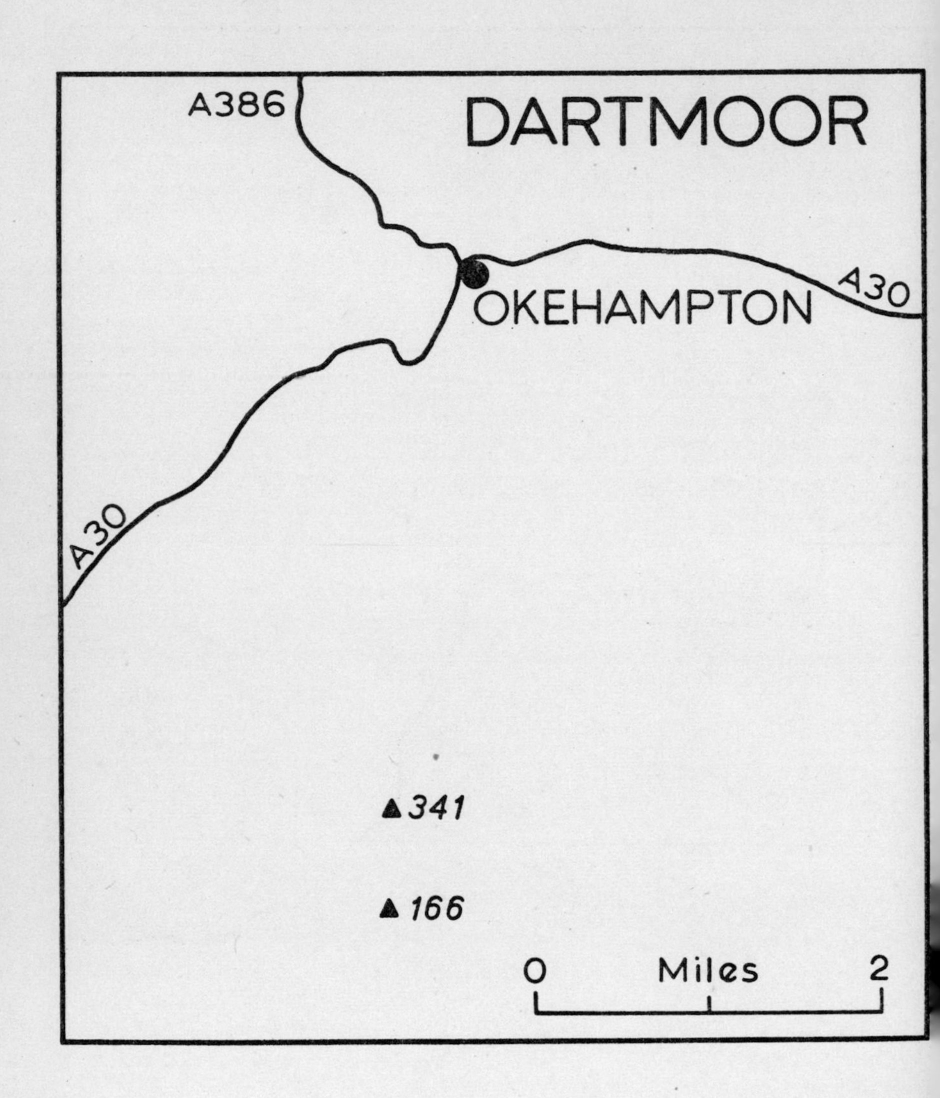
A386
DARTMOOR
OKEHAMPTON
A30
A30
▲341
▲166
0 Miles 2